THE CHURCHES AND RACISM

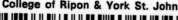

THE CHURCHES AND RACISM

A BLACK SOUTH AFRICAN PERSPECTIVE

Zolile Mbali

SCM PRESS LTD

© Zolile Mbali 1987

British Library Cataloguing in Publication Data

Mbali, Zolile
   The churches and racism: a black South
   African perspective.
   1. Apartheid—Religious aspects—
   Christianity 2. Apartheid—South Africa
   I. Title
   261.7 DT763

ISBN 0–334–01923–0

334 01923 0

First published 1987
by SCM Press Ltd,
26-30 Tottenham Road, London N1 4BZ

Phototypeset by Input Typesetting Ltd, London
and printed in Great Britain by
Richard Clay Ltd,
Bungay, Suffolk

I write this book for my fellow South Africans, remembering especially those who are unable to write or publish a book in their situation, but whose lives are 'living testimonies'. Times are bad now, and they often are for us black people. But we will go on speaking, writing, thinking and acting for our freedom. One day, soon, we shall be free. In the meantime we continue by many different ways in our struggle.

Acknowledgments

First, I must thank Bishop David Jenkins who encouraged me to embark upon this research and offered valuable advice when it was in progress. I also acknowledge with gratitude the funding I received from St Augustine's Foundation, and the small grant from the F.N. Davey Memorial Trust of SPCK. I am grateful to the librarians of Selly Oak, of Leeds and Durham University, and the Colindale Newspaper library. For the research in the latter, I must thank Picton Mbatha who found and photo-copied some of the key articles referred to here. Finally, to my wife Charlotte and our three children, Thandiwe, Ma-Jali and Mandisa, I give thanks. For it is their support and love that kept me going. Without that I could not have proceeded with or completed this study.

Contents

Abbreviations

ABN	Algemene Bank Nederland
AMRO	Amsterdam Rotterdam Bank
ANC	African National Congress
ASF	Anglican Students Federation
BCC	British Council of Churches
BCP	Black Community Programmes
BPC	Black Peoples Conventions
CAA	see UN below
CARAF	Christians against Racism and Fascism
CCSA	Christian Concern for Southern Africa
CI	Christian Institute
CIO	Church Information Office (of the Church of England)
CIIR	Catholic Institute for International Relations
CPSA	Church of the Province of South Africa
DRC	Dutch Reformed Church
EABC	Europe-America Banking Corporation
ECGD	Export Credit Guarantee Department
EEC	European Economic Community
EIRIS	Ethical Investment Research and Information Service
ELTSA	End Loans to South Africa
ESCOM	Electricity Supply Commission
FARI	Foreign Affairs Research Institute
FOSATU	Federation of South African Trade Unions
ICCR	Interfaith Center for Corporate Responsibility
ICI	Imperial Chemical Industries
NCC	National Council of Churches
NGK	Nederlands Gereformeerde Kerk
NHK	Nederduitsch Hervormde Kerk
NIIO	New International Information Order
NUSAS	National Union of South African Students
OAU	Organization for African Unity
OPEC	Organization of Petroleum Exporting Countries
PAC	Pan African Congress

Abbreviations

PCR	The Programme to Combat Racism of the WCC
PCSA	The Presbyterian Church of South Africa
RTZ	Rio-Tinto Zinc Company
SACC	South African Council of Churches
SACHED	South African Council for Higher Education
SADCC	Southern African Development Coordination Conference
SADF	The South African Defence Force
SAIRR	The South African Institute of Race Relations
SASO	The South African Students Organization
SASOL	Suid Afrikaanse Steenkool, Olie en Gaskorporasie (South African Coal, Oil and Gas Corporation)
SODEPAX	Society of Development and Peace
SPROCAS	Study Project on Christianity in Apartheid Society
SWAPO	South West Africa People's Organization
UNCAA	United Nations Centre against Apartheid
UNESCO	United Nations Educational, Scientific and Cultural Organization
WCC	World Council of Churches
ZANU	Zimbabwe African National Union
ZCC	Zion Christian Church

1

A Black Perspective

I was born in 1940 in Orlando West, part of what is now Soweto. I spent my early years at my grandfather's place at Matatiele, at the foot of the Drakensberg mountains, an area where Sotho and Xhosa people intermingle. My Xhosa father was from an important Tembu clan, and my mother is Mosotho. I spent my teenage years in the Transvaal with my clergyman uncle, first at Roodepoort and then at Benoni, where Desmond Tutu was a curate.

My father had died when I was about nine, and my mother was struggling in Natal to earn for the family. In 1957 I had to break off schooling in order to earn school fees for my younger sister. For two years I did labouring work at a railway construction site. Safety was appalling and I saw the skulls of my fellow-workers crushed by rocks. Food was rough and living quarters were cramped. Because of the insanitary conditions I contracted typhoid and had to return to my family in Natal. Whilst I was there, a local priest spotted my educational frustration and encouraged me to borrow books from his collection. The calibre of these priests and their love for the people projected an inspiring image of the church for me. This eventually led to my going to test my vocation at the Modderpoort school run by the Fathers of the Society of the Sacred Mission.

From 1960 to 1971 my education was sponsored by the church, from the Modderpoort school to St Bede's Theological College in Transkei, and from there, after matriculating by correspondence, to Fort Hare for a BA in English and Philosophy. These student years coincided with the efforts to make NUSAS, the National Union of South African Students, inter-racial, and also the inter-racial conferences of the Anglican Students Federation (ASF). Meanwhile, my vacations were spent in Natal, sometimes doing parish work.

In 1968 I was one of the students who benefited from the Uppsala decision of the World Council of Churches to set up the Theological Education Fund to finance the further studies of key students who would return to their home countries to be theology tutors. Thus I was at Oxford from 1968 to 1971 to study for a BA in theology, at The Queen's College, where David Jenkins was Tutor and Chaplain. At that time I was aware of the initial British media reactions in 1970 to the first WCC grants in the Programme to Combat Racism (PCR), headlined by some newspapers as THE CHURCHES' AID TO TERRORISTS.

However, throughout the 1970s, from 1971 to 1981, during the main period covered by this book, I was back in Africa. I went first to the Diocese of Natal, where I worked in the large township parish of Kwa Mashu, near Durban, and then in the sugar plantation area of Tongaat. In 1973-74, I was chaplain and tutor at St Paul's Theological College, Grahamstown, teaching the white students there by day and living in the Fingo township. In December 1974 I left South Africa to go to Botswana. Charlotte, an English girl I had met in Oxford, had got a job there. We married in January 1975 and I took up work in Botswana doing theology by extension.

In Botswana we read South African newspapers, and also got first-hand news from family and friends visiting us or the churches. In 1976, the crisis in Soweto resulted in the outflux of refugees through Botswana. The main agency providing for their welfare was the Botswana Christian Council, whose General Secretary, the late James Ndebele, was one of my closest friends at the time. From him, after his frequent fund-raising trips on behalf of the refugees to Europe, I used to get snatches of news of the WCC.

Then in the spring of 1978 I went to a church conference in Europe. I took the opportunity to visit David Jenkins, to discuss with him my hopes of doing further studies. As he had been working at the Humanum division of the WCC he was the right person to discuss a proposal to study the Programme to Combat Racism from a black perspective. However, I had to return to Botswana, where I had no academic base from which to begin such a study. The war in Rhodesia to the north of us was in the crucial final stage. We knew what was happening in Southern Africa from a grass-roots perspective, but could not see fully what the churches outside were doing, except through the tantalizingly brief summaries of Ecunews, circulated to us via the South African Council of Churches. I saw no way of extricating myself from the diocese of Botswana, where I was working in a rural parish, and moving to somewhere which would enable me to study.

Then in 1981 I got a letter out of the blue inviting me to go to the diocese of Durham. It was from Nick Beddow (he claims that he had a dream about me) whom I had met a few years before at a theological tutors' conference in Zambia. He had moved on to be chaplain to the Bishop of Durham, and had not forgotten my plight. Thus it came about that in 1981 I became the vicar of Preston-on-Tees. I renewed contact with David Jenkins, then Professor of Theology at Leeds University, and embarked on the research which led to this book. But by 1983 I realized that I would need to move nearer a library that stocked WCC materials systematically. Fortunately, St Augustine's Foundation granted me a scholarship to enable me to move near Selly Oak Colleges from October 1983 until July 1984. Thus the bulk of this book was written then. Publication was delayed by the hiatus of moves: I went back to parish work, and David Jenkins moved from Leeds to be Bishop of Durham. However, he has always encouraged me to work towards publication, being aware of the significance of theological thinking that comes from the people in the thick of events, as he once wrote: 'the only valid document to come from the ecumenical movement (is) the living epistles of people'.[1] Being similarly aware of how personal circumstances shape committed theology, I have tried to select my sources mainly from the words of those people at the crux, those under the pressure of personal decision, those who must defend their position so to speak when the shooting has already begun.

Having now disclosed the personal circumstances surrounding the writing of this book, I want to explain the black perspective. Central to my aim is that, more often than not, a lot is discussed about us black people over our heads. But we are not mutes; we have an inherent right to raise our voices and participate in this discussion. In 1980 PCR declared:

> oppressed racial groups should be encouraged to reflect theologically on their present and historical experience of oppression and share this with the wider church.[2]

Racism is not just an academic matter for me, a topic for discussion. It is existential, in so far as I have lived this reality at every moment of my life; from birth till now I have known racism at first hand. It has determined in no small measure the person I am, and the one I am prevented from becoming. People brought up in 'free' countries do not, usually, suffer as individuals for what they write or proclaim; people brought up in South Africa frequently do. Thus there is a radical difference between the writing which comes from people who know oppression and those who belong to the oppressors (even if they become critics of that oppression). Mostly the oppressed are silent, or silenced, in their situation. For South Africans, the penalty for dissent is all too often martyrdom; some are executed after trial under the terrorism laws; many die, like Steve Biko, while in police custody, undergoing interrogation; others, having left the country as exiles, are killed by terrorist methods, such as parcel bombs, which are used to eliminate outspoken opponents of apartheid living in the countries near South Africa.

Black theological perspectives have come into being from within the experience of oppression. Try as he may to find an answer to the problem of racist structures in the society he has to live in, the black man is unable to find it in the traditional academic theology of the West. This blankness of Western theology, this failure to answer his problems, makes it clear that he is on his own, thrown back on his own understanding of the Word of God, in so far as that Word speaks to him in his situation, a situation that no one outside his own experience of 'being black in the world' can enter or meaningfully minister to. Thus the cry 'black man, you are on your own', which heralded the black consciousness movement in South Africa, has theological significance. The black man, as it were, 'came to himself' and awoke from the slumbers of the assumptions that had previously propped him up. He could not be dependent on the white man's analysis of his black situation. He began to discover that making a viable stand over his destiny in the world of inter-cultural and international relationships was not something that would come to him automatically, without struggle on his part.

This emergence of self-awareness among black people made it possible for them to realize that the theology that they had relied upon all along was sectional theology, sectional in the sense that it was a theology largely geared to answering questions posed by the white people in their dealings with the problems that encountered them as white people in the world. They discovered that these problems which were being addressed by white theology were very much tied up with the history of the white people (including colonization) in the context of historical experience and self-understanding as a result of that experience.

In some of the controversies to be discussed in this book there is a hidden assumption that there is 'pure' theology (as practised by Western academics) and theology mixed with politics, as in Latin American liberation theology, black theology and other writings coming from the Third World. Without wanting to enter into discussion at this point about what would constitute 'pure' theology (this side of heaven), I must emphasize that in most of the arguments about the churches and racism the theology involved is contextual, in other words theology arising from the social context of those who proclaim it.

Black people have no hope of attaining the corresponding liberative language for their experience if they rely upon the language of the white community and the concepts it uses to refer to the black experience, for that language and those concepts deal with reality as seen in the white experience of the world. But if black people use their own language and concepts to describe their own situation, if they produce a 'black' theology, their critics can turn round and accuse them of separating themselves from the rest of humanity. And that proves to be just one horn of a dilemma. For if black people then try to meet this criticism by remaining within the ambit of the language used by white people for solving their existential problems, black people may then feel uncatered for.

So what kind of theological communication can take place?

When the World Council of Churches sponsored a symposium on liberation theology in Geneva in 1973, the report on it was published in *Risk* under the title 'Incommunication', to indicate that it had proved impossible at the meeting to fit the discussion into a 'nice intellectual framework' similar to that applied to other Third World fieldwork. The black perspective is firmly contextual. We are always aware of the sociological position of the proponents and opponents of the case in any debate. This is not just an intellectual trick, picked up from the Latin Americans, during the confrontation between Western and Third World speakers. It is to be found even in the village councils of Africa where arguments may be repeated and repeated, because they are given added weight by each man who endorses the propositions from his particular position with regard to the village hierarchy, the chief, and the family under discussion.

I am delighted to point out that there is even a biblical example of this black tendency to contextualize: see the story in Acts 8.34, which seems to me to give the correct line of enquiry for black theologians. The Ethiopian eunuch, who was reading the book of the prophet Isaiah, asked Philip: 'Of whom is the prophet saying this? Of himself, or of someone else?' This is the legitimate question for black people to ask today of theologians. Of whom is this man writing here, of himself, or of someone else? Of his culture, values and society, or those of someone else? Of his own experience, or that of someone else? Is the writer writing about the situation of the white tribe, or of some other tribe?

It is when we begin asking the Ethiopian's question that we see the limitation of much accepted theology, which we have been taught and have venerated for generations. Furthermore, not only does this Ethiopian diplomat set us an example of contextualization in Bible study; he also brings theology into praxis, immediately. He took a decisive initiative, and asked for baptism. It is doubtful whether Philip would have suggested baptism as a matter of course unless the man had shown himself to be ready by asking for it. Similarly, it is hardly likely that racism will ever be significantly checked unless and until black people take the initiative.

2

Portrait of Apartheid

Government without representation

On 4 May 1960, Robert Sobukwe said in a South African court in his own defence:

> It will be remembered that we refused to plead to the charges against us. We felt that we had no obligation to obey the laws made by a white minority. Without wishing to impugn the personal honour and integrity of the magistrate, an unjust law cannot be applied justly...[1]

I set this quotation at the start of this chapter as a reminder that all the laws and the administrative, political, economic and social arrangements of apartheid are set up by the white minority and imposed upon the black majority of South Africa.

The first steps taken on the way to apartheid legislation were to dismantle what few constitutional rights black people had. After 1936, black people (who had hitherto had a limited franchise, based on educational qualifications in the Cape Province) could no longer vote directly for black candidates. They had to choose seven white representatives to speak for them. In 1956, the same thing was forced upon Coloured people. Then in 1959, the all-white population put forward the Promotion of Bantu Self-Government Act, which annulled even this minimal representation, to be followed in 1968 by the Separate Representation of Voters Amendment Act which removed the representatives of the Coloured from Parliament. In the same year the Political Interference Act outlawed multi-racial political activity.

Separate development

The idea of the Nationalists is that each group in South Africa should have separate 'freedoms'. J.S.F. Botha expressed their solution like this:

> Eventually present-day South Africa will harbour eight independent black nations and a white sovereign state, each independent politically and free to associate with one another and the Republic of South Africa for common purpose. Each of the different black nations in South Africa, we believe, should have the opportunity to exercise its basic right to determine for itself its own future. Nothing should prevent each of these nations from becoming independent in the fullest sense.[2]

However, in putting the black view, Chief Albert Luthuli dubbed apartheid a 'deceit concept' and remarked:

> There is really no possibility of anyone developing 'along his own lines', as is often suggested. But in practice 'developing along your own lines' turns out not to be developing along your own lines at all, but developing along the lines designed by the government through the Native Affairs Department. Even in determining the laws that govern us in our development, there is no attempt to consult those affected. There is no contact between governor and governed, at the present moment. 'Developing along your own lines' has come to mean 'developing along their own lines': the government's lines. The essence of developing along your own lines is that you must have the right to develop. Its essence is freedom and – beyond freedom – self-determination. This is the vision we hold for our future and our development.[3]

The majority of black people living within urban areas are against the Bantustan system. They regard themselves as South Africans, entitled to citizenship of that country, and they would prefer a franchise for the South African Parliament to citizenship and polls for Bantustans.

Resettlement

It is difficult to estimate the number of those who have been affected by forced resettlement. Those endorsed out of the towns are only a proportion of those moved about the country to fit in with the apartheid map of black spots and white areas. One estimate was that they would amount to about two million people by 1982. Accurate census is difficult because those who consider themselves in danger of being endorsed out of an area are not likely to come forward with information about themselves, and in fact do everything possible to avoid the attention of officialdom.

Rather than inaccurate statistics, it is the human stories that are most revealing of the effects of this apartheid programme. These movements are sometimes enforced for strategic reasons, from areas required for dams, motorways, army bases or no-go areas near the frontier where infiltration might take place. Sometimes the plan changes, as in the tragedy of the Makgatho tribe. In 1964 they were ousted from their traditional place and moved. Believing this resettlement area to be permanent, they established sturdy houses, churches, schools and flourishing agriculture. In 1978 they were informed that the area was badly situated, too close to the great North road, and they were to be moved again. A Makgatho man named Philemon, on contract work in Johannesburg, heard in 1979 of the latest removal and travelled back to the rural area in search of his family, whom he found sheltering with a nearby tribe. He went back to his deserted house, removed possessions, doors, windows and roofing, and disappeared. He was then found four days later, hanging from a tree near his ruined homestead.[4]

Health reports indicate the bad effects of this enforced movement of people. The outbreak of cholera in the homelands 'must be viewed in the context of the web of migrant labour, forced resettlement, overcrowding, poor housing and inadequate services'.[5] The amount and quality of land allocated to blacks cannot support the overcrowded settlement. A survey by Kupugani, the organization concerned with malnutrition and attempts to counter it, at the end of 1972 found:

Malnutrition was reported as the rule: 75-80% of the children examined at the two hospitals in Pondoland, in the Transkei, were found to be suffering from it. Many of the children die or are permanently brain-damaged as a result. It is widely recognized that apart from increasing poverty, the forced system of migrant labour, which involves the separation of families from their major income-earner, and the destruction of the traditional family and community responsibilities, is a major cause of starvation and disease in the Bantustans. About half of all the children in the Ciskei are being stunted in their growth through malnutrition. In Kwa Zulu, a study of malnutrition warns that it is changing the traditional Zulu physique: people are becoming small, stunted and mentally enfeebled.[6]

The attitude of the government to the people being thus moved about is that they are the superfluous appendages of people working in the white areas. For instance, Mr Fronemann, the Minister of Justice and Planning, was quoted as saying:

> We settle many elderly people. If they are doing nothing in the white homeland, they may just as well be doing nothing in the black homeland.[7]

Such reports show that the resettlement is a barely disguised dumping policy, because white South Africa needs the labour but does not want to pay the social costs of its apartheid policy.

Economic privilege

Apartheid is supposed to be based on the rationale of 'separate, but equal'. Blacks are supposed to be immigrants in the white areas while they have employment, which is usually on limited contract basis, and low pay because they are supposed to have alternative means for their families in the farms of the homelands. This might have been the situation a century ago, when subsistence farming was flourishing in tribal areas, but the economic facts are rather different today. The Gross Domestic Product of the homeland economies is a tiny fragment, under 5%, of the overall GDP of South Africa, and that indicates the degree of underdevelopment and poverty and the extent of regional dualism. It has been reckoned that only 8% of the rural population of South Africa lives by subsistence farming. So by far the greater part of the income of those who live in the homelands has to come from outside. So the homelands are areas that constitute cheap labour pools for white-owned businesses situated on or near their borders.

It is also important to realize the grip which the state has on the South African economy. The economist Francis Wilson has remarked:

> In South Africa, where public expenditure is approximately one quarter of the gross domestic product; where investment by the state accounts for approximately half of all gross fixed investment; and where approximately one third of all economically active whites are employed by the state, analysis of the state is crucial in understanding the behaviour of the economy... the state plays an active part not only

as investor or employer, but also as central banker, controller of the money supply, and shaper of the country's educational structure and – through such diverse factors as educational and pass laws – of the patterns of its labour supply.[8]

Is the state then more powerful even than the rich mining firms? Some accuse the firms of sheltering behind apartheid laws, because, in any case, as Francis Wilson's detailed book on the subject shows, they profit greatly from the cheap migrant labour. However, mining magnates like Harry Oppenheimer have also publicly argued against apartheid on the grounds that it restrains economic growth. But there is also the argument that it is not only the apartheid laws, but also the pressure-groups of the white workers that sustain the system. For instance, the government does not actually legislate the wage levels, but the restrictive legislation on employment conditions makes it impossible for Africans to achieve the same economic status as whites. In particular, the restrictions on apprenticeship and training make it impossible for Africans to qualify for higher status jobs. The white unions themselves are vigilant to ensure that unionization of the black labour force is a slow and risky process. After a series of strikes, the government reluctantly agreed to register some black unions, but some of the black labour leaders do not trust the new system of registered unions; and trust is increasingly being eroded by repeated harrassment and arrests of such labour leaders.

There are about 1,500,000 blacks working in town on contract. This is migrant labour from the homelands. These contract workers are not allowed to bring their families with them and have to live in hostels. Family life suffers. Legislation has been proposed to remove some of the restrictions on job opportunities, but the proposals do not apply to migrant labourers, who make up fifty per cent of the labour force. Reform would simply increase the gap between those in the Homelands and those with rights of access to the core region.

So the economic reason for apartheid can be seen as cheap labour. The existence of cheap labour sustains the high standard of living of the whites.

Oppressive laws

In 1972, the Christian Institute reported:

There is no longer any doubt that South Africa is a police state. There are police informers, detention without trials, and unexplained deaths in police cells with strong evidence of torture at the hands of the police.[9]

To one who has never experienced the South African situation, it may seem incredible that the victims of this apartheid seem to be doing nothing to improve their lot. So it must be stressed that the reason for their apparent docility is that they are prevented from active dissent by stringent legislation, which has even been duplicated in the homelands. Thus an Act has been passed in the homelands giving authorities power to ban any organization that they consider undesirable, an Act modelled upon such earlier Acts as the Suppression of Communism Act and the Unlawful Organization Act of 1960 in South Africa. This Act is meant to suppress all forms of detectable dissent, for the term 'Communist' in South African legislation means anyone holding views contrary to that of the ruling party.

The Terrorism Act of 1967 is of such severity that it carries the death penalty. Furthermore the definition of terrorism is so broad that anyone considered to be endangering national security may come within its reach. For example, campaigning against investment policies or the labour laws of South Africa is dubbed economic sabotage and the campaigners are called 'terrorists' or 'Communists'.

Trials under the Terrorism Act are usually covered by the international press. The deaths in detention before trial are not forgotten; in particular the deaths of Steve Biko in 1977 and Neil Aggett in 1981 are still remembered and discussed.

In addition, there are hundreds of cases of pass law offences. Every African must carry a pass-book, which is the instrument by which the authorities control work-seekers and residence rights in the urban areas. In 1979 an average of 750 people a day were arrested on pass-law offences.[10] It is therefore hardly surprising that a society which has such laws, as well as much social violence engendered by poverty and resentment at inequality, has one of the highest ratios in the world for people in prison as compared to population, and also a very high rate of legal executions per year.

Militarization

The South African Defence Force has grown into a powerful force of nearly 500,000 men. Conscription is compulsory for whites, and after initial military service men are liable to be called up again in emergencies.

This force is use in 'operational areas', which mean Namibia and Angola, as well as along the borders of South Africa in the northern part, and it is also used on occasion to contain revolt within South African townships. South Africa's defence budget in 1979 was R1857 million, double the 1975 figure.[11] In 1979 there were reports in the press that the USA had some evidence that South Africa had conducted nuclear tests.

Press censorship

There are various ways in which the state has increasing control to curb the press. Whenever a paper has become too bold in its criticisms of apartheid, eventually such criticism is suppressed either by banning the newspaper, as happened with *The World*, or by prosecuting the editor, as happened with Percy Qoboza, and with Donald Woods who had to flee into exile. New controls have been imposed as the incidents of sabotage increase, so that people are kept in ignorance about the security situation, or are given information only through the government spokesmen.

In 1986, the government became alarmed at the impact on the publicity overseas of TV programmes showing the fighting in the townships, and the harsh actions of the military or police. There was a clamp-down on foreign correspondents, especially film crews. Since then, there has certainly been a reduction of such news. But the overseas public should not be deceived by such a manoeuvre into assuming that all is quiet in the townships. The South African régime is treating the foreign public to the same sort of censorship it has tried to impose for years within the country, with the aim of 'out of sight, out of mind', which is the attitude of many whites to the black townships. To counteract this the British Council of Churches and other church agencies have set up the weekly bulletin *Southscan* to get uncensored news from South Africa.

Race laws

Finally, it is necessary to point out that the whole system of apartheid depends upon classifying people according to their colour and racial features. This classification will then determine where they may live, what jobs they may do, whom they are forbidden to marry or have sex with, and what schools their children may go to. Needless to say, such a system can cause great heartache, especially in families of mixed descent, or where an anomaly occurs.

Legislation keeps the races apart as far as possible. In public places, either social custom or local laws enforce racial separation. On the railways, there are separate carriages for non-whites, and separate entrances at most large stations. In Johannesburg, the trains from Soweto come in under the main platforms reserved for whites. In many towns throughout the country, black people have not been able to sit on the park benches or use the public libraries, though this was later relaxed in the 1970s in some places. In many towns the shop-keepers serve black people at a separate counter, sometimes eveen by a hatch into the yard with the black customers queueing outside. In most places, it is assumed that a white customer should not have to queue behind black customers, even when both are making similar purchases. In churches, the Group Areas Act ensures that in fact different church buildings are used by different races. In towns, the Catholics and Anglicans have managed some mixed worship. But in Afrikaner churches mixed worship, even at funerals, arouses fierce controversy and hostility.

Because of all this it is in fact very difficult for white people, even those relatively few liberal and humane white people still living in South Africa, to meet black people. Intense social pressure is exerted by hardliners against 'kaffir boeties' (i.e. Kaffir brothers). In such a society, truthful dialogue between white and black people is hard to come by, and hard going when it occurs.

3

The Programme to Combat Racism

The setting up of PCR

The most publicized response to racism made by the churches took the form of the Programme to Combat Racism. So it is the discussion which that sparked off that I shall be using to illustrate the issues in which Christians become involved in their attempts to do something about such a blatantly racist practice as apartheid.

The World Council of Churches' concern over racism goes back to the General Assembly held at Uppsala in 1968. Section IV of the Uppsala Report reads:

(a) Racism is linked with economic and political exploitation. The churches must be actively concerned for the economic and political well-being of exploited groups so that their statements and actions may be relevant. In order that victims of racism may regain a sense of their own worth and be enabled to determine their own future, the churches must make economic and educational resources available to the underprivileged groups for their development to full partici-pation in the social and economic life of their communities. They should also withdraw from institutions that perpetuate racism. They must also urge that similar assistance be given from both the public and private sectors. Such economic help is an essential compensatory measure to counteract and overcome the present systematic exclusion of victims of racism from the mainstream of economic life. The churches must also work for change of those political processes which prevent the victims of racism from participating fully in the civic and governmental structures of their countries.[1]

(b)...The churches must eradicate all forms of racism from their own life. That many have not done so, particularly where institutional racism assumes subtle forms, is a scandal.[2]

Racism was defined as:

> ...ethnocentric pride in one's own racial group and preference for the distinctive characteristics of that group; belief that these characteristics are fundamentally biological in nature, and are thus transmitted to succeeding generations; strong negative feelings towards other groups who do not share these characteristics, coupled with the thrust to discriminate against and exclude the outgroup from full participation in the life of the commmunity.[3]

It is clear from this that those who were at Uppsala in 1968 realized that the issue was not just the problem of negative feelings between people of different races, but racism as it reinforces contemporary political and economic arrangements, and the way in which in turn these structures bolster racism. Thus it would be naive to attack racism without acknowledging its political and economic dimensions, or to assume that racism can be eradicated simply by moral exhortation.

Following these impressive statements, the World Council of Churches prepared for concrete action through a consultation in May 1969 in Notting Hill, London. Forty Christian leaders, lay and clergy, met there, along with twenty-five additional consultants. Seven participants and two consultants were from Africa, and there were several blacks among the participants from the USA and the UK. Only two participants were from Eastern block countries: a noteworthy fact in view of the way in which opponents of the WCC tend to brand it as Communist.

There is a full account of the Notting Hill Consultation and the way in which it saw the issues in the report written by John Vincent which was published in 1970.[4] John Vincent also describes how late on the afternoon of the penultimate day the consultation was interrupted by a small group of young 'black power' people who read a 'Declaration of Revolution' putting forward the most radical issues, such as the way in which the churches controlled economic power and used it for exploitation; the need for a transfer of that power by force (with the famous quotation from Malcolm X, 'power grows out of the barrel of a gun'), a demand for publication of lists of the financial investments of all member churches of the WCC; and specific demands for money for named liberation organizations. The consultation devoted considerable time to this, at the expense of discussing the reports of some of its working groups, so that WCC staff members had to do the final work on the material that was to be submitted to the various divisions of the WCC for comment before it went to the WCC Central Committee at Canterbury, England, in August 1969.[5]

Because the Canterbury mandate resulted in the setting up of the Programme to Combat Racism it is important to see what it actually said.[6] To highlight the key issues I have italicized the words and phrases which seem to me to be most striking and important.

II. *Recommendation regarding an Ecumenical Programme to Combat Racism*

1. Since its inception, the WCC has consistently denounced the sin of racism. This issue is not new to us. But today it rises with a new and terrifying urgency. The WCC has offered a strong lead in the past, but its studies and statements generally have evoked neither adequate awareness nor effective action. Further, recent study and dialogue have served to open the dimensions and implications of the problem never before realized. Thus the struggle against racism as it rapidly intensifies is now confronting the churches with a challenge to deeper understanding, fresh commitment and *costly redemptive action*.

2. The Consultation recommended to the WCC and its member churches lines of action for an ecumenical programme to combat racism. However, more important than any recommendation, it *pleaded for a profound and renewed commitment from the churches – and specifically from the World Council of Churches – to offer a convincing and moral lead* in the face of this great and growing crisis of our times.

To make the commitment quite concrete in the life of the World Council of Churches, the following propositions were put for adoption:

A. The Scope and Focus of a New Ecumenical Programme to Combat Racism

1. Racism is not an unalterable feature of human life. Like slavery and other social manifestations of *man's sin*, it can and must be eliminated. In the light of the Gospel and in accordance with its principles and methods, Christians must be involved in this struggle and, wherever possible, in association with all people of goodwill.

2. Racism today is not confined to certain continents or countries. *It is a world problem. White racism is not its only form.* It is recognized that at this moment in some parts of the world, like Asia and Africa, other forms of racism and ethnocentrism provide the most crucial

problems. There is a strong element of racism in current forms of anti-semitism as well as in the discrimination against the lower castes in India.

3. It is the coincidence, however, of an *accumulation of wealth and power in the hands of the white peoples*, following upon their historical and economic progress during the past four hundred years, which is the reason for a focus on the various forms of *white racism* in the different parts of the world. People of different colour suffer from this racism in all continents. . . .

4. There was a period when 'colonialism' was the main feature of white racism. Some areas still suffer in this way. While many formerly colonial people have become independent, they still suffer from the aftermath of 'colonialism', part of which is the struggle for power between communities and tribes.

5. It is further recognized that the fight against racism in all its forms must be set within the context of the struggle for World Community, including World Development.

B. *Rationale for an Ecumenical Programme to Combat Racism*

1. Growing tensions and conflicts between the races demand urgent action; time is running out. The pervasiveness, persistence and viciousness of racism has challenged many Christians. But a sense of the impotence of the churches to achieve reconciliation has immobilized many others. Many have even despaired.

2. We have sadly to recognize that in spite of the battle that has been fought against racism by the churches, mission agencies and councils of churches, with often heroic personal sacrifice, racism is now a worse menace than ever. We have also sadly to confess that churches have participated in racial discrimination. Many religious institutions of the white northern world have benefited from racially exploitative economic systems. Many church members are unaware of the facts of racism and of the involvement of their religious and secular institutions in its perpetuation. Lacking information about institutionalized racism and about the possibility of developing sophisticated strategies to secure racial justice, Christians often engage in irrelevant and timid efforts to improve race relations – too little and too late.

3. In our ecumenical fellowship there are churches from all parts of the world, some of which have suffered from these racially

exploitative economic systems. What is needed is an ecumenical act of *solidarity* which would help to stem the deterioration in race relations. To do this our action must cost something and must be affirmative, visible and capable of emulation.

4. The issue of reparations has been raised by some groups in the USA and the WCC Consultation at Notting Hill. It cannot therefore be avoided. Many of the churches which are confronted by this demand belong to our ecumenical fellowship, and are called upon to make a meaningful response to this issue. *The concept of reparations, however, is inadequate, for it seeks simply to apportion guilt* for the past and highlights a method of action which leaves out of account the need for acts of compassion, brotherhood and community which go beyond any financial payment. The Gospel speaks to us of *the cost of reconciliation both to those who have suffered and those who have inflicted suffering.*

5. We call upon the churches to move beyond charity, grants and traditional programming to relevant and sacrificial action leading to new relationships of dignity and justice among all men and to become agents for the radical reconstruction of society. There can be no justice in our world *without a transfer of economic resources* to undergird the redistribution of political power and to make cultural self-determination meaningful. In this transfer of resources a corporate act by the ecumenical fellowship of churches can provide a significant moral lead.

C. Call to Member Churches for Self-Examination and Release of Resources

1. We call upon the churches to confess their involvement in the perpetuation of racism. Churches should make an analysis of their financial situation in order to determine the degree to which their financial practices, domestic and international, contribute to the support of racially oppressive governments, discriminatory industries and inhuman working conditions. The impact will be greater if this is an ecumenical act.

2. The forces seeking to liberate non-white peoples from the oppressive yoke of white racism have appropriately demanded the participation of religious institutions in restoring wealth and power to people. We urge churches to make land available free or at low cost to racially oppressed groups for community and economic development. Churches which have benefited from racially exploit-

ative economic systems should immediately allocate a significant portion of their total resources, without employing paternalistic mechanisms of control, to organizations of the racially oppressed or organizations supporting victims of racial injustice.[7]

After sections discussing the administrative implications of the programme the document moved on to the question of finance. A special fund was to be set up with $200,000 from WCC reserves:

This special fund to be distributed to organizations of oppressed racial groups or organizations supporting victims of racial injustice whose purposes are not inconsonant with the general purposes of the World Council...[8]

The Executive Committee was authorized to decide which organizations should receive the Special Fund grants, as advised by the International Advisory Committee.[9]

The Special Fund (Arnoldshaim 1970)

The way in which the Special Fund was to be distributed was discussed at a meeting of the Executive Committee of the WCC meeting at Arnoldshaim in West Germany in September 1970. The minutes make it clear that the Committee's concern was a redistribution of power.

There can be no justice in our world without a transfer of economic resources to undergird the redistributions of political power and to make cultural self-determination meaningful.[10]

This fund made headlines in the press, and people not otherwise interested in the doings of the WCC formed opinions about it, as if assuming that the WCC was the special fund and nothing else. The grant of $200,000 was to be distributed among nineteen named organizations. Southern African liberation movements received the most, and the rest was distributed among various groups in Asia, Latin America, Australia and the Caribbean. The principles and criteria of this distribution were those of the Canterbury meeting. They laid down that the grants were to be used for humanitarian purposes only, and that that they were intended to strengthen the organizational capacity of the oppressed. All these stem from the Notting Hill Consultation criteria.

There was a new departure here: whereas the church formerly relied upon charity in its giving, the PCR grants marked a new approach of solidarity with victims of racism. This posed a dilemma to the WCC. How could it avoid being identified with a partisan approach towards the liberation movements? In other words, how could the church, through the Special Fund of the WCC, help the people involved without being identified as taking sides?

Despite growing criticism, it became clear that for the churches to remain neutral would be interpreted as condoning the evil of racism. This was the overriding consideration, and on the basis of it the WCC felt compelled to support the grants rather than risk appearing to acquiesce in racism. The amount of money involved did not amount to a 'redistribution of power', but it was a powerful 'symbolic act' which stirred up much debate in the churches and, via the Press reports, among the general public. These debates were part of what might be termed 'a learning experience' or journey in awareness for many who have endeavoured to consider seriously the issues involved and the people that those issues press upon.

Addis Ababa 1971

In response to the furore of debate, the Central Committee of the WCC meeting at Addis Ababa in 1971 put forward a new resolution:

> The churches must always stand for the liberation of the oppressed and of victims of violent measures which deny basic human rights. [The Central Committee] calls attention to the fact that violence is in many cases inherent in the maintenance of the *status quo*. Nevertheless the WCC does not and cannot identify itself completely with any political movement, nor does it pass judgment on those victims of racism who are driven to violence as the only way left to them to redress grievances and so open the way for a new and more just order.[11]

The PCR staff then prepared a paper that gave some background material to the PCR's Special Fund, so that the Central Committee could determine whether to continue with it or not. The main outline of what the PCR staff recommended was:

1. The Fund made the WCC move beyond charity and involve itself – even if only symbolically – in redistribution of power.

2. The Fund acted as a leverage: several groups, organizations and governments had been influenced by the WCC to make grants to liberation movements.

3. The struggle against racial oppression had intensified and the need for humanitarian programmes had increased; the financial and moral support of the WCC could not now be withdrawn.

4. Discontinuation of the Fund would create the impression that the WCC no longer stood by the Canterbury decision to support directly the racially oppressed.

5. The grants had started the educational process among Christians about the churches' role in a world of racial oppression. This process was without precedent and had to be continued.

6. The grants had helped to start a process of growing confidence of oppressed people *vis-à-vis* the churches' commitment to justice.

7. Pledges and plans for future support of the Fund were encouraging.[12]

Since the Addis Ababa Central Committee was considering the reactions to the first allocations decided upon at Arnoldshaim, it decided that the debate about violence and non-violence was a major issue, especially as critics of PCR were accusing the WCC of condoning violence because the grants helped groups which were engaged in armed struggle. Thus they decided to set up a two-year study project to examine this issue, under the Church and Society Working Committee.

The two-year study of violence and non-violence

Introducing the study programme, the Church and Society Department pointed to the widespread call for clearer thinking about the kinds of action appropriate to Christian participation in social conflict and especially about the potentialities and problems of violence and non-violence. The two-year programme was aimed at:

(*a*) furthering the church's reflection on the ethical dilemmas posed by violence and non-violence in the struggle for justice and peace;

(*b*) contributing to the search for strategies of action which will minimize the sum-total of violence in conflict situations.[13]

This introduction went on to indicate that the question of violence and non-violence had occupied the modern ecumenical movement for a long time, going right back to Archbishop Soderblom and the Life and Work conferences of 1925 and 1937, so that the ecumenical movement could never be said to have ignored the problem of violence.

However, violence had been discussed almost exclusively in terms of international conflicts between sovereign states, and the dimensions of the problem indicated by the writings of Karl Marx and the Russian Revolution, namely the use of violence as an instrument for achieving greater social justice, had been neglected. Not until the Third Assembly of the World Council of Churches in New Delhi in 1961 had a step forward been taken, particularly in a focus on non-violence. This new focus issued in a statement on violence and non-violence at the 1966 Church and Society conference in Geneva:

> Violence is very much a reality in our world, both the overt use of force to oppress and the invisible violence perpetrated on people who by the millions have been or are still the victims of oppression and unjust social systems. Therefore the question emerges today whether violence which sheds blood in planned revolution may not be a lesser evil than the violence which, though bloodless, condemns whole populations to perennial despair. Christians who have, in fact, participated in revolutionary process which involve violence and defiance of law with an uneasy conscience look to the church for understanding and guidance. Other Christians resist such action with an uneasy conscience. Still others are complacent as long as 'law and order' prevail.
>
> It cannnot be said that the only possible position for the Christian is one of absolute non-violence. There are situations where Christians may become involved in violence. Whenever it is used, however, it must be seen as an ultimate recourse, which is justified only in extreme situations. The use of violence requires a rigorous definition of the needs for which it is used, and a clear recognition of the evils that are inherent in it, and it should always be tempered by mercy. It must also be recognized that there is no guarantee that the actual results of the use of violence will be those that were intended, nor that violence, once released, can be controlled by its initiators. However, there are certain basic ethical principles which must be related creatively to the specific situation in which a Christian finds himself, and the final decision must emerge from working out these two elements...[14]

However, the Fourth Assembly of the WCC at Uppsala was hesitant and reluctant in its response to the question of violence and non-violence: the drafts for sections prepared in advance of the assembly were more open to violence as a Christian option than the final reports. Section II observed that there were revolutions in various parts of the world and that in such areas some Christians would follow revolutionary action: the question whether the Christian community could support such action was just posed and left at that. Section III commented that even law and order might be violence of some kind, in that it might provoke violent response and resistance, and Section IV said: 'those who would condemn Christians who have borne the risk of shedding blood' must not forget 'the bloodshed of the *status quo*.'[15]

The Geneva study paper saw four options in working for the transfer of power:

1. The use of channels of power and influence available for change in the given structures of government, industry, technology, etc.
2. Non-violent strategies of pressures on the given structures.
3. The creation of new social structures to form alternatives to the present ones.
4. Strategies of violent struggle against existing structures.

It then set out further questions on these options and proposed that the two-year study should proceed with a focus on 'several specific conflict situations' – Southern Africa being the first listed.

After two years, the Church and Society Department reported back to the Central Comittee. It stated the need for repentance in churches which have supported unjust power and profited from the poverty of others, using force against those which differed from them in ideology. It then referred to the dilemma faced by millions of Christians as to whether to join in a violent movement to overthrow an unjust order or to remain passive and thereby responsible for continuing injustice. Christians cannot remain content:

...merely with binding up human wounds. The causes of suffering in the collective selfishness and unjust structures of society must also be attacked in the name of Christian love.[16]

It described the situation in South Africa:

...many Christians support a government representing a white minority that imposes its will upon a black majority by coercion, threats and frequently overt violence, to protect their privileged status because they are afraid of total loss and anarchy should the present power structure crumble. Other Christians seek to oppose and change the government policies in some respects, but face well-nigh complete frustration in their non-violence and legal efforts. In the same country many black Christians and even some whites find themselves pinning their hopes on or taking part in liberation movements which aim at the overthrow of present oppressive authority, as the way to justice and freedom. These movements, which in other countries in Southern Africa have liberated territory and set up *de facto* governments of their own, use many tactics ranging from education to military action.[17]

Amid some further discussion about Christian attitudes to power some important points were recognized: the goal of resistance to unjust power 'should not be the destruction of an enemy but a more just order within which different groups... agree to live in peace', and: 'no human institution or movement is without sin. Those who uphold the powers that be as well as those who attack them bear their various measures of guilt for the evils of society.'[18]

The report set forward three distinct points of view on violence and non-violence:

(*a*) Some believe that non-violent action is the only possibility consistent with obedience to Jesus Christ and object to success-criteria as theirs is 'witness to the transcendent power of God in Jesus Christ'.

(*b*) Some are prepared to accept the necessity of violent resistance as a Christian duty in extreme circumstances, but they would apply to it criteria similar to those governing a just war.

(*c*) Some find themselves already in situations of violence in which they cannot help but participate... the problem is to humanize the means of conflict and to build structures of peace wherever possible within it.[19]

However, it failed to reach agreement on the dilemma 'Violence or non-violence?' It referred to 'vast possibilities' of non-violent strategy which deserved WCC support but also asserted that non-violent action is highly political, may be extremely controversial, and is not necessarily bloodless:

Often violent and non-violent struggles are mixed together. A non-violent movement may produce peripheral violence... an armed struggle may also have non-violent dimensions such as education designed to persuade and win over the enemy.[20]

Equivocal though the study group was between violence and non-violence, it knew where it stood on apathy:

Certainly the fact that some Christians are acting violently for justice and peace whilst others are acting non-violently is a problem. But the greatest problem is that most of those who name Christ as Lord are not consciously acting on the matter at all.[21]

While the study programme was in progress and being published, there were a number of violent incidents in Southern Africa: in Portuguese Africa the assassination of Amilcar Cabral, the liberation leader of the Cape Verde islands (January 1973) and the slaughter of 180 people in Wiryamu (December 1972); in Namibia flogging, torture and arrests; in South Africa, the shooting of fourteen miners at Carletonville during a strike (September 1973).

Nonetheless there had been criticism of and opposition to the Special Fund grants, especially from the South African churches. Eleven representatives of the South African member churches went to Geneva in August 1973 for talks with the PCR. Some indication of the thinking of the South African churches can be deduced from the following motion put to the WCC General Assembly in Nairobi by Philip Russell, Anglican bishop in South Africa:

> We recommend that the churches do not support the Programme to Combat Racism and the Special Fund unless an assurance is given that no assistance will be given from the Special Fund to organizations that at the time of their application are such that their course of action is likely to cause the inflicting of serious injury or the taking of life.[22]

Various members argued against this motion, including the representative of the Reformed Church of the Netherlands, who had recently met with South African Reformed Church representatives. They had expressed these conclusions:

> 1. The humanitarian support from PCR should be continued unless it can be proved that this support has been used for the support of violent action.
> 2. If this support were to be withdrawn, it would be regarded in South Africa and elsewhere as a capitulation to the white DRC and an abandonment of the cause of the victims of racism.[23]

When Bishop Russell's motion was put to the vote, it was defeated: 62 were for, 22 abstained and 325 were against.

In 1976 there was an uprising in Soweto, primarily as a result of the state's insistence that Afrikaans (and not English) should be the medium of instruction at all black schools. This was resented by the black people, who saw Afrikaans as the language of the oppressor; use of the language would signify acceptance of the domination of whites over blacks. This uprising caused an exodus of young refugees to the frontline states. Other WCC agencies, via local councils of churches, were heavily involved in giving humanitarian aid and scholarships to these young South Africans. Some of these young people went on to join the military cadres of the ANC or PAC.

From about this time, there was also a small but significant trickle of white conscientious objectors into exile. The churches in South Africa began to take note of the issue of conscientious objection, and we shall consider this issue in more detail in due course.

International concern about the military plans of South Africa intensified when the news broke that South Africa had been planning to detonate a nuclear device in the Kalahari in July 1977. The facts about this are still unclear, mainly because Western countries were keen to continue their nuuclear collaboration with South Africca, which they insisted was purely commercial. However, more and more documentation about the South African military build-up and nuclear programme began to emerge, especially after the UN mandatory embargo on arms to South Africa, passed on 4 November 1977. I do not intend at this stage to go into the details of this debate, but it is important to bear it in mind when weighing up what was said in Western countries about the violence/non-violence debate.

Meanwhile a number of atrocities in the Zimbabwe war, especially in 1978, received sensational reporting. However, it is noticeable that the incidents in which whites were the victims were given more coverage in the Western press than the many incidents in which blacks were the victims. The biggest press coverage was given to the massacre of the eight British missionaries and four of their children by a guerrilla gang at the Elim Pentecostal mission in the Urumba mountains on the night of 23 June and to the shooting down of a Viscount by the Patriotic Front, followed by a massacre of the survivors. At about this time the PCR grant of £43,000 to the Patriotic Front from the WCC Special Fund was announced. It had in fact been decided upon after soundings late in 1977 and early in 1978, and was made to assist the Front in providing medical services and looking after the large number of refugees in Zambia and Mozambique. But the Western press saw it as a 'grant to guerrillas'. However, when the 1978 applications came up, the Patriotic

Front was not awarded a grant, although SWAPO, fighting in Namibia, got £62,500.

The matter of grants to guerrillas was still a hot issue at the Jamaica meeting of the WCC in January 1979. There had been a critical vote in the General Synod of the Church of England, and the Salvation Army and the Presbyterian Church in Ireland had suspended membership, while the Protestant Church of West Germany had expressed severe criticism of the SWAPO grants. However, the Central Committee endorsed the view of the Review Committee of the WCC that the administration of the Special Fund 'has so far been in accordance with the established and accepted criteria set by the Central Comittee'.[24]

The General Secretary in his report countered the criticism thus:

> ...the Fund supports movements in Southern Africa which are engaged in armed struggle with military and security forces of the racist regimes in the course of which innocent people, including children, are killed. Several churches and groups have raised the question of supporting violence which cannot be the action of the Church. It seems to be easier to tolerate the violent institutions and practices of the racist regimes, which claimed to be upholding Christian civilization and which are maintained by external economic investments and military support, than to understand the violent struggle of the oppressed who have been deprived of every non-violent means of travailing for their liberation, and have been forced as a last resort to take up arms. How are we to evaluate the relationship between violence of oppression and violence for liberation?[25]

Political bias

At Addis Ababa in 1971 the Central Committee of the WCC considered the reactions to the first PCR Special Fund grants and issued the following statement:

> The churches must always stand for the liberation of the oppressed and of victims of violent measures which deny basic human rights. It calls attention to the fact that violence is in many cases inherent in the maintenance of the *status quo*. Nevertheless, the WCC does not and cannot identify itself completely with any political movement, nor does it pass judgment on those victims of racism who are driven to violence as the only way left to them to redress grievances and so open the way for a new more just order.[26]

The criteria for the Special Fund grants laid down by the International Advisory Commission included that the grants were to be used for humanitarian purposes. One question raised in the debate, e.g. by the Swiss churches, was whether the church should help victims or political organizations. Some were uneasy about unmonitored grants. The WCC was trusting that the recipient organizations would use the grants for humanitarian purposes, not guns. An argument from the realists is that there is no difference, as aid for the humanitarian part of a budget would release an equivalent amount of funds within the organization for more weapons. Thus this debate is connected with the violence/non-violence debate. The worry about unmonitored grants may also be seen as part of the issue of solidarity: the WCC had chosen a method involving trust and solidarity which contrasted with the practice of other missions and development agencies giving aid in the same regions on more paternalistic terms and with careful monitoring.

The full text of the Criteria is:

1. The purpose of the organizations must not be in conflict with the general purposes of the WCC and its units, and the grants are to be used for humanitarian activities, i.e. social, health and educational, legal aid, etc.

2. The proceeds of the Fund shall be used to support organizations that combat racism rather than welfare organizations that alleviate the effects of racism and which would normally be eligible for support from other units of the WCC.

3. (*a*) The focus of the grants should be on raising the level of awareness and on strengthening the organization capability of the racially oppressed people.

(*b*) In addition we recognize the need to support organizations that align themselves with the victims of racial injustice and pursue the same objectives.

4. The grants are made without control of the manner in which they are spent, and are intended as an expression of commitment by PCR in the cause of economic, social and political justice, which these organizations promote.

5. (*a*) The situation in Southern Africa is recognized as a priority due to the overt and intensive nature of white racism and the increasing awareness on the part of the oppressed in their struggle for liberation.

(*b*) In the selection of other areas we have taken account of those places where the struggle is most intense and where a grant might make a substantial contribution to the process of liberation, particularly where racial groups are in imminent danger of being physically or culturally exterminated.

(c) In considering applications from organizations in countries of white and affluent majorities, we have taken note only of those where political involvement precludes help from other sources.

6. Grants should be made with due regard to where they can have the maximum effect: token grants should not be made unless there is a possibility of their eliciting a substantial response from other organizations.[27]

The underlying concern of some of the critics from Western churches is that the movements supported by PCR are Marxist-inspired and anti-Western. This concern surfaces when questions are asked suggesting that the prime concern of campaigns against injustice and oppression should focus on the Eastern bloc, against the repression there. 'Why pick on South Africa? What about Afghanistan?' In a Western European context this approach can be countered by the demonstration that the collaboration of the West with South Africa is far greater than that with Afghanistan, and that campaigns about South Africa therefore have greater potential effectiveness. But in a forum like the WCC which includes representatives of Eastern-bloc churches, the question would be more even-handed. One problem is that the focus of the question is wider than racism as such, as it is directed against many sorts of repression attributed to Communist regimes. I have not come across a version of the question in documents specifically related to the WCC which identifies issues of *racism* as such behind the Iron Curtain, such as the treatment of Soviet Jews.

The accusation of political bias on the part of PCR gained momentum in 1978 when the Smith regime in Rhodesia was trying to set up a moderate ANC government rather than the 'Marxist' government that might result if the Patriotic Front gained power. Critics, especially from Britain, did not think that one political party should be favoured by the PCR Special Grants over any other. In his report to the Jamaica Central Committee meeting in 1979, the General Secretary of the WCC countered the criticism thus:

In situations, as in Southern Africa, where groups representing oppressed people have opted for cooperating with the racist regimes for a so-called peaceful solution without touching the structures of racist oppression, it is considered a dubious political act for the

Council to support other groups of the racially oppressed which demand that all parties should seek a peaceful solution in terms of full participation of the whole people, both black and white, in their destiny and the immediate dismantling of the racist structure. By its actions the Council has risked taking sides in a difficult situation on the basis of an assessment of the existing situation in the light of the Council's clear stands.

... it must also be said that the debate has been mainly in certain Western countries which are most heavily involved in maintaining the racial systems in Southern Africa.[28]

This last point had already been noted elsewhere. Headquarters secretaries in the British churches and the British Council of Churches contrasted the response they got to comments and criticism relating to other areas of WCC activity with that which they got to PCR. In the former case discussion was easy and rational; in the latter the questioner or critic became identified with the oppressors in such a way that reasoned discussion became impossible. Which brings us back to the point I made right at the beginning of this book. Can there be a political theology without a political bias? In a contextual debate, is any questioner disinterested?

The investment debate

From the 1968 Uppsala Assembly onwards, the churches had been urged to withdraw investments from institutions that perpetuated racism. A directive from the Central Committee to WCC staff committees and member churches to analyse their involvement in racism as expressed in investment policies, employee training and promotion and the ownership and control of property and church-related institutions was concerned with the churches as property-owning and investing institutions. However, the churches were also urged to look at the wider political implications of this emphasis. They were to:

(*a*) Investigate and analyse the military, political, industrial and financial systems of their countries;

(*b*) Develop individually or in co-operation with other churches, strategies and action programmes to redirect these systems...[29]

After Addis Ababa in 1971, PCR decided to make the investment issue a priority topic. A symposium was held in February 1972 on the Cunene River scheme, a project which, dependent on overseas investment and skills, was strengthening white power in that part of Africa. This symposium recommended a campaign, through stockholder action, boycott and disinvestment, to get the companies and banks involved to withdraw from the scheme. Although the campaign never got going in full, it was a rehearsal for the larger campaign of disinvestment. In April 1972, PCR sponsored a consultation in Washington on the investments issue. The venue was chosen because the Protestant churches of America had already done much work in analysing the involvement of American firms in Southern Africa. PCR was in contact with the Corporate Information Centre of the NCC in the USA which had developed criteria for investment policies. This Washington meeting prepared for the Utrecht decisions of August 1972, when the following resolution was passed by the WCC Committee:

The World Council of Churches, in accordance with its own commitment to combat racism, considering that the effect of foreign investments in South Africa is to strengthen the white minority regimes in their oppression of the majority of the peoples of this region, and implementing the policy as commended by the Uppsala Assembly (1968) that investments in institutions that perpetuate racism should be terminated:

(i) *instructs* its Finance Committee and its Director of Finance: to sell forthwith existing holdings and to make no investment after this date in corporations which, according to information available to the Finance Committee and the Director of Finance, are directly involved in investment in or trade with any of the following countries: South Africa, Namibia, Zimbabwe, Angola, Mozambique and Guinea Bissao; and to deposit none of its funds in banks which direct banking operations in those countries.

(ii) *urges* all member churches, Christian agencies and individual Christians outside Southern Africa to use all their influence including stockholder action and disinvestment, to press corporations to withdraw investments from and cease trading with these countries.

In the context of the multiple strategies recommended at Addis Ababa the Central Committee is aware of and appreciates proposals to achieve racial justice in Southern Africa through reform (e.g. the preliminary statement by the Council of the Evangelical Church in Germany). The Central Committee is nevertheless convinced that the policy of withdrawal already commended by the Uppsala Assembly needs to be implemented now.[30]

In response to enquiries received by the WCC following this resolution, PCR prepared the booklet *Time to Withdraw*, which sets out the policy alternatives:

The Argument for Increased Involvement

To promote increased investment and accelerated infusions of technological expertise, in the belief that the economic growth thus stimulated will inevitably alter the economic conditions and social structure, and ultimately lead to the involvement of blacks (Africans, Coloured and Indian South Africans) in the political process.

The Argument for Reform

To press business interest to raise black wages, offer training and better promotion opportunities for black workers and plough back a portion of their profits into educational and other benefits for the black community.

The Argument for Withdrawal

(defined as termination of investment links by corporations)

To stop providing direct economic and material support to the white minority regime and advocate the withdrawal of investment and the severing of economic links as the consistent moral alternative which at the same time offers solid support to Southern Africans committed to winning their freedom.[31]

These alternatives were then analysed in the light of data about the South African economy. After analysis had shown that the first two approaches did not necessarily lead to significant improvement for the majority of people in South Africa, the pamphlet concluded:

If indeed investment in South Africa assists in maintaining the overall system of white control then the only legitimate demand possible by those wishing to challenge that control is that the companies withdraw from South Africa.[32]

It was also pointed out that for more than a decade African voices of resistance had called for the economic isolation of that country until its racial policies had changed and that this campaign was an expression of solidarity with oppressed people.

In 1973 the WCC Finance Sub-committee meeting in Bangalore

realized that the Utrecht resolutions were too vague for implementation. For example, 'direct banking operations' had been taken to mean banks with branches in South Africa, like Barclays. But it was realized in 1973 that the banks were providing, through international lending operations, considerable direct support to the South African government. The Interfaith Center for Corporate Responsibility (ICCR) in the USA got hold of information about a large (£90m) loan by the Europe-America Banking Corporation (EABC) to the South African government and its agencies. Until the ICCR had published the fact, the loan had been secret. The Bangalore meeting asked WCC staff to undertake further study of the banks and Southern Africa.

The WCC commissioned Counter Information Services of London for this study, and the results were published in 1974 under the title *Business as Usual: International Banking in South Africa*. In May 1974, PCR passed the following resolutions:

(i) The PCR Commission requests its staff to present to the Central Committee in August 1974 a short list of certain banks involved in Southern Africa, highlighting their role in strengthening the racist regimes. Particular attention is to be drawn to the part they play in the provision of loans and banking operations, the undergirding of internal arms industries and trade in weapons, the encouragement of white migration and tourism.

(ii) The WCC should instruct its Finance Department not to bank with any of the banks listed in (i) above.

(iii) The PCR should also publicize the role of the whole international banking system with regard to Southern Africa. In this context, PCR should draw attention to ongoing national and international campaigns related to specific banks and encourage churches to support and participate in them.[33]

Correspondence with the banks listed in the Berlin resolutions continued. In the Netherlands, the AMRO Bank and ABN were the targets of campaigns by Pre-Paid Reply and other anti-apartheid groups. The political parties of the opposition also got involved. Eventually AMRO became the first of the listed banks to concede to anti-apartheid campaigns, and state that it had decided to stop granting loans to the South African Government. ABN became the second Dutch bank to write to the WCC that it had also decided to stop such loans. In 1977, PCR published the material about the bank loans campaign, including the letters exchanged with the banks, AMRO in particular.

In August 1974, the Central Committee, meeting in West Berlin, resolved to seek assurances from the Europe-America Banking Corporation that they would stop granting loans to the South African Government and urged all member churches, Christian agencies and individual Christians to use all their influence to press those banks on its list and other banks participating in the loans to cease lending to the South African government and its agencies.

The Fifth Assembly of the WCC at Nairobi reaffirmed this economic campaign by PCR:

> South Africa, which highlights racism in its blatant form, must retain high priority for the attention of the member churches. Apartheid is possible only with the support of a large number of Christians there. We urge member churches to identify with and wherever possible initiate activity and campaigns to halt arms traffic; to work for the withdrawal of investments and the ending of bank loans; to stop white migration. These issues have already been urged by the WCC and we recommend them for urgent action by the member churches. Their implementation would be an effective non-violent contribution to the struggle against racism.[34]

The point was further pressed home at the Central Committee meeting in Jamaica the next year.

The next major relevant WCC event was the 1980 Consultation in the Netherlands which had a working party on the Economic Basis of Racism. Amid statements of wider focus is the following one on PCR and South Africa:

> PCR should continue to focus specifically on isolating South Africa economically. It should also continue its work on disinvestment of banks and corporations from South Africa. The debate stimulated by this work has highlighted the nature of the corporate ethos of business corporations and brought out into the open the need for corporate accountability. It has also brought home to Christians the implications of their commercial involvement, and thus it has been of great educational benefit to the churches.
>
> We therefore further *recommend* that other specific strategies with regard to the economic isolation of South Africa might include:
>
> 1. The development of new means for gaining information on the operations of banks and corporations in South Africa;
>
> 2. That other vulnerable areas in these economic relationships be

identified such as the transportation of oil to South Africa, export guarantees by governments, and boycott of South African Airways by non-African states.[35]

It should be realized that the declarations of the WCC during the 1970s were the public expression of a good deal of detailed monitoring that was being carried out both by church-related organizations and by other bodies. The UN had called for mandatory sanctions in 1968, and the UN Centre against Apartheid has been a continuous source of detailed monitoring documents. Student activists have sustained the demonstrations against banks like Barclays. A small group of committed individuals have gone yearly to shareholders meetings of some companies to make an anti-apartheid protest. Throughout the 1970s, these groups, and the WCC, were clarifying what was involved in the disinvestment campaign and learning how to answer the excuses of those sceptical about it. For example, a recent leaflet from Christian Concern for Southern Africa (CCSA) advises that while institutional investors with less than £25m in the offending companies should pull out, those with larger shares should attempt disengagement, i.e. persuading the company to pull out of South Africa, but they should publish these negotiations so that there could be no doubt about their aims. The same leaflet also argues against the Church Commissioners' plea of the need for a balanced portfolio by laying out some clear criteria, to do with the size of each company's South African operation, and the type of activity they are involved in, with strategic operations regarded as the most urgent to pull out of.

1986 showed some results from the labours of the economic pressure groups. Sanctions against South Africa were put on the political agenda in such a way that even the governments most opposed, such as those of Britain and the United States, were forced to consider them. In the United States, mainly because of the growing strength of the black caucus, it looked as if stronger sanctions measures would have to be implemented, which would leave the British government isolated in its opposition to sanctions. However, regardless of what sanctions were likely to be legislated into being, some firms were already making the decision to pull out. The announcement by Barclays Bank to this effect was hailed as a major triumph. So the WCC pronouncements of the 1970s were being translated into significant action.

Communication

When the first grants by PCR were announced in the press in 1970, many newspapers made much of the fact that the money was going to organizations engaged in armed conflict. The first news many church people had of the grants was through these headlines in the secular press. Criticism was voiced that the original announcement of the grants was deliberately provocative and widespread publicity for quite a small part of the programme, and it was suggested that even members of the Canterbury meeting which approved PCR did not get the impression that violent revolutionary organizations were the original focus of that meeting.

Was something wrong, then, with PCR's methods of communication, both internal and external?

An examination made in 1974 suggested that systems of disseminating information could be improved within the WCC and that PCR had not been given an adequate theological background; the issues were fully debated that year at the Central Committee meeting in West Berlin. Communication continued to be a major cause for concern in WCC circles, and this is evident from the various WCC/PCR documents of the 1970s.

When the Vorster government was compelled to admit that it had for years been spending millions in undermining opposition newspapers commercially, buying favourable reports from Western journalists and engaging in other 'dirty tricks' (the so-called Muldergate scandal, named after the then South African Minister of the Interior and Information, Dr Connie Mulder), among the details that emerged was a counter-information campaign against the WCC. This produced even greater concern about the public image of PCR, and the following statement was issued by the Central Committee meeting in Jamaica in 1970:

> There was unanimous agreement that well-financed propaganda agencies in the media, hostile to PCR and the WCC in general, were distorting the member churches' understanding of PCR's work. Mention was made in particular of the recent scandal in South Africa which exposed the clandestine efforts of the South African government to influence news agencies in the Western world.
>
> We were concerned that member churches should be helped to question the sources of information about PCR's activities and to examine press reports with critical judgment; for example, information issued by racist government agencies or censored by them, as well as

by private organizations and published in the religious and secular press. Attention should be given to terminology such as 'execution', 'assassination', 'guerrilla', 'terrorist', etc. Also, in our own dissemination of information, the very diverse activities of PCR which are not limited to Southern Africa or the Special Fund should be given greater prominence.

We were also of the view that although the adverse image and understanding of PCR nees to be changed, the purpose and thrust of PCR itself are still valid. We are hopeful that with member churches alerted to the areas of distortion and misrepresentation, even greater support for PCR and the Special Fund would be forthcoming.[36]

The General Secretary in his report also made a point of the information gap:

... the manner in which the fund has been administered has been a matter of concern. Requests are processed through the PCR Commission, decisions are made by the WCC Executive Committee, whose meetings are not public, and the grants are announced through the public media with brief descriptions. It is assumed that the various background documents and pamphlets which have been published from time to time will have been read and will explain the actions of the Council. The experience of the last grant to the Patriotic Front of Zimbabwe has shown that it cannot be assumed that the religious and secular media will provide the necessary background to the grants or even that church leaders will be sufficiently informed about it. In a highly complex and confused situation as in Southern Africa, the action of the Council has not been readily understood. An information and communication gap exists here which must be squarely faced.[37]

Regional consultations preparing for the 1980 Consultation on Racism also called for more information – and for more theology. The African Consultation held in Nairobi in April of that year asked:

1. To establish an effective communication network within the African continent to support the fight against racism. Special attention should be given to material in the French and Portuguese languages, as well as effective interpersonal contact throughout the continent.

2. To support programmes for a contextual theology, and to engage in reorientation, reflection and retraining in the church on a regional, national and local level.[38]

Once again we see requests for more information and more theology coming together, as with the European critics of Arnoldshaim.

By this time, Africa was becoming increasingly aware of the need for a New International Information Order (NIIO), and there were gatherings of African secular journalists disussing the problems of the African media. The main themes of this discussion were the control and ownership of the media (public or private?) and the reliance on news items from the Western-dominated news agencies. The Tunisia 1978 Conference on NIIO declared:

> Developing peoples (are) victims of domination by the news media, which transgress their most deeply felt cultural values, systematically distort their way of life, restrict their freedom of action and in the end subject their interests to those of imperialism.[39]

Also in 1978, a UNESCO meeting in Paris on NIIO produced a declaration entitled:

> Declaration of fundamental Principles concerning the Contribution of the Mass Media to Strengthening Peace and International Understanding, to the Promotion of Human Rights and to Countering Racialism, Apartheid and Incitement to War.[40]

The assumption here is that the press should not be neutral about racism, but should be anti-apartheid and anti-racist.

The problem of distortion of African news goes both ways. Not only is the inflow of news – even news about other African countries – distorted by going via the Western agencies, but also news coming out of Africa is forced to fit Western categories, as Tom Mboya once pointed out:

> The news coming out of Africa is often, if not always, related to the already biassed and prejudiced mind that keeps asking such questions as: 'Is this pro-East or pro-West?' Very few, if any, of the world's press ask such logical, in our view simple, question as 'Is this pro-African?'[41]

4

PCR and the Churches in South Africa

So far we have been looking at the effects of PCR on the world scene. It is now time to turn specifically to its effect in South Africa. As we do so, it will be important to have at the back of our minds the broad spread and diversity of the church there, in terms of denominations and the colour classification of apartheid society. Several things should be remembered here:

1. Church membership statistics are difficult to obtain and denominational figures are unhelpful in any comparative table because churches vary in their understanding of membership. The figures opposite are therefore based on the 1970 government census.

2. Many churches no longer divide their membership into racial categories.

3. Census figures are usually inflated by about one-third actual membership and one-half active participation.

4. The Gereformeerde Kerk is divided into separate white and African synods with one umbrella General Synod. The Lutherans are divided into several different churches, one of which is mainly white. The Presbyterians are divided into three main churches, two black and one multi-racial, predominantly white. African Independent is a category covering more than 3000 different groups.

5. The Nederduitsch Hervormde Kerk split from the Cape church at the time of the Trek and became the church of the Transvaal trekkers' Republic. It then split again six years later, when the Gereformeerde Kerk was formed. The missionary efforts of the DRC/NGK produced the Sendingkerk, for Coloured members, the NGK in Afrika for blacks and the Reformed Church in Africa for Asians. The term Dutch Reformed Church usually refers to this whole group.

Church membership[1]

	African	Asian	Coloured	White	Total
Anglican	940,000	6,000	330,000	400,000	1,676,000
Baptist	170,000	2,900	19,000	47,000	247,000
Congregational	185,000		150,000	20,000	355,000
DRC/NGK				1,500,000	1,500,000
NGK in Afrika	900,000				900,000
NG Sendingkerk			500,000		500,000
Reformed Church in Africa		1,000			1,000
Gereformeerde	25,000	800	3,900	120,000	149,700
Lutheran	750,000	360	83,000	40,000	873,360
Methodist	1,500,000	2,500	115,000	360,000	1,977,000
Moravian				100,000	100,000
Nederduitsch Hervormde	25,000		1,600		26,600
Presbyterian	330,000	300	7,500	120,000	457,800
Roman Catholic	1,330,000	1,400	200,000	305,000	1,836,400
African Independent	3,500,000				3,500,000

The racial composition of a particular denomination should be remembered in looking at its response or lack of response to PCR. Because I have focussed this study on PCR I have not referred to the Roman Catholic Church, simply because it is not a member of the WCC. Of course that does not mean that the Roman Catholic Church has not made any pronouncements on racism in South Africa: on the contrary. However, the story of that must be told elsewhere.

In discussing the responses of South African churches to PCR I shall divide them into two groups: the Afrikaner churches (i.e. NGK/Dutch Reformed, Gereformeerde and Nederlandse Hervormde) and the mission churches, including all the churches which originated in European mission efforts.

The Afrikaner churches

These churches are in fact Calvinist in origin, and the mutation of the original Calvinist ideals into the political programme of the present Nationalist Party of South Africa makes a fascinating story which has been told in another book.[2] For our purposes it must be enough to go back to 1936, when Dr N.Diederichs, at that time a professor of political philosophy in the Free State, wrote a thesis on Nationalism which reversed the Calvinist emphasis on individual rights. He argued:

Nationalism rejects this concept of freedom... on the grounds of its doctrine that the individual in itself is nothing, but only becomes itself in the nation as the highest (human) community.[3]

The theological grounding of Afrikaner political thinking is evident in his assertion:

The highest, ideal order, that nation-transcending territory where nations meet each other in a complementary way, cannot be seen in other than a religious light. In religion every human life, every nation, discovers its grounding and meaning. Without a religious point of relationship and an ultimate object, the universe, the nation and the individual would be incomprehensible, senseless and purposeless... On every particular nation especially there rests this special task to accept its providential role as a nation, and by realizing it to play its part in the ultimate attainment of the godly purpose of the universe.[4]

This type of Afrikaner political theology must not be forgotten when considering the action the South African government has taken against 'political' clergymen. This is not a struggle of spiritual Christians against worldly Christians or Bible disciples against a social gospel: both sides invoke theology and Bible texts to justify their actions.

Within the Afrikaner churches, the objections to apartheid started in the 1960s, several years before the WCC concern of 1968 or PCR as such. The Dutch Reformed church was at that time a member of the WCC, but the Anglican Archbishop Joost de Blank wrote to Dr W. A. Visser't Hooft:

The future of Christianity in this country demands our complete dissociation from the Dutch Reformed attitude... either they must be expelled or we shall be compelled to withdraw.[5]

The WCC then offered to sponsor a consultation at Cottesloe in Johannesburg in December 1960. However,

Although the Consultation was ecumenical and multi-racial, it was essentially a white affair – at its core, a group of anguished white clerics setting out to listen to each other and to pay polite attention to the small minority of their black colleagues.[6]

Not surprisingly, these white clerics were still attached to ideas of Christian paternalism, or 'trusteeship', as they called it. The point that the black representatives were able to contribute was that unsatisfactory social conditions, not 'agitators', were the cause of current unrest. In addition, although Bantu were generally law-abiding, 'they did not feel bound by laws which they have no hand in making' – a point important in the trials of Sobukwe and Mandela.

The significance of Cottesloe is that it is the last time that the Afrikaner churches and the mission churches met to consider their Christian vocation in South Africa and were able to *agree* – sufficiently, at least, to issue an agreed statement. As the churches involved were not of the pietist tradition, they were able to agree that the church was to 'make known the Lordship of Christ in every realm of national, social and personal life', so there was no withdrawing from politics into a sacred zone of purely ecclesiastical or mission affairs.

They boldly tackled the racial problem with the statement:

> It is our conviction that the right to own land wherever he is domiciled and to participate in the government of his country is part of the dignity of the adult man, and for this reason a policy which permanently denies to the *economically integrated* non-white people the right of collaboration in the government of the country of which they are the citizens cannot be justified.[7]

It was a fragile unanimity which was splitting apart even before the final drafts were drawn up. The underlined words, vital to the DRC understanding of the statement, were omitted from the published version. The DRC spokesmen, who were collaborating in the formation of National Party policies, had slipped in the phrase 'economically integrated' because this would then exclude migrant labourers, and ultimately, as they envisaged with the Bantustan policy, all non-whites, from the polity they were creating. To the apartheid legislators, most non-whites were not economically integrated: even if they toiled in the white areas for most of their working days, they 'belonged' to a homeland, even if the connection had to be traced back via a grandparent's birthplace. Once the DRC churches saw that the vital phrase 'economically integrated' was not in the final version, the DRC churches reacted against the anti-apartheid tenor of the documents. Their synods rejected the Cottesloe statements. They withdrew from the WCC. The church authorities moved against the two main proponents of the Cottesloe statements who came from the DRC, namely Professor Geyser and Beyers Naude.

There was much sensational publicity about these two: first Geyser had to seek justice in the Supreme Court over his ecclesiastical standing in the Hervormde Kerk. Beyers Naude, who had been profoundly influenced by the ecumenical fellowship he had found in the planning stages of Cottesloe, tried for two years both to work for a reassessment of apartheid doctrine within Afrikanerdom and to work ecumenically for race relations. It was impossible to keep a foot in both camps, and in 1963 he publicly resigned from the key Afrikaner organization and secret society, the Broederbond, and admitted that he was responsible for betraying Broederbond secrets at the time of Geyer's trial. This was a scandal of betrayal in the views of many Afrikaners. Geyser and Beyers Naude became the two leading founders of the Christian Institute in August 1963, but by this time the number of DRC clergy willing to support Naude publicly had dwindled to less than a dozen. It is scarcely surprising that when he sought permission from NGK authorities to take up the post of Director of the Christian Institute he was told that he would have to choose between that and the NGK ministry. He chose the Christian Institute.

As he left the ministry of his church he pleaded from the pulpit:

> O my church, I call this morning in all sincerity from my soul – awake before it is too late. Stand up and give the hand of Christian brotherhood to all who sincerely stretch out the hand to you. There is still time, but the time is short, very short.[8]

From henceforth Naude found it increasingly difficult to worship with NGK congregations. Finally, he ended up worshipping on Sunday with a small black congregation. The NGK had successfully insulated itself from anti-apartheid criticism coming prophetically from within its own Calvinist tradition.

For the rest of the 1960s, the Christian Institute continued to be the voice of conscience to the churches. Its membership and activity were still mainly directed towards the white congregations, and those of the mission churches rather than the Afrikaner churches.

The mission churches

The protest of the mission churches against the Nationalist Government programme of apartheid was heard from the 1950s onwards. But it is important to realize that the hierarchy of these churches was all white, and the synods were dominated by whites. For instance, a major priority for those of us who were theological students in the 1960s was to attempt to get black caucuses going at major church conferences and synods.

We had to debate through a structure set up by white missionaries and still largely dominated by them. Although some blacks achieved high positions in the 1960s, notably Seth Mokitimi in the Methodist church and Alphaeus Zulu as a bishop in the Anglican church, the synod pronouncements of the mission churches at this time cannot be assumed to represent the views of the black members of those churches. The whites had the stronger voices in the debates, and they did the final draft wording and publicity.

Trevor Huddleston, who felt the force of the church hierarchy during his own outspoken stand against apartheid, wrote revealingly:

> It is but rarely in history that the hierarchy takes prophetic initiative against evil. Perhaps because its chief function is to guard the truth rather than proclaim it.[9]

In short, one expects to find caution, not prophetic courage, in the pronouncements of the mission churches.

The Christian Institute, however, was prophetic, and attached to it were some of the most radical members of the mission churches. As social issues were the main task, denominational allegiances were irrelevant. Following the Geneva Church and Society Conference of 1966, the two South Africans present at that conference, Beyers Naude and Bill Burnett (later Archbishop of Cape Town), worked through the Christian Institute and the South African Council of Churches (SACC) to sponsor a National Consultation on Church and Society in 1968. However, the findings of the gathering, that Christians should work for change through the existing structures, were, to say the least, hopelessly out of date. The existing structures were the very thing that the blacks were opposed to.

The next important initiative by SACC and the Christian Institute was the 'Message to the People of South Africa'. It is a document in which many vital issues were set forth with brevity and clarity. It gives the theological basis for the Christian struggle against apartheid. Here is an extract from it, indicating its main thrust:

> (i) ...The Gospel of Jesus Christ declares that God is the master of this world, and that it is to him alone that we owe our primary commitment.
>
> (ii)...The Gospel of Jesus declares that the Kingdom of God is already present in Christ, demanding our obedience and our faith now.

(iii)...The Gospel of Jesus Christ offers hope and security to the whole man, not just in man's spiritual and ecclesiastical relationships, but for human existence in its entirety. Consequently, we are called upon to minister to the meaning of the Gospel in the particular circumstances of the time and place in which we find ourselves. In South Africa, at this time, we find ourselves in a situation where a policy of separation is being deliberately effected with increasing rigidity. The doctrine of racial separation is being seen by many not merely as a temporary political policy but as a necessary and permanent expression of the will of God, and as the genuine form of Christian obedience for this country. It is holding out to men's security built not on Christ, but on the theory of separation and the preservation of racial identity; it is presenting the separate development of race groups as the way for the people of South Africa to save themselves. And this claim is being made in the name of Christianity.

(iv) We believe that this doctrine of separation is a false faith, a novel Gospel. It inevitably is in conflict with the Gospel of Jesus Christ, which offers salvation, both individual and social, through faith in Christ alone. It is keeping away from the real knowledge of Christ; therefore it is the church's duty to enable our people to distinguish between the demands of the South African State and the demands of discipleship.

(v) The Christian Gospel requires us to assert the truth proclaimed by the first Christians who discovered that God was creating a new community in which differences of race, language, nation, culture and tradition no longer had the power to separate man from man. The most important features of a man are not the details of his racial group, but the nature he has in common with all men and also the gifts and abilities which are given to him as a unique individual by the grace of God; to insist that the racial characteristics are more important than these is to reject what is most significant about our humanity as well as the humanity of others...[10]

Six hundred clergy signed the message, and it was endorsed by the member churches of the SACC with the exception of the Baptists. It put the issues squarely before white Christians in South Africa, but its impact was only felt among a small minority of activists.

Meanwhile, the Notting Hill conference in London and the Canterbury meeting were expressing support for militancy against apartheid. The SACC responded to the Notting Hill proposals. Whilst not defending apartheid, the SACC lamented the means proposed for combatting racism, but significantly added:

> Our social order in South Africa is already to a considerable extent based on violence... The conclusion reached by the WCC consultation on racism in London, that force may be resorted to by Christians in order to dislodge entrenched injustice, has been reached, at least in part, on account of the failure of the churches.[11]

But the churches, through the SACC, registered their unease at the way in which the section 6 of the WCC Uppsala report urges 'the use of means usually associated with the civil power in the struggle against racism'. The appeal of the SACC was presented to the WCC Central Committee personally by Bill Burnett, but it made no difference. The decision to set up PCR was made.

Dr Carson Blake, the General Secretary of the WCC, visited South Africa in early September 1970. He met with the leaders of the member churches of the SACC and even had cordial discussions with the estranged Dutch Reformed churches. Indeed he was invited to return for further discussions. However, within a week relationships changed drastically following the announcement of the Arnoldshain grants.

The reactions from South Africa were furious. The Afrikaans churches denounced the grants and confirmed their rejection of the WCC. The English-speaking churches joined in the denunciations but refused to withdraw from the WCC. Referring to this refusal, Mr Vorster told the National Assembly:

> I would be neglecting my duty as head of government if I did not take action against them, if I allowed churches which are members of the WCC, and wished to remain members, to send representatives to conferences of that body, and if I failed to take action... against clergymen who allow pamphlets (explaining the action behind the grants) to be distributed at their churches on Sunday...[12]

The churches faced not only the Prime Minister's bellicosity but also opposition from within their own membership to the WCC grants, which were seen as legitimizing organizations seeking to topple the South African government. As a result, those churches which still remained members of the WCC were seen as anti-South African, identified with violence and revolution. Withdrawal from the WCC was demanded by 'patriotic members'. And in this mood the annual synods of the mission churches met.

The Presbyterian church, the first to meet, gave a courageous reply:

(the Church's) only Lord and master is Jesus Christ, and it may not serve two masters. Its task is not necessarily to support the politics of the government in power, but to be faithful to the Gospel of its Lord and to seek justice for the afflicted and liberty for those who are oppressed.[13]

The other churches followed suit, with the result that:

1. All decided to retain their membership of the WCC.
2. All criticized the WCC for its implicit support of violence in making grants to the liberation movements.
3. All strongly criticized racism in South Africa.
4. All desired further consultation with the WCC.
5. Most decided not to send funds to the WCC as a sign of protest.[14]

These decisions relating to the WCC might by themselves have assumed a different tone had the churches been able to reach them independently of the South African government's strong reaction. But as it was they were the actions of a frightened church – fleeing the impending wrath of the government. As an indication of the government's sternness on this point, it was then made illegal to send any funds to the WCC. The government also set out stringent conditions under which any future visits by WCC representatives to South Africa might be made. Thus when the member churches followed up the decisions of their synods by trying to arrange a consultation with the WCC about the theology behind the PCR grants, they had to request government permission. Unfortunately the leaders who were delegated to see Mr Vorster described the intended consultation as a confrontation, between the South African churches and the WCC. This term was seized upon by Mr Vorster and the press. The Prime Minister is reported to have said that the government was:

...not prepared to allow the visiting delegates to go further than the International Hotel at Jan Smuts Airport and to stay longer than the actual duration of the confrontation.[15]

This uncompromising reaction by Mr Vorster blocked the possibility of any further fruitful consultation between the member churches and the WCC for the time being.

The determination on the part of all the churches to remain members of the WCC was a courageous step which asserted their independence from the secular power of the day. However, the Pretoria government was not displeased with their criticism of the apparent support to racism in PCR and by the decisions not to send funds to the WCC. After all, verbal protests were nothing new, and any consultations with the WCC could easily be controlled by the government. This was the period when visa and passport control on important individuals came to be increasingly used, the main example being the withholding of Bishop Tutu's passport when later he became a link person with the WCC. The decision by the churches to withhold funds was playing into the hand of the government, which then moved to make it illegal to transfer funds, a technique later developed into the definition of an 'affected organization', not allowed to receive foreign funds either. It is this sense of ubiquitous government blocking mechanisms at any significant move to bring about worthwhile debate that inevitably engenders frustration and anger amongst black people.

The South African government also took action against anti-apartheid clergymen. Adrian Hastings comments:

> The leadership in some churches, notably the Presbyterian and Anglican, came out in mutual condemnation of the grants, so reinforcing the basic sense of where they finally stood, while the more radical clergy, who, like almost all Africans, found themselves unable to do this, could not rather easily be proceeded against as crypto-Marxists threatening the security of the country.[16]

The government moved to take action against 'political' clergymen, without evoking much worthwhile protest from the South African leadership of the churches. Two mission priests were deported. Cosmos Desmond, who had written a book about the resettlement camps, was banned. The Dean of Johannesburg, Gonville ffrench-Beytagh, was arrested and put on trial in 1971 in connection with the humanitarian funds he dispensed to the families of political prisoners. Thus the South African government moved against the most outspoken individuals from the mission churches in the same way in which it had coped with the earlier crisis in the DRC churches in the 1960s: by the method of extrusion and isolation it cut off the prophets from their respective churches by various procedures such as banning, deportation or arrest, and also tried to cut the churches off from the oikoumene, the world-wide fellowship of churches that supported them both morally and financially. It was a method almost totally successful in the case of the Afrikaner churches after Cottesloe, but it has not so far totally succeeded as applied to the mission churches, who have up to now tenaciously maintained their links with the oikoumene.

Meanwhile, as a result of the 'Message to the People of South Africa', and even before the furore about the Arnoldshaim grants began, the Study Project on Christianity in Apartheid Society (SPROCAS) had been launched. Although there were a few token blacks on the commissions, it was mainly a white dominated affair.

> Strongly inclined towards a liberal cast of mind, seeing capitalist organizations as essentially progressive forces capable of incremental reforms, and with a strong faith in education, the great majority of commissioners had little understanding of... a process of change in which the poor were given power.[17]

The comment of Steve Biko in connection with SPROCAS reveals that in the black viewpoint, too, the parameters of the SPROCAS mandate were basically too conservative:

> Between these extremes, they (liberals) claim that there lies the land of milk and honey for which we are working. The thesis, the antithesis and the synthesis have been mentioned by some great philosophers as the cardinal points around which social revolution revolves. For the liberals the thesis is apartheid, the antithesis is non-racialism, but the synthesis is very feebly defined. They want to tell the blacks that they want integration as an ideal solution. Black consciousness defines the situation differently. The thesis is in fact a strong white racism and therefore the antithesis to this must, *ipso facto*, be a strong solidarity amongst the blacks amongst whom this white racism seeks to prey. Out of these two situations we can therefore hope to reach some kind of balance – a true humanity, where power politics will have no place. This analysis spells out the difference between the old and new approaches. The failure of the liberals is in fact that their antithesis is already a watered-down version of the truth whose close proximity to the thesis will nullify the purported balance. This accounts for the failure of the SPROCAS commissions to make any headway, for they are already looking for an 'alternative' acceptable to the white man. Everybody in the commissions knows what is right but all are looking for an 'alternative' acceptable to the white man. Everybody in the commissions knows what is right, but all are looking for the most seemly way of dodging the responsibility of saying what is right.[18]

Although SPROCAS had no political effect on South Africa at large, it did, however, stimulate some experiments in the churches. For instance, the church commission had criticized the churches for failing to promote inter-racial dialogue. I was working in the Diocese of Natal when a twinning programme aimed at promoting this inter-racial contact between congregations was initiated as a Lent exercise. But there were problems. The hospitality was mainly from the white side, and except for a few determined individuals, it petered out, frustrated by practical obstacles such as the long routes round to the townships, and the lack of telephones to make the arrangements or change them. Return hospitality by the blacks was almost impossible, especially as the township houses are small, and moving around unfamiliar streets after dark could be a problem. In this way a brave experiment was defeated by the social barriers inherent in South African society. However, other changes adumbrated in the church commission, such as improved salary scales for black clergy, began to be implemented. There was increased promotion of some blacks into positions of importance to express the multi-racial church, for instance the appointment of Desmond Tutu to be Dean of the cathedral in Johannesburg. I do not want to suggest that SPROCAS caused these changes, but it reflected upon changes that were already beginning to take place in the mission churches.

Meanwhile, individual white Christians and groups with a social conscience were continuing with protest against the social and economic evils of apartheid. In particular, David Russell and others made a well publicized protest against the resettlement camps. There was protest against migratory labour, articulated especially by Francis Wilson, a labour economist, who led a pilgrimage to Cape Town to draw attention to this aspect of apartheid. There were various initiatives in adult education for blacks, by the South African Council for Higher Education (SACHED) and Turret, the section in it which offers correspondence courses. But admirable and courageous though these efforts were, they have to be put in the tradition of white paternalism, of whites doing things for blacks. Black consciousness had some grave reservations about such white initiatives:

Instead of involving themselves in an all-out attempt to stamp out racism from their white society, liberals waste lots of time trying to prove to as many blacks as they can find that they are liberal. This arises out of a belief that we are faced with a black problem... The problem is white racism and it rests squarely on the legs of the white society. The sooner liberals realize this, the better for blacks. Their presence amongst us is irksome and of nuisance value. It removes the focus of attention from essentials and shifts it to ill-defined philosophical concepts that are both irrelevant to the black man and merely a red herring across the track. White liberal must leave the blacks to take care of their own business while they concern themselves with the real evil in our society... white racism.[19]

The White Community Programme tried to tackle precisely this problem, targeting on the liberal establishments such as the churches, opposition political parties, the business community, white trade unions and youth organizations. The SPROCAS 2 (Special Project for Christian Action in Society) labour programme tried to inculcate awareness of employment practices by sending out some questionnaires to all such organizations. The responses from within the white dominated churches indicated that as employing institutions, with servants and labourers, they followed the norms of apartheid society.

Meanwhile, as well as SPROCAS, there was another initiative at the SACC, which decided in 1971 to set up the Committee and Divison of Justice and Reconciliation, originally on a three-year basis. The account of this in papers from the SACC states:

Leading representatives of the SACC repeatedly interpreted the WCC resolution of 1970 a a challenge to the South African churches to become active in the areas of social justice in South African society. Their statements received consideration in the SACC member churches and stimulated thought on what could be done. A variety of programmes were started in the different churches and committees on racial justice were set up. In this context a request of the Methodist Church of South Africa was considered by a consultation of church leaders in the setting of an ecumenical Committee on Justice and Reconciliation.[20]

The first paragraph of the mandate given to this new division reads:

One of the creative responses to the controversial World Council of Churches decision of 1970 in terms of their Programme to Combat Racism was a commitment by the South African member churches... to intensify their witness to justice and reconciliation in church and society.[21]

It is important to note here the tribute to the WCC 1970 grants. In spite of Mr Vorster's attempts to block dialogue with the WCC, the action of the grants had had repercussions within the churches in South Africa.

As this account of the actions of the small minority of white anti-apartheid Christians indicates, at that time the premise of their discussion and actions appears to be that there was still time for peaceful change. Hence it is not surprising that even anti-apartheid whites initially reacted against the PCR grants, assuming that they endorsed violent change. It is not that these people refused to consider the thorny question of violence, for within SPROCAS there are passages of discussion about the violence of the *status quo*. Yet it must have been galling to those who with great zeal were searching for the peaceful transformation of society, by appealing to the good will of their mostly unheeding fellow-whites, to be made aware by the grants that the WCC and Christians abroad appeared to ignore this good will, and assume that there was already a conflict and the time had come to take sides. As Peter Randall, Director of SPROCAS, bitterly asked: 'Have white South African Christians finally been written off as beyond redemption?'[22]

The mandate of the new SACC Division of Justice and Reconciliation contains some striking words:

> There can be no reconciliation without righteousness, and therefore we must reject any 'cheap' form of reconciliation which avoids the costly way of justice, repentance and forgiveness... Justice must be done in the Church, and done specifically and concretely, if there is to be that trust and understanding which produces true reconciliation.[23]

This contains some of the basic ideas of the (mostly white) Christian anti-apartheid discussion of the time, justice and reconciliation always being yoked together, and justice to be done 'specifically and concretely' (as in some of the SPROCAS proposals) so that there could be reconciliation. There was a recognition that this might be 'costly' – some in the churches had already experienced the reaction of the state, in deportation, banning, arrest, etc. It was a view that did not, as yet, seriously take into account the need for dialogue with blacks. It is true that the most far-seeing individuals, like Beyers Naude at the Christian Institute, were beginning to open up dialogue with black churchmen, consultation that eventually produced Black Community Programmes alongside the white programmes already described. This consultation also gradually led to the opening up of the ecumenical hierarchy to blacks, so that by the end of the decade the SACC was led by a black General Secretary, Desmond Tutu.

However, the most significant encounter occurred at the All Africa Council of Churches meeting in Lusaka, when representatives of the SACC met South African exiles. Perhaps for the first time these white liberal Christians encountered the viewpoint and the arguments on which the original PCR was based, i.e. the premise that a conflict already existed, and that there were Christians on both sides. John Rees, the General Secretary of SACC, reported back on this encounter to the annual SACC gathering held at Hammanskraal:

> The representatives of the liberation movements had made a deep impression on him and on other participants from South Africa. In these movements, there were many convinced Christians. A Methodist preachers' association had been formed in one area to serve Methodist freedom fighters. Practising Christians in liberation movements were not aware of a contradiction between the violent methods they used in the fight against South Africa and their Christian faith. They had taken their decision to join the liberation movements in the full awareness of being Christians and of being responsible to God for their actions.[24]

These black Christians had made specific demands for changes within South African society, such as the abolition of influx control, job reservation and migratory labour. In discussion about this at Hammanskraal, it was decided that since there was no possibility that the churches could initiate changes in these matters, instead they should make proposals on 'matters in which they had a realistic possibility of action'.[25] Thus came about a motion about conscientious objection to military service, which is compulsory for all whites in South Africa. Previously there had been concern about conscientious objectors, but this mainly stemmed from concern at the plight of the few individuals involved, at this stage mainly Jehovah's Witnesses and Quakers. But the proposal made by Douglas Bax at Hammanskraal introduced a new cutting edge into church/state relations. It stated clearly that it is wrong to defend by force an unjust society, thus implying that the military activities of the South African Defence Force in operational areas (mainly Angola and Namibia) would not bear moral scrutiny. The motion was passed. Adrian Hastings describes the reactions:

> It was a courageous counter-move to the moral and patriotic

nationalism whipped up in reaction to the World Council grants and was bound to produce a further outcry. 'I want seriously to warn those who are playing with fire in this way,' declared the Prime Minister, '...to rethink before they burn their hands irrevocably...' His brother, Dr J.D.Vorster, Moderator of the NGK, added that the SACC was 'playing into the hands of leftists', while Edward Knapp-Fisher, Anglican Bishop of Pretoria, rejecting the resolution, said that '...to insist that our society is so unjust that no one can be justified in taking up arms to defend the country seems to be ill-conceived and unwarranted'. He was joined by the leaders of the Presbyterian and Methodist churches.[26]

The value of the Bax motion was that for the first time in South Africa whites were being challenged by fellow-whites on this matter. The drawback was that the motion put the painful burden of decision on to young seventeen-year-olds who were about to be conscripted into the SADF. Very few of them were in a position to consider all sides of the question and make a mature decision. However, the number of articulate conscientious objectors increased. Meanwhile the South African government, in response to the Hammanskraal motion, made it illegal for anyone to promote conscientious objection in South Africa.

Within ecumenical circles there was the constant challenge of the discussion about South Africa stimulated by the PCR abroad. For example in 1976 the Lutherans declared that the South African situation was a *status confessionis*, and that the rejection of an oppressive system is an obligation of faith. In 1977 the WCC sent to the SACC the pamphlet *South Africa's Hope – What Price Now?*, which referred to the Lutheran discussion and also to events such as the death of Steve Biko. This stimulated discussion within South Africa about the concept of just revolution, and the SACC produced a study paper which cautiously redefined the terms until the discussion theme mutated to justifiable resistance.[27] However, it asked some penetrating questions of white Christians as to what extent their attitudes to violence/non-violence were a cloak for inaction, and whether they were prepared to bear the cost of resistance to injustice. This line of discussion produced proposals in 1979 about 'positive non co-operation',[28] some of which were based on the techniques advocated by peace activists from abroad. It is suggested that white Christians could defy restrictions of seven listed types, such as restrictions on worship, on publication, on education. It also has the jolly and naive suggestion that a positive affirmation campaign of car stickers and lapel badges with the slogan 'I am South African' or 'We are one nation' was the kind of thing everyone could cooperate in.

Such idealism about positive non-cooperation had no discernible political effects, but the 1979 discussions should not be discounted altogether. First it is clear that the thinking within these SACC conferences was being influenced by discussion abroad. Secondly, it shows that white Christians were painfully coming to redefine the terms of their situation. They were now fully aware that a Christian interpretation of injustice was involving them in conflict with the state. Furthermore they were now aware that those opposing apartheid from within the liberation movements could give Christian arguments for their action.

Black reaction

We must now backtrack to 1970 in order to trace the effects of PCR on black Christians. The mood of the 1970s was well expressed by Barney Pityana:

> It is the black people themselves who must work out the priorities in terms of their overriding aspirations.[29]

From this black perspective, the PCR debate was as yet one which concerned white South Africans, and did not have to evoke black opinion:

> It is difficult to believe that Black Christians were comparably upset (by PCR). Only Bishop Alphaeus Zulu, Anglican Bishop of Zululand and one of the Presidents of the WCC, publicly raised his voice, and then circumspectly. The South African churches, he believed, had not been consulted, and the 'SACC should lodge its protest and demand to be heard'.[30]

Pro Veritate had the good sense to regard Bishop Zulu's response as atypical of blacks and to wonder what the silent majority was thinking.

> One may find that our black Christian brothers viewed the WCC decisions very differently.[31]

This insight would have been confirmed by a visit to the Federal Seminary at Alice where the students celebrated long into the night on hearing of the WCC grants. Bishop Zulu, perhaps by now gauging black reactions, changed his stance:

Very few whites in this country are committed to non-violence and there is no reason why there should be any more among blacks.

After the disillusionment that followed the quelling of black resistance movements in the middle fifties, it has become unreasonable to gain support for the hope of a non-violent solution. The harshness with which discrimination is enforced by law and custom makes a black man look simple and naive if he continues to believe and talk of non-violence ever becoming effective. This is a fact even though nobody speaks of violence.[32]

We have seen the disillusion expressed by some black spokesmen like Steve Biko over the well-meaning attempts by white people towards avoiding violence by paternalistic projects. It is from within that disillusion that a new vision was sought by the black community, which flowered into the black consciousness movement.

The theological aspects of the black consciousness movement were expressed by Pityana in an article written in 1972. He began by pointing out that black consciousness and black theology are intertwined. The entire lives of black people are permeated by religion, hence the added significance of black theology for the self-awareness of black people. It leads to 'a quest for new values and definitions that are meaningful and appropriate for black people and which give substance and significance to their lives'.[33] Pityana points out that the coming of Christianity brought about a real upheaval within African values. This in turn led to the break-up of the structures of tribe and family, especially as a result of what came with Christianity, namely the money economy. The effect of this prepared the ground for the dehumanization of the black man at the hand of colonial rule. This dehumanization made it possible for black people to regard their imposed inferiority as natural, even in their own country.

The early church was never prepared to face the serious encounter with all those elements that stifled the national development and happiness of the black people. It is a realization of this great myth designed to rob the black man of his soul and his human dignity. It was brought about by the white settler with the assistance of his handmaiden the church, through blood and tears, in suppression and humiliation, through dishonest means, by force and subjugation of the sons of the soil. It is the liberating effect of this self-knowledge and awareness that we refer to as black consciousness.[34]

In other words, what black theology was doing was to direct black attention to the role of the church in its subjugation. Hence the linking of black theology and black consciousness. This linkage in turn cuts the bond, as it were, of the black man's dependence on white interpretations of the gospel.

The church as presently constituted is still foreign to the soul of the black man. He will not bring forth his love, thought-patterns, fears, social relationships, attitudes, philosophical dispositions, needs, aspirations, etc. The church of the people must have its roots deeply established in the history and traditions of those who profess it. It is the black people themselves who must work out the priorities in terms of their overriding aspirations. They alone can do so by reason of their emotional and intellectual involvement in the struggles and sufferings of their people.[35]

There was a hostile reaction from some white theologians to black theology. None of the Afrikaner theologians who contributed to a book on *Black Theology*[36] viewed it in a positive light, but one essay 'recognized Black Theology as a judgment on White Christianity in South Africa'.[37] The writer admitted:

Black theology is a painful reminder... that we have been unable to give these black people the Christ of the Bible, because they cannot see this Christ in their lives.[38]

Another writer called black theology 'the scream of a child'[39] and then said that it was necessary to ask what pain had caused the child to scream. The predominant tone of the DRC comment on black theology was to view it as reactive, and exponents of it were chided for being unappreciative: 'all the many things (whites) have done and are doing are not being given due honour.'[40]

However, the exception to this Afrikaner mistrust of black theology was, as might be expected, Beyers Naude. As I have already said, even while the whites were otherwise ignoring possible black reactions to PCR, the Christian Institute together with some of the staff at SACC were beginning to take note of black consciousness leaders. Aided by money from abroad, they were able to assist in the setting up of BCP (Black Community Programmes). But in May 1975 the Christian Institute, the White Community Programme and the BCP were all declared 'affected organizations' by the government, which passed a new law for the purpose of closing down such projects. They moved in to close organizations financed from overseas. At the time the Christian Institute was receiving 75% of its funds from overseas. BCP had already embarked on some useful grassroots projects under the influence of black consciousness ideas, but most of these were forced to close with the loss of the money. However, contrary to government expectations, the suppression of the BCP, with the killing of Steve Biko and the scattering of black consciousness exiles abroad, had the effect of giving it publicity on a worldwide basis.

Nor were the voices of black protest silenced in South Africa. In March 1978 Desmond Tutu became General Secretary of the SACC. He had worked for the WCC Theological Education Fund ten years previously (another of the programmes set up as a result of decisions at Uppsala in 1968) and had maintained his ecumenical contacts even when he returned to South Africa. On one of his trips abroad while he was working for the SACC Tutu made a statement about the boycott movement. This was a challenge to the churches within South Africa and the SACC took up the matter, issuing a statement in 1978 which called on the churches to examine their investment policies and see 'what influence they can bring to bear' to produce improvements in labour relations, the right to family life for all workers, and so on.[41] In 1979 Desmond Tutu was asked on Danish television about his views on the boycott. His candid response angered the Pretoria government and a cabinet minister demanded his apology. The government was trying to isolate Tutu at this time as a trouble-maker, and that is how his remarks were often presented in South African newspapers, as if he spoke on his own account rather than as a representative, not only of the views of black people but also of the SACC. Over the Danish incident the SACC refused to allow this isolation manoeuvre, and issued a strong statement.[42] First, it stated that it shared 'his wholehearted commitment to work for change without using arms', an implicit reminder that the boycott movement was at least a non-violent option. It also pointed out that 'a full and responsible discussion of alternatives to armed violence is impossible in South Africa because of the law'. It also considered his statement and stated that a retraction of it 'would constitute a denial of his prophetic calling'. The statement concluded with firm support for Tutu's position:

We will not allow any single member of the Body of Christ to be isolated for attack when we are sure that his primary commitment reflects, as does Bishop Tutu's, those values for which each of our member churches firmly stands. In this matter, therefore, the state is dealing with all the member churches of the SACC.[43]

The South African government, in conflict with the churches, tried the method it used successfully after Cottesloe with the dissidents within the ranks of DRC, that is, isolation and expulsion. The methods used against leading anti-apartheid clergymen in the mission churches, against the Christian Institute, against the black consciousness movement, and against the SACC, all fit this pattern. However, in spite of this, the anti-apartheid prophets continue uncowed, especially Beyers Naude, who has withstood it all from Cottesloe until his new present position at the SACC.

In contrast to the 1960s, when the leading spokesmen within the churches were nearly all whites, in the 1980s the significant voices are of black church leaders. Dr Allan Boesak, as a leader of the Sendingkerk, a mission offshoot of DRC for Coloured people, has been able to make some trenchant criticisms of the ideology of apartheid from within the framework of Calvinist theology. In fact the black reformed churches have been able to stay in fellowship with the World Reformed alliance from which the DRC churches have been excluded by their racist ideology. Dr Allan Boesak has even been elected leader of this world-wide Reformed fellowship. Unfortunately he too has suffered from attempts to isolate him, as agents of the Nationalist government tried to implicate him in a sexual scandal, hoping to get him suspended from his church position – unsuccessfully, as it turned out.

So there has been and continues to be a two-way dialogue between the WCC and Christians within South Africa. The WCC formed its programmes as a result of consultations which included South African Christians, both those still able to work within the country and those in exile. In one important instance, the matter of conscientious objectors, the dialogue did not go via Geneva but took place at the level of an African ecumenical conference. Statements made by PCR have influenced or stimulated church action in South Africa, especially through the SACC. To the beneficiaries of apartheid within South Africa those courageous individuals who become spokesmen for the churches on anti-apartheid matters may seem like eccentrics and 'agitators'. But *it is vital for the churches to see through the extrusion methods used by the state, and refuse to allow it to work, by issuing strong declarations of solidarity, as the SACC did with Tutu. The individuals involved should not become prophets without churches, prophets unsupported by the Oikoumene.* I consider the passage in italics to be of the utmost importance, not just for South Africa, but for any country where the church's witness is either inhibited by the state or subtly undermined by seemingly plausible 'patriotism' or even 'state security'.

In 1985 the Kairos document was published, signed by over 150 prominent people, both black and white, from South African churches, including some from the Afrikaans churches. The first four chapters are directed at types of theology, both the state theology which bolsters the government and church theology which colludes in more subtle ways, such as being more concerned about reconciliation than justice, and advocating non-violence while failing to condemn state-sponsored violence. The chapter on prophetic theology argues that the majority of the people of South Africa regard the government as a tyranny, and there is a Christian tradition of the right to resist tyranny. The chapter ends with a message of hope even as the crisis deepens. The next chapter, headed 'Challenge for Action', states unambiguously: 'Christians, if they are not already doing so, must quite simply participate in the struggle for liberation and for a just society.'[44] It advocates transforming normal church activities with prophetic theology; it also says that special campaigns and programmes will be necessary. There is a section on civil disobedience. There is also a section on the church's duty to give clear moral guidance, not just a message of caution, but also to motivate and challenge people. Finally, towards the end, it says: 'Although this document suggests various modes of involvement, it does not prescribe the particular actions anyone should take.'[45]

It is too early to judge what effect this document is having on people in South Africa. It says that it should be used in discussion groups, which means that whatever debate and activity it is generating is taking place in private. In a way, it is of the same mould as the 'Message to the People of South Africa', a bold statement by an *ad hoc* group of church people. It is interesting to contrast such statements with that of PCR. The South African statements are strong in theological language and moral exhortation, but leave the detailed application to others. In contrast, PCR carried proposals into action which immediately had the effect of focussing the debate. The execution of the proposals that caused the setting up of PCR had direct institutional application – for instance in that the WCC had to begin to discuss with the banks where its own funds were going. The Kairos document gives no concrete recommendations: it says that the churches must give moral guidance, but it does not, for instance, say that there is a Christian duty for white conscripts to avoid serving in the army.

Other statements of the 1980s, notably from the SACC, have been more forthright on what the moral imperatives mean. The SACC in 1984 unequivocally backed the End Conscription campaign, and also the moves to demilitarize army chaplains.

However, in spite of this vagueness on specific questions, the Kairos document is a significant publication to come out of the crisis in South Africa. The fact that it gained the support of 150 prominent church people shows that the churches are learning to respond to the government's attempts to move against the outspoken as if they were isolated individuals. The fact that it comes neither from an individual nor from an institution makes the document difficult for the government to quash by the old methods.

5

Non-Violence

For this chapter I shall also be drawing on material mainly from within South Africa, for that is where the sharp end of the debate is. There matters of principle cannot be left at the theoretical level, for many Christians face a situation which requires difficult, often sacrifical, moral decision-taking. Blacks face the violence endemic in apartheid structures and the pressures to join in anti-apartheid activities, such as school demonstrations, that may turn violent and lead to more drastic action, such as flight into exile to join the active cadres of the liberation movements. On the opposite side, young whites face conscription into an army that is actually engaged, on occasion, against the civilian population.

Black passive resistance

Before the ANC turned to violence, there had been fifty years of passive resistance to oppression, as Nelson Mandela pointed out at his trial in 1962:

> Throughout the fifty years of its existence the African National Congress... has done everything possible to bring its demands to the attention of successive South African Governments. It has sought at all times peaceful solutions for the country's ills and problems. The history of the ANC is filled with instances where deputations were sent to South African Governments either on specific issues or on the general political demands of our people.[1]

In 1913, Sol Plaatje wrote a book entitled *Native Life in South Africa* to protest against the 1913 Land Act which ruled that 'all the blacks who hitherto lived on the Boer areas... would only be allowed to come back to Union territory as servants to the white farming population'.[2] It is an early example of peaceful black response to oppressive legislation. Plaatje estimated that nearly a million black squatters on white farms were affected by this law.[3] These squatters, in many areas the descendants of tribes which had been traditionally in the area before the coming of the whites, had continued to farm the land under white settlers in a system of share-cropping. Blacks who had wanted to buy land in Boer-occupied areas like the Orange Free State under the European land tenure system that replaced the old tribal communal system had been forbidden to do so, and the act legalized the system, crowding black people into demarcated 'native areas' in which the population was becoming too dense for traditional cattle-herding and fuel-gathering needs. The Bantustan policy of the Nationalists is the culmination of this land-grab by the whites. Yet in 1913 there was no armed resistance to the Act. Instead,

> The native leaders have spared neither pains nor pence in visiting the scattered tribes and exhorting them to obey all the demands of the South African government under the Grobler law *pending peaceful intercession from the outside world*.[4]

Educated Christian leaders like Plaatje had a splendid, but futile, faith in 'the Christian world at large' (then on the eve of World War I):

> We appeal to the Churches. We would remind them that in the past the Christian voice has been our only shield against legislative excesses of the kind now in full swing in the Union. But in the new ascendance of self and pelf over justice and tolerance, that voice will be altogether ignored, unless strongly reinforced by the Christian world at large.[5]

Plaatje was one of the Native Deputation to Britain in May 1914 when the matter was raised in the House of Commons, and in public meetings around that country (he lists sixty meetings that he personally addressed). This appeal by Plaatje to the Christian world at large has been repeated through the years by other black leaders, notably Chief Luthuli in the 1950s and Archbishop Tutu today. In Plaatje's statements there is evidence that Christianity had a restraining and pacifying influence on black resistance to white oppression, especially while there was hope of a response from the outside world.

Within South Africa, whenever black resistance has been organized, the government has responded with violence rather than ameliorate the conditions or withdraw the repressive laws. Plaatje described the resistance of black women in the Free State to the pass laws. He went on to see the imprisoned demonstrators at Kroonstad and commented:

> Our hearts bled to see young women of Bloemfontein, who had spent all their lives in the capital and never knew what it was to walk without socks, walking the chilly cemented floors and cold sharp pebbles without boots. Their own boots and shoes had been taken off, they told us, and they were, throughout the winter, forced to perform hard labour barefooted.[6]

This early example of government brutality in response to peaceful African protest was then to be repeated over three generations. For example, in 1927 strikes were repressed by guns and arrests. In 1946 a strike by 100,000 black miners was repressed by force; in 1952 in the ANC anti-pass campaign, 8,500 were arrested; in 1956 when 2,000 women demonstrated against the pass laws 156 leaders were arrested. All these instances have been described more fully in historical studies, but are not particularly well known. That, however, was all to change in 1960, when sixty-seven people were killed at Sharpeville during a peaceful demonstration.

It was at this stage that the confrontational politics of whites against blacks in South Africa reached a turning point. For the first time, after fifty years of peaceful efforts to negotiate, the Pan African Congress and the ANC decided to wage armed struggle against the apartheid government. At this stage, it may be worth taking a look at the perceptions of the South African authorities, both political and ecclesiastical, with regard to the violence and tragedy of Sharpeville.

The DRC issued this statement:

> We, the undersigned ministers of the Dutch Reformed Churches of South Africa, have learned with great concern of the tragic and shocking events in our country during the last few days. We wish to assure all people of all races affected our deepest sympathy. The world-wide unfavourable publicity and repercussions compel us to issue the following statement:
>
> 'Some church leaders and others here and overseas have taken the liberty to comment and to issue some shocking statements before the facts have been determined and released judicially. We wish to appeal earnestly to churches overseas and locally to show a sense of responsibility in this crisis situation. We cannot condone the continuous besmirching of our country, people and church by untrue

and slanted information. We wish to warn the outside world that such irresponsible action, which has continued for years and is still going on in intensity and fury, is precipitating a clash in our country, the end of which is to be foreseen...'[7]

The interesting aspect of this statement is the fact that it is more concerned to defend the good name of South Africa than to lament the deaths that had occurred. Here we see the rationalization, the self-defence mechanism, that people of academic training in moral studies have to employ when confronted with the inhumane results of their ideology. The judicial process establishes the facts. That sounds acceptable if the law courts really do establish truth; but judgments made by apartheid courts over the years tend to skew the facts in favour of government policy. These Afrikaner spokesmen even suggest that the reporting of the fact, the 'besmirching', causes 'the clash'. This fits the usual Nationalist party reaction that 'agitators' are responsible for anti-apartheid incidents, rather than admit that the ideology and practice of apartheid is the main cause of the social unrest.

Another perspective and response to Sharpeville came from the Anglican church, then under the leadership of Archbishop de Blank:

In de Blank's view South Africa faced the gravest crisis in its history as Africans were not only rejecting white oppression; they were also turning away from a Christianity that was only too clearly associated with the injustices of Apartheid. All churches stood condemned, and Anglicans, he confessed, were or should be 'deeply penitent' for their failures... but as a church, and with all other churches except the DRC, they condemned the policies which led to the crisis... unless the DRC now publicly repudiated 'the doctrine and practice of compulsory segregation', the Archbishop argued, the spread of the Christian faith would be seriously endangered.[8]

The merit of de Blank's statement is that at least it refers to the root cause of the violence, i.e. compulsory segregation, but its weakness is that he seems to suggest that a Christian objection to apartheid is that it is holding up the spread of the Christian faith, as though, outside their role as clients for missionaries, blacks had no other autonomous status as human beings. If church leaders appear to narrow religion to head-counting in their congregations, and become obsessed with ecclesiastical survival, the religious vision of human need in its totality, regardless of church allegiance, has been overlooked. Such narrow-mindedness on the part of Christians also cuts them off from others who are protesting at the same injustice from a human rights perspective.

As far as some anti-apartheid movements were concerned, the time for fruitless exchange of words was over and the time for violence had arrived. In 1961 the ANC and PAC decided to form military cadres, and began a strategy of selective sabotage. Meanwhile the government repression of unarmed opponents went on. In 1973 fourteen people were shot dead at Carletonville during a strike in which 100,000 workers were involved. In 1975 the leaders of SASO, a non-violent student movement, were arrested. In 1976, in an uprising by schoolchildren, 649 people were officially listed as shot dead and over 5,000 were arrested. And in 1977 Steve Biko was murdered in prison.

In 1979 the Archbishop of Cape Town, Bill Burnett, stated that unless white people in South Africa abandoned apartheid and replaced it with a more just system, violence was inevitable. The Archbishop acknowledged:

Some would try to transform apartheid by organizing pressure for change in its social structures and some would seek to achieve that end through the written word. Still other Christians would conclude that all peaceful means to achieve change had been tried. He continued that since passive resistance was virtually impossible in South Africa, they might then decide, as some already had, that they should join guerrilla movements beyond South Africa's borders.[9]

These words serve as a reminder of the long history of African peaceful protest in the face of government violence. In spite of all these accidents, the influence of Christian thinking on non-violence emerges in the statements of such leaders as Sol Plaatje and Albert Luthuli, who, in their time, devoted their best efforts to constitutional means of change and appeals to the world at large, as Chief Luthuli expressed it (in the years just before the ANC formed its sabotage cadres):

Who will deny that thirty years of my life have been spent knocking in vain, patiently, moderately and modestly at a closed and barred door? What have been the fruits of moderation? The past thirty years have seen the greatest numbers of laws restricting our rights and progress, until today we have reached a stage where we have almost no rights at all.[10]

White resistance

As I indicated in Chapter 4, conscientious objection has now
become a matter of debate in some South African churches. It is
important to understand this debate in the context of the growing
militarization of South Africa during the 1970s. A study published
by the Catholic Institute for Race Relations chronicles this military
expansion.

> After 1960 and the international reaction to the Sharpeville massacre,
> particularly from the newly independent African States, Pretoria
> embarked on military expansion. The end-point was the most powerful
> and sophisticated military machine on the African continent and in
> the Southern hemisphere.[11]

This militarization gave rise to what was termed 'total strategy', which
meant the military preparedness of the whole white population against
possible external or internal attacks against South Africa by those who
were supposedly engaged in a 'total onslaught' against the *status quo*,
against Christianity and the survival of the white race. Under pressure
of such fears, the defence budget has been increased from R40 million
in 1959/60 to R2,900 million for 1982/83. Universal conscription for
white male citizens was decreed in 1967. The South African Defence
Force (SADF) increased from 78,000 in 1960 to 494,000 in 1979. The
South African army of occupation in Namibia is estimated as 100,000
troops. Periods of national service have been increased. In 1982, young
white South Africans were required to do two years initial service, to be
followed by 720 days to be spread over twelve years. Under the Defence
Act of 1957, conscientious objection was allowed for by an exemption
clause under section 97(3):

> A person who *bona fide* belongs and adheres to a recognized religious
> denomination by the tenets whereof its members may not participate
> in war, may be granted exemption from serving in any combatant
> capacity, but shall, if called upon to do so, serve in a non-combatant
> capacity.[12]

The incidence of conscientious objection or war resistance increased
during the 1970s. In 1978, the Ministry of Defence informed Parliament
of the following figures:[13]

	Number failing to render military service	Prosecutions
1975	3,314	605
1976	3,566	916
1977	3,844	532

The difference between those who failed to report for service and those prosecuted represents those who evade service either on the run inside South Africa or by going into exile. It is impossible to tell how many of those who evade conscription do so for ethical, political or religious reasons. Indeed, many are probably confused about their motivation or are unwilling to challenge the pressures of social conformity. Thus some, especially those from wealthier families or those with relatives overseas, in Britain, for instance, could choose to go abroad during the time their call-up papers were due. At first there were liberal exemptions or postponements of service for those who were studying. But as the procedures for call-up were tightened in accord with increased military operations, so the debate about conscientious objection became sharper. There was pressure to amend the Defence Act to allow for different types of objectors. This amendment, of 1983, lists three types of religious objectors and makes provision for them:[14]

1. Those who object to fighting *per se*, but not to service in the Defence Forces. These will be assigned non-combatant duties within the Defence Force, of the same term in length as normal combatant service.
2. Those who object to combatant duty, to maintenance tasks of combative nature and to wearing uniform, will have a specially assigned role within the Defence Force of one and a half term's length.
3. Those who object to any form of service or training in the armed forces will have to do community service twice as long as the normal service.

The provisions under 3. are new in that under the old Act, quoted above, there was no provision for community service instead of military service. Also new in the 1983 measure are the tough penalties of imprisonment for those who base their objection on political grounds, rather than on their membership of a recognized pacifist denomination.

What are the arguments used by the conscientious objectors who have been thus legislated for?

Jehovah's Witnesses

The first war resisters to be imprisoned were the Jehovah's Witnesses. In 1973, for example, out of 159 imprisoned for twelve months in the detention barracks, 158 were Witnesses.[15] They were imprisoned because they refused to serve in the SADF in any capacity. They also resisted with great courage within the military prison any attempts to impose upon them a military-type regime, such as the wearing of uniform, ceremonies with the flag, etc. Their religious position has been described by Adrian Hastings:

> Witnesses await the imminent return of Christ to establish the kingdom; in the meantime they see all governments as the expression of the power of Satan and, while willing to pay taxes and keep the peace, they refuse to participate further in political life – to join a party or vote, to sing the national anthem or salute the flag. It is not surprising that they are unpopular with governments, particularly young governments sensitive to any slight. In Africa Witnesses are most numerous in Zambia and Malawi and Nigeria; in most other countries they are few. Several independent governments have banned their activities, but where they are not numerous they can fairly be ovrlooked. In Zambia this was not the case, for their numbers have been very considerable both on the copperbelt and in Lumpa province, and in 1967 they appeared to be offering UNIP and the state much the same sort of challenge as that presented by the Lumpa church a few years earlier... UNIP youth were soon hounding them in many places and during the latter part of 1968 forty-three kingdom halls were burnt down and much damage done. Some Witnesses were killed and many more fled into the bush.[16]

This account of the Jehovah's Witnesses in independent black states of Africa reveals the non-political basis of their protest and so explains why the South African authorities evidently do not see such views as threatening and why they were willing to make provision for Witnesses in the amendments to the Defence Act. Their resistance to military service does not stem from views on violence or non-violence, but from their beliefs about power and authority. It is an other-worldly theology which sees *all* political systems as evil and so poses no particular ethical or religious critique to the South African government any more or less than to the government of an independent black-ruled state. Nonetheless their protest was a nuisance to the authorities, and the SADF had some difficulties in the organization of the military detention camps in which the Witnesses were held because of their refusal to wear camp uniform. Occasionally the English liberal newspapers carried reports of this. At a time in the early 1970s when there was almost no other public discussion about the position of conscientious objectors, these few Witnesses detained in military establishments served to highlight the possibility of principled and persistent resistance.

Society of Friends

The Friends fit under the original exemption clause of the Defence Act. The theological position of their Society is traced in an excellent booklet by Horace G.Alexander, *The Growth of the Peace Testimony of the Society of Friends*, published in 1939 on the brink of the Second World War. It opens with a statement of pacifist principles by George Fox:

> We utterly deny all outward wars and strife, and fightings with outward weapons, for any end, or under any pretence whatever; this is our testimony to the whole world. The Spirit of Christ by which we are guided is not changeable, so as once to command us from a thing as evil and again to move into it; and we certainly know and testify to the world that the Spirit of Christ, which leads us into all Truth, will never move us to fight and war against any man with outward weapons, neither for the kingdom of Christ nor for the kingdom of this world.[17]

This religious position, originating at the end of the era of religious wars in Europe, is a repudiation of the Crusade idea of war 'for the kingdom of Christ'. It also rejects any kind of religious justification for national wars, 'for the kingdoms of this world', on the grounds that the Spirit is not 'changeable'. What this seems to be is a refutation of the currently held view of the 'just' war, which held that sometimes, in specifically defined conditions, war was justifiable. George Fox is arguing against the permissibility of that 'sometimes', 'and again to move into it'. What he is proclaiming is a total and consistent pacifism for the Friends. In no circumstances are wars and strife to be justified by the Friends. This is a rather different position from that of the Jehovah's Witnesses. While the Witnesses draw on their theology of power and the coming kingdom of Christ, the Friends focus more on the nature of peace and the gifts of the Spirit. While Witnesses avoid political controversy, the Friends actively enter into peace-making dialogue. The international record of the Friends, whether at the time of the Crimean War, the wars of imperialism, the two World Wars, or more recently the Falklands war, is consistently pacifist and international in vision. Their response is not other-worldly. They enter vigorously into the debate and suggest peace-making actions, backing them up with money, committees and publications. On the international scene, Quakers were influential in the formation of the League of Nations. They linked with other pacifist churches such as the Mennonites and the Brethren to present a statement to the World Council of Churches, 'Peace is the Will of God'.

Along with their pacifism, they have a deep commitment to 'point out the moral issues which are so often obscured in political discussion'.[18] Hence they have always been involved in the Human Rights movement, whether this has taken the form of anti-slavery movements, prison reforms or action over refugees.

Individual pacifists in non-pacifist churches

The provisions of the old Defence Act did not allow exemption to pacifists who are not members of a recognized pacifist church. However, within the non-pacifist churches, such as the Anglican church, there are pacifist organizations like the Anglican Pacifist Fellowship:

> We, the communicant members of the Church of England, or of a church in full communion with it, believing that our membership of the Christian Church involves the complete repudiation of modern war, pledge ourselves to renounce war and all preparation of war, and work for the construction of Christian peace in the world.[19]

This is consistent pacifism, similar to that of the Quakers, but the Anglican church, like the other mission churches, does not demand a pacifist position from its members. Historically the Anglican church is closely linked to the nation-state in its origins, and has always appeared to subscribe to the 'just war' theories about the morality of military service by Christians. But it has not often been called upon to enunciate doctrines of peace and war as applied to actual political situations. In South Africa, as I have already pointed out, the socialization of young white males via segregated schools straight to military conscription inhibits the asking of too many questions about the morality of war. The mission churches know only too well that within their membership, consisting of both black and white, there is no uniformity of opinion about the morality of peace and war in general, and divergent interpretations about the actual war operations for which the South African state has imposed conscription. The CIIR book comments on this:

> Most of the major denominations do not hold a pacifist position nor do they demand a pacifist approach from their members. Yet nearly all their members urge the use of peaceful methods of change and have shown a growing willingness to denounce the use of violence to maintain the *status quo*.[20]

Such denunciation was brought into sharper focus by the courageous stand of Charles Yeats, who was foremost among young Anglicans in taking a consistent pacifist position. He was sentenced to twelve months in prison for refusing to serve in the SADF on the grounds that he was a Christian and a member of the Anglican Pacifist Fellowship. The *APF Newsletter* quotes a comment by the British Council of Churches Division of Affairs on Charles Yeats' case:

> It is significant that Christians within and without the country (South Africa) see the significance of the stand taken by Yeats and express solidarity with those who abhor the way of violence. The most unanimous white Christian response in South Africa condemning participation in a violent revolution appears to black Christians to be particularly hypocritical when the way of oppression through violence is already embraced by the white community. Charles Yeats has highlighted the hypocrisy and pleaded for a consistency of approach to this problem. During a recent visit to the United Kingdom, Bishop Desmond Tutu of the South African Council of Churches expressed his perplexity that a Christian community who had generally endorsed the necessity of violence when resisting Hitler became generally pacifist when viewing the armed struggle of black South Africans in resisting the oppression of apartheid. The stand of Yeats is an attempt by white Christians to take Bishop Desmond Tutu's call for consistency seriously. It is also a stand in conformity with the teachings of the Anglican church.[21]

Thus Yeats was a pioneer, in that his case forced Anglicans, in particular, to examine the religious and ethical principles involved. However, in so far as his position was one of consistent religious pacifism, and close to that of the Friends, such a case would now fall into one of the three categories allowed for in the new amendments to the Act, and he would face community service rather than prison.

Political or selective conscientious objection

The South African authorities are more lenient towards total and consistent conscientious objection because it does not necessarily entail criticism of the apartheid system or question the rightness of the particular military operation in which the SADF is engaged. The position of those who move from arguments about a just war to criticism of South Africa's Namibia operations is more difficult and more challenging to the authorities. This position was that expressed in the resolution that Douglas Bax put forward at the SACC Hammanskraal Conference which argued that the criteria of a just war rule out any war engaged in in order to defend an unjust and discriminatory society, and that the armed forces of South Africa were defending an unjust system of government. Since then several objectors have based their pleas not on consistent or total pacifism but on a selective protest against the injustice of the war in Namibia and Angola.

The arguments of Billy Paddock, an Anglican who is not a pacifist, summarized in *Seek* in January 1983, speak for themselves:

(*a*) *The declaration of war must be made by a legitimate authority*

Paddock argues that the war in South Africa and in Namibia has never been declared. That the war has been entered into without the authority of Parliament as should have been the case, but was an executive decision by the Cabinet. That, moreover, in the case of Namibia, not only does the South African government have no legitimate authority in that land, but is a *de facto* illegal occupying force in Namibia which is not part of South Africa.

(*b*) *The war has to be for a just cause*

The war in South Africa was one that was being waged against black and other South Africans who had decided to flee the country, as a result of the oppressive exploitative laws. That many of those who fled were students who had fled the country, as a result of the troubles arising from enforced Afrikaans teaching in the schools in 1976 and 1977. That far from the war being fought for a just cause against an external threat, it was a civil war. In the case of Namibia, South Africa was the invading force, and this meant that SWAPO had the vindication of fighting a war intended to regain justice.

(*c*) *The war has to be motivated by a right or good intention*

Paddock states that South Africa has been seen as an unjust society, with much oppression ever since the white people first arrived in that country. Racism and exploitation are very evident in the labour policies of the country. The South African Defence Force is *per* the admission made by one of its generals (Magnus Malan) defending apartheid.

(d) The war should have a reasonable chance of success

Here Paddock quotes General G.J.J.Boshoff, who said, '(the war) is eighty per cent socio-economic and only twenty per cent military. If we lose the socio-economic struggle, then we need not even bother to fight the military one.' It was in promoting this view that the SADF initiated a programme for 'winning the hearts and minds' of the oppressed, in what it called the Civic Action Programme. The enduring hostility to the South African army, as seen in Namibia, indicates that this policy has failed. This in turn can, via inference, indicate that the war does not have a reasonable chance of success.

(e) The war should be waged only as a last resort

The case of the reluctance of South Africa to arrive at a settlement with SWAPO is mentioned as an instance illustrating that South Africa has not exhausted all attempts at arriving at a peaceful solution to the dispute. That instead South Africa is afraid that such a settlement would enrage the right wing in its party, and bring about a backlash, as the government of South Africa would be seen as having sold out on Namibia. And so South Africa maintains its stalling tactics over Namibia, though perfectly aware that in the end the United Nations will have to initiate and enact a settlement over Namibia.

(f) That war should be conducted in terms of proportionality (In other words, the beneficial results of the war should outweigh the harmful aspects of the war.)

Paddock argues that in the past three years (up to 1962) the defence budget figure amounted to twenty per cent of the total South African budget, This means that shortages have resulted in those departments that provide facilities and services to the population of South Africa as a whole. And he concludes by saying that 'this war economy... halts the development of the country for the benefit of all'.

(g) The war has to be conducted with just means

Here Paddock refers to reported instances of misconduct by the troops of the SADF.

(h) The war must bring about a just peace

Paddock concludes by referring to Pope Paul VI, who said, 'If you want peace, work for justice.' Paddock states that the SADF is fighting in defence of apartheid. The Anglican church and the Roman Catholic church have critized apartheid as indefensible because of its unjust and exploitative nature. Thus, even if the military forces of the present South African government were to win the war (a possibility which Paddock thinks is unlikely) a just peace would not result from such a victory. The hated apartheid would then still be enforced and the injustice it engenders, such as detentions without trial, death while in police custody and forced removals, as well as the exploitation of black labour under white domination.[22]

From such forthright argument it is easy to see why the South African government has imposed the severest penalties, under the new amendments, on selective conscientious objectors with views similar to Billy Paddock. They are sometimes termed 'political' objectors, even though there is a religious basis to their arguments. Indeed that is why they are more of a challenge to the state. If their arguments were purely political, they could be isolated as 'communists' and 'agitators', but instead the arguments are from within the traditional theories about peace and war in the mainstream churches, traditions which the Reformed churces also claim. So the claim that the Namibia-Angola operations are unjust is a challenge not only to the government but also to the Afrikaner churches which give it moral support. I have yet to come across a serious attempt by South African theologians who support apartheid to answer these arguments about the just war point by point.

The bishops of the Anglican church have been directly challenged here by the Anglican Students Federation. In 1982 ASF wrote to the bishops of CPSA asking whether the war in Namibia could be regarded as a just war. *Seek* of September 1982 quotes from the bishops' reply:

It could be argued that participation as a National Serviceman in the Namibian war is lawful because 'the magistrate' has commanded it. That in turn raises the political and judicial question as to whether 'the magistrate' in this case, namely the South African government, is the legitimate authority in South West Africa/Namibia...

A question we would wish to pose, therefore, is this: is it proper for the bishops to declare in relation to particular conflicts whether they are just or unjust? Is it not right, instead, for them to seek to set forth the considerations which will help each individual to make up his mind for himself?... The answer is that each individual must act according to a well-formed and well-informed conscience. It is not for the church in its official capacity to identify wholly with one view or another.

The ASF in an eight-point resolution about this reply found it:

> difficult to accept the stance of much of the letter... (and) difficulty in reconciling this committed stance against the *status quo* (as shown in the Bishops' 1980 Christmas letter which stated that they were 'wholly opposed to apartheid') with a less committed stance on the violence used to support it. They asked the Episcopal Synod to appoint a commission to produce material 'designed to help young South African Christians to make a 'well-informed' decision in response to conscription by the SADF or in response to the possibility of serving in a guerrilla army.[23]

A Cape Town priest, the Revd Sydney Lockett, wrote to the bishops that their letter revealed a 'bias in favour of SADF' and 'in the light of the fact that church members are being legally forced to fight for one side, the silence of the bishops constitutes a serious failure in pastoral responsibility'.

The *Seek* editorial of September 1982 takes up the argument at this point:

> The really complex decision is: Violence or non-violence in opposition to government violence? Our view is that the non-violent response is the most creative one, and one that should be pursued with greater seriousness than in the past. With actions, rather than words.
>
> ...it is one thing to say that the church must not decide for its members... it is quite another thing to say that our bishops should not state their understanding of God's word on important moral questions.
>
> In the end, it is the individual's duty to decide. But our bishops do give leadership on moral questions like abortion, divorce and apartheid – and so they should. Why not on the question of the Namibian war, especially when this leadership is requested by some of those faced with deciding about their participation in that war?

These arguments from the editorial are about the role of the individual in relation to the church authorities. Here we see the CPSA trying to steer a middle course between the Catholic view, with the papal encyclicals which give quite specific rulings on specific moral questions, and the Protestant view of the individual conscience guided by the Holy

Spirit and scripture. The bishops know that they lead a divided church. Yet the ASF want firm pronouncements as if from a united church, whose leaders speak for and guide their flock. Incidentally, the bishops' views on the Namibian war are becoming clearer after their 1983 visit to the war zone in Ovambo-land where they were so appalled at what they saw and heard that they made public a resolution to call for the withdrawal of all military presence from Namibia as soon as possible.[24] What this implies for individual Anglican conscripts serving in Namibia is not stated.

The ASF objects to the stance where the bishops are refusing to give moral support to conscientious objection, presumably because this could play into the goverment's hands and allow the extrusion strategy (see Chapter 4) to operate in isolating individual dissidents from their churches. Such isolation is designed to render the protest less contagious. It denies the proclaimers of such dangerous arguments a voice in the synods and papers of that church.

Another challenge which Douglas Bax put forward in his resolution at the SACC Hammanskraal Conference was that chaplains should be withdrawn from the SADF. When the motion was put before the provincial synod of CPSA it was defeated by 38 to 34. Comments ranged from Mr Matobane, on the black side, who said: 'South Africa should get out of Namibia and allow SWAPO and the people to settle their affairs' to the Dean of Bloemfontein who said that the motion was 'almost a denial of the incarnation. God did not withdraw from the world because of an immoral and unjust social order, but became totally involved.'

This reference to the incarnation shows the problem of Anglicans facing moral choices in an unjust society. The main tradition of the Anglican church, from its English origins, lies in the close association of the church with the nation state. This leads some to the view that the church should defer to the state and leave politics to politicians, a view which will be analysed in Chapter 6. Another way of aruging from within this incarnational tradition is to say that it demands close and serious attention not only to the general principles but also to the particularities of each specific case. The bishops' fact-finding trip to the war zone is thus within this incarnational understanding, as are the arguments of Billy Paddock.

6

Status Quo Theology

In 1979 the Provincial Synod of the CPSA announced:

> That this synod respects the fact that some Christians feel themselves called to be pacifists, others to defend the Republic of South Africa in the armed forces and others to leave its borders to take up arms to achieve what they believe will be a more just ordering of society.[1]

It is worth noting that this significant statement appeared under the heading 'World Council of Churches', as if to acknowledge that the WCC was stirring the church to clarify thinking on the topic of violence and non-violence. The previous chapter considered the arguments and the actions of the pacifists, as given in the first of the three options listed in the statement. I shall now go on to discuss the second option, that is, the justification for service in the armed forces. In order to understand how Christians view their participation in some of the more vicious situations in South Africa's wars, it is necessary to explore the theological roots and assumptions of South African society.

South Africa: a sacral society

In an interesting book on church-state relations, Leonard Verduin writes:

> In a sacral society there is unanimity on the religious plane, the plane on which man's deepest loyalties lie... in a sacral society it makes no sense to speak of 'church' and 'state': these institutions are as yet undifferentiated.[2]

He then goes on to give various examples from different tribes like the Navajo Indians and the Romans of Cicero's time. After that he outlines how various Belgian and Dutch theologians have tried, within the Christian tradition, to differentiate between church and state and comes up with a terminology of what he calls *preliminary* and *subsequent* grace.

> We must look upon the civil power as the creature of this preliminary grace... of a grace that swung into action before redemptive grace went to its assignment... This preliminary grace... utilizes resources that are residual, or backward looking; in this respect it differs significantly from subsequent grace, which utilizes resources that are anticipatory or forward-looking.[3]

He explains:

> Traditional theologies all too frequently have been flat, ignoring the progressive quality of God's gracious dealings with a fallen world.[4]

He further asserts:

> A flat theology cannot develop a suitable doctrine of the State. It must either picture the state as an entity that lies outside the grace of God, and is thus essentially demonic... or it must subsume the state under the program of redemptive grace. Either of these alternatives, however, leads to wholly unacceptable conclusions.[5]

He follows through with a footnote which applies these ideas to the South African situation:

> Flat theology... has never been able to 'think' the separation of church and state... in such a situation it becomes quite unthinkable for the church to do anything but rubber stamp whatever the state does. (Footnote: An outstanding example of such rubber stamping may be seen in the policies of the Reformed Churches of South Africa in our time. South African society is still an essentially sacral society.[6]

At the heart of apartheid is the Calvinist religion of the Afrikaners. People from more secular societies, or pluralist ones where no single religion in particular dominates, find it difficult to perceive or comprehend the close links between the NGK (DRC) Church and the Nationalist Party of South Africa. It was a church minister who founded the Afrikaans Cultural Association that eventually developed into the Nationalist Party which took over government in 1948. The same leading Afrikaner families straddle both church and state offices, for example John Vorster, the Premier, and his brother the Church Moderator. From within such a church/state nexus, it is not surprising to find a cabinet minister declaring:

When the Party is no longer in good standing with the churches, it will be finished.[7]

The 'Party' here means the Nationalists and 'the churches' here means the DRC churches. The Party does not mind what other churches have to say about the government. The 'mission' churches from within South Africa have been criticizing policy for several years, to no avail. Even less does it mean other churches in the ecumenical movement, especially not as expressed in the WCC, which the Nationalist Government has long identified as an enemy. Other churches from within the Calvinist Reformed tradition have also tried to take up the dialogue about apartheid. But increasingly the DRC churches are alienated not only from their kindred churches in the Netherlands but also from the churches they have nurtured, such as the Sendingkerk of South Africa, which, under the leadership of Allan Boësak, has remained within the World Alliance of Reformed Churches, while increasingly critical of the DRC. Thus what the cabinet minister's statement implies is the very close connection between apartheid policies and allegiance to the churches that buttress the apartheid state. It is Christians who are voting for the Nationalists, and their Christian sons who join the SADF to fight in Namibia. As the Nairobi WCC Assembly declared in 1975:

Apartheid is possible only with the support of large numbers of Christians there.[8]

In view of the close links between some of the churches and the political party in power, the argument that religion has nothing to do with politics is ludicrous when applied to South African affairs.

The kind of theology behind the apartheid policy makers has recently been made more available to the English speaking world by a book entitled *Apartheid is Heresy*, in which a number of South African theologians set out their critique of apartheid theology and practice.[9] Chris Loff's essay in nineteeth-century church history reveals how the church hierarchy of the NGK gradually succumbed to acceptance of church segregation, though there were some ministers with integrity who tried to oppose the boycott of black baptized members by their white congregations, giving scriptural and theological grounds. Although in 1829 the Synod had declared that there should be no segregation, it seems that this decision was 'never translated into practice'.[10] The church yielded to the prejudices of the 'weaker' brethren, i.e. the majority of the whites. Biblical texts were searched out to justify such segregation. The last two contributions to *Apartheid is Heresy*, by Willem Vorster and Douglas Bax, are a critique of the NGK exegesis of some of them: Gen.1.28; Gen.11.1-9; Deut.32.8 and in the New Testament Acts 2.5-13: Acts 17.26. These texts are found in a NGK synodical report of 1974 entitled *Human Relations and the South African Scene in the Light of Scripture*. The report declares:

> A serious warning must be issued against the marked tendency which has always existed, namely to link up an understanding of the Bible with current tradition. The danger then exists of the scripture being interpreted according to what the 'historical situation' prescribes and therefore on a selective basis.[11]

Willem Vorster comments:

> It is exactly on this score that the report is self-contradictory. Clearly the 'historical situation' out of which the report grew is taken as a grid through which the Bible is read.[12]

This book, as well as previous work initiated by the Christian Institute, reveals how false theology contributes to the justification of apartheid. Thus since the theologians of the church can quote texts to 'prove' the biblical justification for apartheid, there is no reason why an ordinary youngster of the same church should have any qualms, on Christian grounds, over defending apartheid by obeying military call-up. Even when he is exposed to some of the atrocities of the war zone, any instinctive feelings of abhorrence or of compassion can be suppressed by the strong sense of duty, instilled by upbringing, that the fight is for the Volk and such a fight is right, just as it was for the forbears who drew up their laager in the veld. Furthermore, as will be shown in a later chapter, the fighting is not only justified on such grounds as the right of necessary defence, but is also seen as a crusade against Communism, the Communists being atheists and therefore the enemies of white Christian civilization. From such a cultural mainspring of ideas, coercion and violence, even outright invasion of other countries becomes justified, not reluctantly as a necessary evil, but confidently with the underlying assumption that God is on the side of the Nationalists, just as the NGK is. Thus the Calvinist heritage of the Afrikaners is the opposite of the view that the church has nothing to do with politics. As de Klerk's important book shows, Calvinism as received by the Afrikaners and transformed or distorted to fit their experience as pioneers and colonists give them a strong idealism in politics, that the Kingdom of God on earth requires radical restructuring of society. The ideals of apartheid fit in with such Calvinist yearnings. A government which works for the 'solution of the Bantu problem' is working for something sanctioned by theology.

Bearing in mind the social dimensions of the Calvinist heritage, it is therefore interesting to note the comments of other South Africans who come from the same church traditions but have reached opposite convictions about apartheid. Dr Beyers Naude is the outstanding example of an Afrikaner churchman opposing apartheid. He issued this warning:

> If we, as the white population, do not take note and do not take seriously the legitimate claims and aspirations of the black population, then it would necessarily lead to estrangement, to bitterness, and a polarization between black and white which can lead to conflict, which can possibly lead to violence in this country, and we as whites should be sensible enough to see this development and to recognize the legitimate claims of our black population, to intercept it, in time through negotiations to come to a sensible agreement about political and social order in which the black community could feel they have been granted an equal place in our society.[13]

This plea to give black people in South Africa a place in society matches the arguments of Robert Mangaliso Sobukwe. In a sacral society, the sacred authority given to law is based on the assumption that everyone is part of the same polity, which is patently not the case in South Africa. Under the Calvinist scheme, church and state are two facets of the same polity, members of one being members of the other. From such sacral assumptions, ministers of religion have every right, indeed a duty, to speak out about the moral or religious significance of political actions. Here Beyers Naude, as an Afrikaner Calvinist by origin, is speaking out as a prophet in a sacral society.

Similarly, Dr Boesak, coming from the black section of the Dutch Reformed Church, is equally insistent that politics cannot be split off from religion:

> To keep politics out of religion (or out of preaching) is to break the wholeness of life. It is to put an impermissible limitation on the

restorative and renovative work of the Holy Spirit. 'Compartmentalism,' so writes Max Warren, 'is the essence of heathenism.'

Without realizing it, we have drifted back into the polytheism against which the prophets of the Lord waged their great warfare. The real essence of heathenism is that it divides various concerns of human life into compartments. There is one god of the soil; there is another for the desert. The god of wisdom is different from the god of wine. If a man wants to marry, he must pray at the temple; if he wants to make war, he must pray elsewhere. All this is precisely where the modern paganism of our secular society has brought us today. Certain portions of our life we call religious. Then we are Christians. We use a special language... we call that our Christianity... and there we stop. We then turn to another department of life we call politics.[14]

Like Beyers Naude, Boesak is here asserting the preacher's duty to speak out on social and political questions.

This brief survey of statements from Dutch Reformed churchmen demonstrates that religious arguments are vitally significant, indeed central, to the apartheid debate. So it is inappropriate for Christians abroad, whose theology has been formed by different national experiences, to assert that religion has nothing to do with politics, or that the World Council of Churches should not be allowed to continue a debate with South African churchmen at several consultations such as Cottesloe, begun by, and within, the sacral way of thinking. People who are offended by the fact that the WCC has taken sides, that it is partisan, should also note that ideas of balance, compromise and political pragmaticism, strong though they may be in Anglo-Saxon tradition, are eclipsed within Calvinist idealism by the strong sense of God being on the side of the just. The problem within South African Calvinism is that there are divergent views, as I have explained, about what constitutes a just society.

Casuistry in an imperfect society

In the previous section we saw how distorted Calvinist theology can persuade white South African Christians that it is their duty to fight for South Africa's apartheid society. However, different justifications for readiness to perform military service have been offered by the English churches, from within the Anglo-Saxon tradition of the church of national compromise. As an example of this I have selected an article by a CPSA clergyman, the Revd D.G. Damant, of George, who contributed to the same issue of *Seek* as Billy Paddock. To follow his arguments it is necessary to quote nearly all the article. It was printed on the same centre-page spread as Paddock's arguments, with an introductory paragraph in heavy type:

> Down the ages the Christian Church has produced a considerable volume of casuistical literature on the problem of the Christian's duty in a situation of armed conflict, and the solutions have varied from the militancy of the Crusaders to the pacifism of the Quakers (always with the authority of duly selected biblical texts).[15]

So Damant seems to be asserting that there is a justifiable position between the militancy of the Crusaders and the pacifism of the Quakers, a position which justifies readiness to serve in the SADF, something of obvious concern to his white parishioners whose sons are liable to call-up.

> Pacifism as such has never been endorsed by our church. Quite the contrary, in fact, since Article 37 states: 'it is lawful for Christian men, at the commandment of the Magistrate, to wear weapons and serve in the wars'.
>
> On the other hand, not since the seventeenth century have we been very keen on Holy Wars ('For God, for the Cause, for the Church, for the Laws, for Charles King of England, and Rupert of the Rhine). In general, while we have recognized the evil of war, we have followed the principle of choosing the lesser of two evils and given general consent to the concept of 'the just war'. We have also recognized the right of the state to maintain a standing army or 'Defence Force' in times of peace (or 'undeclared war') and to man it with volunteers or by conscription, and we have always provided such forces with spiritual guides or chaplains.
>
> What has casuistry to say to young South Africans who are called up for military service when they are being told that such service bolsters an undemocratic and unjust society, and that the need to defend their country has only arisen because of particular political policies? (This point of view results in their being classified as 'selective conscientious objectors', objecting to military service only under particular conditions, but being ready to render it under other circumstances.)
>
> In the first place casuistry must remind them that as citizens they have a duty to obey the state as a matter of conscience (Romans 13.5;

I Peter 2.13). In an age when subordination to authority is seen as outmoded and unnecessary this is a principle which needs to be stressed very firmly.

Divine authority is reflected in the home, in the family, in society, and in the state – a hierarchy of order which the individual is in no way entitled to flout merely because he feels inclined to do so. Rebellion against lawful authority has always been condemned in Christian ethics, and in the strongest terms.

Only if the authorities have become enemies of God instead of his servants can refusal to obey them be justified (Acts 4.19).

But at what point does the secular authority pass from being God's servant to being his enemy? Who is to be the judge of this? Is it possible for any human institution to be consistently perfect? If the church itself is imperfect, and yet demands loyalty from Christians in God's name, can the imperfect state not do the same? If the imperfect state as we know it perishes, what guarantee or even likelihood is there that its successor will be any better? Might it not be very much worse? (Certainly we might expect a marked reduction in the level of tolerance of dissent in a Marxist state compared to what we now enjoy!)

Also whatever his political views may be, the Christian accepts without a second thought all the benefits which the structures of the state afford him: security, education, health services, economic stability and so on.

These carry a reciprocal obligation to discharge the duties which society demands of him, and by the time he is old enough to render military service, he is very deeply involved indeed in this 'social contract'.

Patriotism, too, has some claim to be considered as a motivating factor, as long as we remember with Edith Cavell that, by itself, it is not enough.

Firstly, the young man who conforms to the requirements of the law will find he has many opportunities to be of service to his fellow men of all races while he is in uniform, and to continue to work and witness for a better society in which all may have a fair share of opportunity and prosperity.

On the other hand we must never underestimate the agony of mind which a conscientious objector had to undergo before he comes to his decision when motivated by genuine religious commitment and love of his Saviour; but he must be completely convinced that his stand rests on sound exegesis of Holy Scripture and on matters of fact or certainties, and not on assumptions and value-judgments which are open to doubt or differences of assessment.

He must beware of being influenced by predictions of the probable course of events, and Utopian goals which have yet to be realized anywhere else on the face of the earth. He must also be careful to allocate the blame for his predicament fairly.

To be prepared to shed the blood of your fellow man is no light thing, but why does he place you under this fearful necessity?

Is it not because he has accepted Chairman Mao's dictum that power grows out of the barrel of a gun? Is it not because he has associated himself with organizations which have deliberately chosen to go about imposing their will on the unwilling by methods of terrorism, torture and acts of violence on the innocent and unarmed? Ought he not to be curbed? Has the state not the duty to put a stop to his activities?

More especially if it can be shown that the state is taking steps to meet legitimate grievances to the dissidents, then its right to fight terrorism and its right to mobilize its citizens in active service to this end cannot be questioned.

In asserting his casuistry of the *status quo*, Damant appears to be anti-fanatical: 'Not since the seventeenth century have we been very keen on Holy Wars,' he intones. But the tone is misleading in so far as it gives the impression that *this* war is being fought on cold pragmatic grounds, whereas in South Africa the government sells the idea that the war is being fought as a crusade against Communism. Damant himself identifies the enemy as Communist, with his disparaging remarks about the Marxist state, and the influence of Chairman Mao on the enemy. His remark about 'the level of toleration of dissent' grates on the black reader who is painfully aware of the sectional, i.e. racial, bias of the law's toleration, and who would ask if such partisan enjoyment of toleration is moral or Christian. The identification of the enemy as Communist slides easily from anti-Communist rhetoric to Holy War notions, especially as Marxism is officially atheist. Damant ignores the motivation of 'the enemy', while seeing them as power-hungry Maoists rather than as disadvantaged fellow South Africans taking up arms as a last resort, to redress the imbalance in a society that gives them so much pain. Thus towards its end Damant's article, which starts out with anti-fanatical pretensions, veers towards the crusade idea of war, with the stereotyping of the enemy as Communist.

The tone of pragmaticism is also misleading if considered in the light of what the Nationalist government is actually doing. Damant acknowledges that in an imperfect world imperfect choices have to be made. The opposite of being a realist is to be a Utopian, which Damant warns against. In Damant's categories the realists are those who obey the government (which increasingly likes to claim that its policies are the only realistic ones), while the Utopians are on the other side, the freedom-fighters. But it is important to keep in mind that the Nationalist party ideology is based on Calvinist Utopianism, as I argued in the previous section. The government is attempting to mould South African society to its ideology by a determination to impose apartheid, the Afrikaner Utopia, in spite of the fact that the real world of the South African economy has been forcing blacks and whites into a mutual interdependence for more than a century. Thus there is ideology in both camps, and it is hypocrisy to pretend otherwise.

Several of Damant's justifications are based on assertions of fact. He suggests that whereas values are open to doubt, facts are what can be dependend on. My comment on this is, however, that in the South African situation the interpretation of facts is very much dependent upon the allegiance of the debater, for example with regard to what is happening in the 'border zone'. Damant implies that the enemy is associated with organizations which use terrorism, torture and violence on the innocent and unarmed. It has been asserted by several fact-finding tours, especially those organized by the charities, that these are the very methods used by the SADF against unarmed civilians in Namibia. Billy Paddock also used arguments about *facts*, but on the opposite side to Damant. He refers to the reported failure of the SADF to win the hearts and minds of the people.

> Reports of what occurs in the operational area indicate that it is commonly accepted that in searching out SWAPO guerrillas, the security forces stop at nothing to force information out of people. They break into homes, beat up residents, shoot people, steal and kill cattle, and often pillage stores and tea-rooms. When the tracks of SWAPO guerrillas are discovered by the security forces the local people are in danger. Harsh measures are intensified. People are blindfolded, taken from their homes, and left beaten up and even dead by the roadside. Women are often raped...[16]

Such testimony gives us the context, and is an example of what 'facts' can do on both sides of the ongoing confrontation. The question arises as to who is judging whom. Damant insists that the other side is linked with coercive organizations – 'power grows from the barrel of a gun'– while Paddock asserts that the South African government is precisely such a coercive and bullying system. This leads to the conclusion that 'matters of fact' are more open to 'differences of assessment' than Damant cares to admit. He seems to live in a world where everybody holds the same opinion on any given set of facts, a homogenous society which suppresses dissent by custom, convention or stronger measures – exactly what apartheid has done in the white enclaves of South Africa. Yet he seems to be aware that there can be diverging views about values. But he has not probed to discover how values can shape views about facts, even to the extent of suppressing news about some and exaggerating others. For is it not the case that we live in a world in which there are many covert forces behind what we may call 'facts', which, hidden though they may be, are no less determinative of the way moral choices are made and events move. Chapter 9 will analyse in greater detail the workings of the South African government manipulation of facts. Still basing his arguments on 'facts', Damant then refers to the government's forthcoming measures. It is important to note carefully the wording at this point because the factual nature is *conditional*, referring to a future that has not yet become a reality:

> ...if it can be shown that the state is taking steps to meet legitimate grievances...then its right to mobilize its citizens in active service... cannot be questioned.

Such a generalized statement makes no sense in the context in which it is set. Damant must be aware of the fact that whilst apartheid may win the consent of the majority of the white electorate, it is not supported by the overwhelming voteless black majority, The very fact of being denied a vote by the government that is to take the measures, as Sobukwe asserted at his trial, is one of the most basic grievances. Damant never specifies what steps the government might be taking. If he is referring to Namibia, then one is compelled to remind him that free and fair elections had not been held in that country at the time of writing, nor have they since – so the conditional future of his concluding paragraph becomes a hazy basis on which to base a moral choice. If he is referring to South Africa, then the black population still remains comprehensively unconsulted. As Damant is as unspecific as the government as to what steps are envisaged, this in turn makes it impossible for anyone to look for the factual verification entailed in his conclusion. Thus an article which began by insisting that it is important to relate moral choice to particular circumstances concludes by being vague about actually what set of circumstances is being referred to. In short, Damart's pragmaticism is hollow, and not as closely linked to 'facts' as he pretends.

Besides this false pragmaticism, another pillar of Damant's arguments is 'sound exegesis of scripture'. In the introductory paragraph he admits that Christians quote scripture in support of different views, but then in the body of the article he also uses the Bible, referring to Rom.13.5; 5.1; I Peter 2.13 in support of his arguments for upholding the present government. He is honest enough to give the contrary text to Acts 4.19, which suggests that the Christian may have to defy authorities that have become the enemies of God. But he points out the difficulty of judging human institutions. What are the criteria by which it can be decided when a secular movement/government/church has become God's enemy? The crux of his argument appears in the question 'If the Church itself is imperfect, and yet demands loyalty... can the imperfect state not do the same?' The conflation of church and state in this argument reveals its origins in a sacral society. But it does not represent any progress at all towards the answer to the question how the citizen is to recognize when the imperfect has become downright evil. In Damant's moral scheme are there no intermediates between the imperfect and the evil? Does he object to the formulation of any such criteria – by human rights charters, WCC statements or whatever? By the end of the paragraph his position is revealed: he supports the *status quo* for fear of what might come instead; the Marxist state might be *worse*. So he does reveal some criteria for better or worse, and the issue he picks on is 'the level of tolerance of dissent'. It would be difficult to find a scriptural text to justify choosing this issue above others. Furthermore, as I have pointed out, this statement reveals a false perception about how the government actually does treat dissenters in South Africa. Thus a section of the article that began with a scriptural aura ends with snide speculation about putative Marxist states. This shows the futility of trying to base arguments on Bible texts when the real concerns of the moment cannot be encapsulated in reading a particular verse. The text of Acts does not present us with a universal charter by which we can distinguish good governments from bad governments. What it does is to show us how certain characters in the New Testament story about the drama of redemption and evangelism that is now operative in the world responded as the persons they were – rather than as the normative way in which they intended their successors to respond in all similar situations for all time. For howsoever we may wish it, the fact remains that none of us can ever duplicate the motivational situation, as well as theological impetus and moral decisions, that applied on those particular occasions. This type of biblicism, which gives a false scriptural aura to arguments whose real roots lie elsewhere (in this case in a fear of Marxism), is baneful and to be avoided.

Obligations to an imperfect government

Damant's article veers between the theology of a sacral society and the pessimism of a church that has given up the struggle to bring into being the kingdom of God on earth. His statement 'Divine authority is reflected in the home, in the family, in society and in the state' shows the assumptions of a sacralist, but elsewhere his casuistry appears to doubt the divine presence in any human institution: 'the church itself is imperfect'. Such innuendo avoids the challenge of considering whether some institutions, policies or power structures are more imperfect than others. Some are imperfect but tolerable, some are intolerable. Many blacks have decided that the South African apartheid system is intolerable and so have taken up arms against it. According to Damant's philosophy, the state is always to be obeyed, however unjust.

Several church thinkers have argued that the debate is not really about violence and non-violence, but about the use of power. David Gill has commented:

> The tendency to pose the issue as violence versus non-violence must be corrected. In a social conflict, more than in international conflict, the two cannot be presented as if one were the alternative of the other. The term violence of the *status quo*, which becomes current in recent discussion, points to the structures when they are not effectively challenged. An Australian Quaker, for example, documenting the Aborigines, emphasizes that 'Those one in six aboriginal children who die in their first four years of life in the Northern Territory are just as dead as if they had been killed by bullets or bayonets. Institutional violence in this country is "doing violence" to Aborigines, and to our professed values of everyday life.'[17]

Gill then makes a suggestion to clarify the debate in a way highly relevant to the South African situation as well as to the Australian example:

> Instead of this false dichotomy between violence and non-violence,

the discussion should fix us on identifying and evaluating the various forms of coercion which may be effective in a variety of different situations.

This is exactly the sort of intermediate definition that Damant declined to give, because of his view that the *status quo* is better than the uncertainties of the future. Gill also quotes a precedent for his argument from the SODEPAX report of 1969, which discussed 'the organization of power to effect social changes in the direction of greater justice, which is at the same time effective and also least violent in terms of human life and bloodshed'.

This is in line with the Arnoldshaim WCC statement, which affirmed:

There can be no justice in our world without a transfer of economic resources to undergird the redistribution of political power and to make cultural self-determination meaningful.

Jürgen Moltmann clarifies what such a redistribution would mean in terms of white racism:

White racism is by far the most dangerous form of racism, because through it social, economic and political structures are organized and defended which are at variance with the Universal Declaration of Human Rights. In such countries, racism is not simply an ethnic group-phenomenon, but an instrument of domination which secures political, economic and cultural privileges for the whites, and makes second-class humans of black and coloured people, unless they can be designated 'honorary whites', like the economically powerful Japanese. For this reason the race question here cannot be solved solely by a change of individual conscience but only by changing the racist power structures, in order to achieve a redistribution of power from the powerful to the powerless. Conversely, however, such a redistribution of power will not be achieved unless people get rid of racist mentality, any more than the institutional abolition of slavery in the Southern states of the United States of America a hundred years ago really eliminated the racist mentality of many whites there. Racism is, in this connection, both a form of ideology and a manifestation of the institutions of power.[18]

Thus far, it has been argued that violence and non-violence take institutional forms, especially under the influence of racism. Some people have coined the term 'structural violence' to refer to what we have in South Africa. For instance, J.G.Davies writes:

> Structural violence shows itself when the resources and power are unequally shared and are the property of a restricted number who use them not for the good of all but for their own profit and for the domination of the less favoured. 'When a system,' says Thomas Merton, '... without resort to overt force, compels people to live in conditions of abjection, helplessness, wretchedness, that keeps them on the level of beasts rather than of men, it is plainly violent.' To make men live on the sub-human level against their will, to constrain them in such a way that they have no hope of escaping their conditions, is an unjust exercise of force. Those who in some way or other concur in their oppression – and perhaps profit by it – are exercising violence even though they may be preaching pacificism. And their supposedly peaceful laws, which maintain this spurious kind of order, are in fact instruments of violence and oppression.[19]

In other words, in the kind of society that prevails in South Africa, pacifism is not a straightforward choice away from guilt about aggression. This is because the pacifist, noble and courageous as his stance may be, cannot claim thereby to counter the effects of violence in the society of which he is part. The violence of the society is supported by institutional power, power derived from those who vote for that system, and thus authorize the government in its policies of repression and racist discrimination. The pacifist is limited in his ability to stop this from happening. In a different institutional system it could, conversely, be the racist who is limited. To illustrate this, it could be pointed out that in Britain there are people who hold views not dissimilar from those of South African whites towards black people, but whereas the white South Africans have awarded themselves the legal power to impose their racism on the rest of the population of South Africa, their counterparts in Britain do not have that legal power.

In all this, analysis of the South African situation draws us to the conclusion that it has to do with power, and how power is used sectionally. The black section of the population, who do not have that power, may eventually use coercion to obtain it. Similarly, the white population, spurred on by fear of that eventuality, are programmed by upbringing and early induction into the military to defend the *status quo* at all costs. Within this confrontational situation, pacifism is difficult to sustain in any meaningful way, except by opting for exile. Military service appears, not as the citizen's duty to a benign state, as it is represented in Damant's article, but as the furtherance of a violent system.

It is when the actual features of the South African situation are scrutinized that *status quo* theology is seen to be inappropriate. In spite of this background reality, reactions to PCR from some churches abroad continue to reveal national church-type perceptions about the role of the state. In their social thinking some Western churches seem to have a mental set formed by their own historical experience, a kind of stereotyping which they then transfer to South Africa, without considering the facts. I have already shown how Damant's advocacy of obedience to the state dissolves into a hazy set of unfulfilled conditions. *Status quo* theology seems prone to this type of stereotyping regardless of facts; assuming that it does not, usually, imply that might is always right, or allegiance to government (however evil), then it requires some application of moral criteria to the particular situation. Does this then weaken by moral relativism this type of justification? Must each society evolve its own criteria? I am wary of this conclusion, as it sounds like another version of 'South Africa is unique', a plea that is used by apartheid apologists to brush aside human rights criteria. So I do not wish to assert that the situation is so very different in various parts of the world, or periods of history, that it is futile to make comparisons. Indeed such comparisons are very useful as a way of testing moral consistency, of making sure that moral or theological criteria are not getting distorted by instincts of national interest, by false peceptions and forms, or the exigencies of the circumstances. What I am trying to assert is that moral judgment, even casuistry of the Damant variety, should be based on honest inquiry into the facts. With regard to debates that cut across national perceptions, as does PCR, it must be realized that it is misleading to try to transpose political philosophy, or rather political theology, without investigating how far those societies are comparable. I have already discussed one such example, the assumption that the church has nothing to do with politics, which cannot be assumed to apply to the sacral society of Afrikaner-dominated South Africa.

Another assumption made by *status quo* advocates is that the state is benign, and that to obey it, even by actions that induce moral unease, is preferable to allowing social disorder to get out of hand. The hidden premise of such a way of thinking is that 'terrorism' is what disturbs an otherwise peaceful society. But it is what one may call mental laziness to fail to investigate whether such a society really is peaceful or not, for the *majority of* its people, or if the underlying injustice is so dehumanizing that rebellion is inevitable, The word 'terrorist' has strong emotive connotations, and different associations in different countries. In West Germany, the Baader Meinhof group was stirring up political confrontation in the 1970s. For British people, as well as memories of colonial Kenya and Malaya, there is the continual example of the IRA and Ulster violence. I am not qualified to comment on the political implications of terrorism either in Germany or in Britain, but at least in one respect, that of the sheer numbers of people involved, South Africa is a different question. In South Africa, during the 1970s, at least seventeen million black people were being governed without their consent by a regime which is certainly more violent in its methods than those of either Ulster or West Germany. So even on the criterion of 'the greatest number', South Africa has rightly been in the forefront of moral debates about the politics of violence.

Another example of inappropriate transfer of *status quo* arguments can be seen in a report of a working party of the United Reformed Church, commended by the WCC 1973 Study of Violence and Non-Violence.[20] In some of its paragraphs, it commends various non-violent methods, or ways of mitigating violence. In some parts, for instance in paragraphs about policing a riot, it seems to assume that better crowd-control techniques would lessen violence in a country like South Africa – as if the problem were just one of crowd-control, like an over-excited football crowd, rather than a social conflict going back two centuries. This part of the discussion exemplifies the Anglo-Saxon tendency to assume that superior techniques can solve any problem. But today, it is obvious that this style of thinking avoids underlying social realities. Violence in South Africa is unlikely to be halted for long by crowd-control techniques borrowed from a society with a very different calibre of police. The shootings at the peaceful protest at Uitenhage in 1983 revealed to the outside world what kind of police force South Africans have to suffer.

Another assumption of the *status quo* thinkers that was current in the 1970s was that evolution is better than revolution. For example, on 4 September 1970, *The Daily Telegraph* lamented the fact that the Arnoldshaim grants showed 'the removal of all hopes of evolution in favour of revolution'. This preference for evolution is ignorant of the type of arguments about the violence of the *status quo*, as quoted from Moltmann and Davies, that were being expressed with regard to PCR. Meanwhile, the South African government greatly favours this advocacy of evolution as it deflects attention from the violence of its system. Its politicians and diplomats regularly counter criticisms by claiming: 'We are changing... wait for the announcements... give us a hand.' But time and again, when the promised changes are announced, they turn out to be a further consolidation of apartheid. The most recent example shows that those who think it still possible for blacks to negotiate are increasingly proved wrong. Thus those who still advocate evolution are deceived about the nature of apartheid government. It is inappropriate to recommend a course of action which assumes that there are alternatives and choices which, increasingly, have been shut off.

Non-political theology

The two previous sections have shown the social dimension to theology; now we go on to analyse non-political or apolitical dispositions. Here I have in mind the stance adopted by Christians whose convictions cause them to stand aloof from politics. How this relates to *status quo* theology should soon be apparent.

As we have seen, some churches, notably Jehovah's Witnesses and some Zionist churches, have a consistently other-worldly theology. Members of national church-type denominations, however, like Lutherans and Anglicans, who make selective use of an apolitical plea, deserve to be challenged over their view of God, as a pietistic or other-worldly view of God is inconsistent with the main trends of their theology. A God who is interested only in human spiritual well-being has withdrawn from the totality of life and would seem incompatible with any kind of incarnational theology.

There is a strong tradition among the mission churches, including those of national church origins, that the Christian gospel is primarily about saving individuals and instructing them in the spiritual life. So the missionary in the field can go about his task of evangelizing regardless of the material and social circumstances of his congregations. Hence contributors to missionary societies tend to get confused when the message comes back from the 'mission-field' countries that politics are on the agenda. For example, *The Daily Telegraph* of 13 July 1978 reported the words of a Mr Shaw (there is more to him than meets the eye, as we shall see in Chapter 9):

The rot first became clearly evident in the World Council of Churches in 1973 when a resolution was passed to stop sending missionaries to the Third World and to send the money saved to the cause of political liberation instead.[21]

For British Methodists the problem was acute in 1978 because the same fund, the Methodist Overseas Division, handled contributions both to the overseas churches and to PCR. The Revd Dr W.P.Stevens protested in the *Methodist Recorder*:

This means that those who disagree strongly with, say, the grant to the Patriotic Front have only two real choices: support the Patriotic Front because they want to help the overseas missionary work of the church, or not support the overseas missionary work of the church because they do not want to support the Patriotic Front.[22]

The problem within British churches seems to be that many people in the congregations, especially in the older age-groups, formed their ideas of overseas Christians, particularly in South Africa, from missionary meetings of past years, a period of missionary ascendancy in that part of the world. But some of the missionaries, like Fred Shaw, are closely identified with the privileged white minority.

It cannot be denied that some missionaries, like Trevor Huddleston and the Burgos Fathers of Mozambique, and Bishop Lamont in UDI Rhodesia, have a splendid record of communicating back to the sending and funding countries the aspirations of the black majorities among whom they work. But there is a long legacy of missionary reports which presented Africans as simple people, like children. Many missionaries must have missed out the political implications of their work in telling their stories about Africa back home. The first reaction against the PCR grants shows the collision point between ideas formed by old-style missionary work, concerned to save souls and increase congregations, and the arguments emerging from the new awareness within the mission churches of the social and political context of their growth. The old-style missionary hierarchy had been almost entirely in the hands of whites, both in the field and at headquarters. But the WCC's programme was formed at gatherings of Christians from all over the world, including Africa. So it is important to see the inter-church aspect of PCR: one could almost say that PCR represents the challenge of Third World Christians to the old sending missionary countries.

In Britain, as well as the evangelical mission instincts that recoil from political theology, there is also the viewpoint that was voiced by E.R.Norman in the 1978 Reith Lectures. In those lectures he denounced

Christians who choose a secular political idealism rather than spiritual realities. Several books have been published since then to refute his arguments; in one of them Peter Hinchliff, who also happens to be familiar with South Africa, puts a counter-argument thus:

> The church is not composed solely of bishops and clergymen, and its voice is not heard in the pronouncements of synod alone. The church is the whole people of God and the layman has at least something of this same duty to care for other people as the clergyman. Since Christians are also citizens, the church cannot 'go into politics'; it is there already, by virtue of the fact that Christians have votes to exercise, if for no other reason. The alternative is, if a Christian refuses to be involved in politics – then he should not pay taxes either – for paying taxes is one of the ways in which citizens get involved in the doings of the government – and we are thereby responsible for the doings of the government as well.[23]

A truly other-worldly religion would withdraw from both the duties and the privileges of citizenship. The Jehovah's Witnesses are perhaps the best candidates for this, as their faith, as far as I have understood it, is based on a theology of power, that all authority is from God and therefore their actions, e.g. as conscientious objectors or in other forms of confrontation with government, as in Zambia and Malawi, stem from this essential opposition to human sources of power.

In contrast to other forms of other-worldly theology, the arguments of E.R.Norman seem specious precisely because they emanate from a position within a national church, a church which has as its background tradition a good many ideas carried over from the old sacralist society in which church and state are two aspects of the same community. An even more telling point to notice about E.R.Norman's arguments, however, is that he is not indifferent to politics at all: what incenses him is the leftward bias he detects in the political Christians. So I would regard E.R.Norman and his like as supporters of the *status quo* because their other-worldly arguments are selective and inconsistent.

Christian charity

Alongside the over-spiritual view of salvation in the mission field, there is also a strong humanitarian conscience, sometimes side by side in the same churches. Thus it is thought perfectly proper for missions to engage in such socially useful work as setting up schools and hospitals, and where necessary relieving the suffering of disaster victims, refugees and victims of war. Such activity can be termed humanitarian and fits in with Britain's charity laws. But there seems to be an astonishing confidence that this activity can be kept separate from politics. People who protested about the 1978 PCR grants to the Patriotic Front evoked this magic term charity.

For example, Gervase Bradford wrote:

> On the matter of the recent grant of £45,000 from the World Council of Churches to the Zimbabwe Patriotic Front, the logic of your leader last week entitled 'A Justifiable Grant' eludes me. You seek to equate the sanctions-breaking of 'Western supported enterprises' with a gift of charitable funds to the Front. Possibly some sanction breakers are morally motivated, as (presumably) are the WCC. But these are a small minority, and unlike the WCC, they use their own money. The majority break sanctions for the perfectly respectable, but morally neutral, reason of making profit. The point is that neither this group, nor the more engaged minority, would claim to be acting as a charity. Your justification of the gift in terms of its declared purpose (i.e. humanitarian) seems equally unsound. Given that the resources available to any liberation movement must be considered globally, surely it is clear that expenditure upon 'refugees' (though this is a loaded term with which some might quibble) and open armaments are necessarily interrelated. To put it simply, such gifts relieve the Front of the necessity to allocate funds to meet their welfare and medical requirements and consequently increase their capability for guerrilla activity... Does charity include the murder of Muzorewa's envoys while seeking a ceasefire with the Front?...To gain tax advantages of being a charity it is required that funds of the body claiming such status should be devoted exclusively to charitable purposes...[24]

Even in 1983 I was informed that the Overseas Division of the Methodist Church is still finding it difficult to make their contributions to PCR because of the definition of charity for covenanting purposes.

Those engaged in charity administration in Britain, both for local charities and for overseas purpose, have been troubled for some time by the limitations imposed by the concept of charity. It sometimes seems as if their organizations are allowed to work to alleviate the suffering of victims of social malformation but not to devote efforts to tackling the causes, especially if it means trying to influence public opinion, politicians or even the government of the day. The overseas aid agencies, especially in the 1980s, are now beginning to assert that a change in political awareness in the richer countries is necessary before some of the root causes of poverty can be tackled.

But it was above all PCR in the 1970s which challenged most sharply the notions of apolitical theology and the concomitant assumptions about apolitical charity. Many comments that appeared in the British Press reveal the acrimony of this debate. For instance, on 15 September 1970 *The Times* leader commented:

> Even to give money for non-military use is to invite comment that it will free money for military use. There are other forms of Christian aid, and other ways of fulfilling the Council's Programme to Combat Racism.[25]

In the same issue of *The Times*, the Deputy Director of Christian Aid dissociated that organization from PCR:

> In conveying this decision to Geneva the Board also noted that if in due course certain specific projects to combat racism were identified and funds sought for these particular projects, the Board would be prepared to consider them for financial support on their merits. Any request would have to come within the terms of reference of Christian Aid, which is a registered charity.[26]

The same debate flared up again in the press in 1978 during the worst part of the violence in Rhodesia/Zimbabwe. Again Christian Aid, as shown in Kenneth Slack's letter to *The Times*, was striving to draw a distinction between political actions and humanitarian project aid:

> The World Council of Churches has a right to be heard on the urgent political and international issues of the day. If Christianity has no concern with the common life of men and nations, it is absurdly irrelevant...
>
> The World Council has a vast humanitarian task of united Christian service to the refugees, the disaster victims and the poor. The present acute problem arises from the mingling of the two elements – the political judgment and the humanitarian task.Probably the best course would be for the World Council to revert to handling these matters separately through the Commission on Inter-Church Aid, Refugee and World Service (as to the humanitarian task)...[27]

The *Methodist Recorder* was especially keen to air views on the PCR grants; understandably, as the Methodist Overseas Division is the only

British church which has actually given money to PCR, as contrasted to those that merely talked and criticized. In 1978 David Haslam returned from a visit to the camps in the Front Line states and wrote in the *Recorder* that the grants were inadequate to the task, as he pointed out that they amounted to about 50p per refugee, since ZANU leaders were responsible for about 70,000 refugees and the Botswana Christian Council for another 8,000. He was adamant that the WCC money was being used for purely humanitarian purposes. However, the debate continued in the correspondence column of the *Methodist Recorder*. Irene Runcorn wrote in on 5 October:

> If the officials of the WCC realize, as they must surely do, that their decision is extremely unpopular among Christians and non-Christians alike in this country, should they not reassure us that no further allocation of cash will be made to any country where terrorism is taking place. Where help is needed by the innocent victims of this violence, it should be sent out in kind and administered by our own officials. Prior call on our resources should be for peaceful countries, where it will be used for education, agriculture, medical purposes, and hopefully, too, the spread of the Gospel, which is what it was all about in the first place.[28]

The letter reveals many of the stock prejudices. There is the paternalist preference for distribution by our own people (i.e. white missionaries). Although the letter is mostly about politics and charity, the final remark is about politics and Christian evangelism, thereby revealing the old-style missionary prejudices mentioned earlier, a veritable pie-in-the-sky gospel. The suggestion about only helping peaceful people is an extraordinary one, showing naivety about the political causes of need. It can also be rebutted by a reference to the example of Jesus refusing to be associated only with 'good' people.

Another Methodist correspondent protested on 19 October:

> In fact, of course, the grants to the Fund to Combat Racism are not primarily humanitarian and objective at all. They are intended to be political gestures, packaged as humanitarian actions, in an attempt to forestall and disarm criticism. Our first duty is to say so loud and clear. Such acts of political solidarity may be justified in themselves, but if so they must in all honesty be described and defined as such, and not sold as humanitarian programmes.[29]

The Community and Race Relations Unit of the BCC put out a leaflet in September 1978, still trying to present the humanitarian purpose of the grants.

Question: Isn't there a danger that the grant to the Patriotic Front's humanitarian work will free other funds for military purposes?

Answer: Our experience with this and other African liberation movements, dating back to 1970, gives us no reason to believe that the money we give is used for anything other than the purposes for which it is requested. We invite anyone with evidence to the contrary to let us know immediately. But whether these grants free other funds is a question you could ask of all the churches' aid-giving.[30]

Kenneth Skelton, then Bishop of Lichfield (he had formerly been the Bishop of Matabeleland) spelled out the misconceptions about aid through the churches in his address to the diocese of Lichfield in October 1978:

The argument that guerrilla movements are thereby enabled to save money which can be spent on armaments is a two-edged one. Far greater sums have been, and still are, contributed by the churches in this country, for the relief of suffering and education inside Rhodesia – and the Rhodesian government is thereby enabled to save money likewise – and use it for other purposes. But no word of protest has ever been uttered against those grants.[31]

What this selection of viewpoints from the PCR debate in Britain reveals is that many British people appear to have had an astonishing confidence that there is a clear-cut distinction between humanitarian and political actions in situations where violent confrontation is already taking place. This distinction probably works in a society like mainland Britain, which has been comparatively free of major social injustice and violence for many generations, but if the concept is transferred across to Southern Africa, it does not work in the same way. This is another example of the mind-set of *status quo* thinking.

Furthermore, as emerged from the comments on Dr Norman made earlier, the debaters about the Patriotic Front reveal at times that their preferences are not just for apolitical charity: their main objection was that the grants were supporting the wrong side. In the 1978 letter quoted above, Kenneth Slack advocated supporting the Muzorewa government. It could be asserted, following Irene Runcorn's line of thought, that support should be given to the most peaceful side. However, the Bishop of Lichfield's comment was a shrewd reminder that the same criticism of the Patriotic Front could also be applied to the then government in Rhodesia. In such a situation of war, where news was being manipulated by the Rhodesia Information Services (see Chapter 10), it would be difficult to judge fairly which side was more peaceful.

Some of the people advocating the charity-only approach resented being accused of being one-sided. For example, one of the most vehement of the letter-writers to the British press asserted:

> There is one misunderstanding that is common, but it seems probable that it is wilful. It is the idea that if you do not support the movements concerned, you must support governments against which they rebel and the political *status quo*. To express that fallacy is a sufficient repudiation.[32]

He was writing from Salisbury, Rhodesia. Was he refusing to pay taxes and dissuading the young males in his congregation from obeying call-up to the security forces? I shall have more to say later, in Chapter 10, about the 'fallacy' he refers to; but it is already worth noting that some of the letter writers advocating the 'no politics we're Christians' arguments were in fact financed by the information services of the white régimes.

The sharpest arguments about politics and charity surfaced in 1978, over Rhodesia. However, it is also relevant to take a look at what happens to charitable impulses in South Africa itself. What kind of Christian action for humanitarian purposes – free of all political significance – is possible in South African society? The Christian missions have been centres of education and medical help for generations. In many countries of the world, these functions have been taken over by government, either wholly, or on some arrangement of grants together with a degree of official control. In other words, what one epoch regarded as the proper work of the church the next regards as the job of governments. In South Africa, the take-over was blatantly political; to be able to bring in Bantu Education, the government moved against the mission schools. The Anglican church closed down its schools rather than yield to the National party view of education deemed appropriate for 'Bantu'. In medical work, doctors at mission hospitals complain that resources are taken up treating the results of malnutrition. How, then, can teachers or medical workers regard their work as charity without political causes or consequences? Similarly there are several voluntary organizations in South Africa trying to alleviate the suffering of black people, for example the Black Sash clinics for pass-law victims, Kupugani nutritional enterprises

which seek to combat malnutrition among blacks, and educational classes
such as those associated with SACHED. Some of these activitiies lead
into more overt political activity. Black Sash, for instance, publishes
reports on the effect of the pass laws, and has regular demonstrations
against apartheid. But the white women who are the main voluntary
workers and contributors to these organizations admit that they go as
far as they dare in such activities within the law (or, in some cases, as far
as their husbands allow them). To go any further would jeopardize their
families. Thus in South Africa it is not a charity commission that draws
the line where charity turns to politics: it is the threat of visits by the
Security Police and prison. Because of these limits, such white initiated
enterprises can be called 'charity within the *status quo*', though that is
not to say that the efforts are worthless.

The opposite of this type of charity is exemplifed by the few who take
great risks and make sacrifices in their identification with those who
suffer. Charity in the full-blooded, open-hearted sense implies sympathy
with the victim, and is not limited by fear. Dr Beyers Naude is someone
who has taken the risks and can speak truthfully about the demands of
unconditional charity:

> In order to determine the causes of injustice a person must not only
> have the outward individual facts of the matter, but as a Christian you
> are called upon to identify yourself heart and soul, to live in, and feel,
> the hearts, the consciousness, the feelings of the persons who feel
> themselves aggrieved. This is the grace that the new birth of Christ
> Jesus gives to a person, every person who wishes to receive it.[33]

This position is the opposite of charity within the *status quo*.

Another type of Christian-motivated response to apartheid is manifested in the phenomenon of what might be termed 'the multi-racial
enclave'. Religious bodies are a prime example, and blacks and whites
are allowed to live together in such religious enclosures. The mission
churches have tried to keep open venues where black and white can mix.
In CPSA, the main cathedrals have multi-racial congregations, and
there are centres, such as Diocesan Retreat Centres, where clergy and
laity of the different race-groups meet. But while at such centres,
everyone is aware that social mixing is circumscribed by law. For
instance, the Anglicans had a brave scheme for encouraging teams of
youth workers, both black and white. Naturally enough, one pair wanted
to get married, but because they would have fallen foul of the race laws,
they had to go into exile. I can also speak from personal experience of

such attempts: NUSAS and ASF got into difficulties at their multi-racial conference over such matters as living quarters, joint eating and joint travel, because of apartheid. Now in the 1980s the churches are doing some joint theological training, and again I have had personal experience of the difficulties of trying to work towards a multi-racial institution, at St Paul's, Grahamstown, while facing the entrenched atittudes and prejudices of those brought up in apartheid society. The question to ask is: how far is it possible to sustain such multi-racial enclaves against the social pressures?

Another type of multi-racial enclave is the phenomenon of the international hotel, or the homeland resorts, or Swaziland, which provides the setting for multi-racial sex without prosecution in Mmabatho, the Sun City, sometimes termed Sin City because of its blatant function as the venue for multi-racial relationships forbidden by apartheid laws. The question to ask about this tolerance of multi-racial enclaves is whether they represent the growing points of a new multi-racial South Africa or are just regarded as useful safety valves by a government intent on keeping a repressive system intact. Some see that there are signs of hope in enclaves of multi-racial opportunity. For example, there are now more private schools which accept both black and white pupils though the black pupils tend to be the children of the most privileged. To what extent is it possible to begin to build a new society within the shell of the old?

The WCC Working Party for the 1971 study on Violence, Non-Violence and the Struggle for Social Justice considered as one of its four listed options 'the creation of new social structures which form alternatives to present ones', but then warningly asked: 'What is the relation of these new structures to effective transformation of society? Is this road taken in hope for the whole world, or as an alternative to this hope?'[34] In other words, is opportunity for the privileged going to lead the way for the rest? The black top classes may benefit, while behind this facade the oppression of the rest continues. Mmabatho, Sun City, has the image of a place where rich and glamorous black people disport themselves, whilst in the surrounding veldt life is tough for those less financially endowed. Similarly, the move to allow black pupils into private schools has been interpreted as a manoeuvre to deflect the criticism of the most educated black parents away from the educational slums of the townships. Thus the enclave option can be harnessed to the current policy of the government, to relieve pressure for bigger changes. Those involved in such enclave enterprises, either from charitable, religious or self-help motivation, should constantly ask if their chosen enclave is truly the vanguard of social change or being used to shield the *status quo*.

7

Theology of Solidarity

Solidarity

The critics of PCR show that they are unable to believe that humanitarian action is possible among the freedom movements. They allege that grants to such movements enable the movements to buy more weaponry, hence the 'guns for guerrillas' headlines in 1970 and 1978, the years of most controversy about the PCR grants. Bishop Skelton's arguments quoted in the previous chapter show that with regard to Zimbabwe in 1978 the argument should be applied to both sides. Any money contributed to help war casualties either of the Rhodesian Government or the Patriotic Front might be releasing funds for war material and supplies. But the argument, if looked at in terms of actual money (50p per refugee, as Haslam pointed out), was not really about money at all, but essentially about the principle of solidarity.

Solidarity is a key concept in the documents of the WCC about PCR. For example, the 1971 WCC Central Committee stated:

> The Commission on the Programme to Combat Racism will be responsible for working out World Council policies and programmes on combating racism, giving expression to solidarity with the racially oppressed.[1]

It is significant that the word 'charity' is avoided. Charity has gained a loaded meaning which includes paternalistic attitudes towards those assisted by it. It is often limited to aid for individual needy cases, or to projects that can be controlled and monitored by the donors. It is sometimes undertaken with more attention to the immediate relief of sensational cases, especially the ones that make an impact in a TV sequence, than to the long-term context of the victim's predicament.

Donor satisfaction, in the sense of relieving guilt feelings by some action seen to be done, is sometimes given higher priority than the actual needs, or even expressed wishes, of the victims/recipients. Thus it has been seen as an activity undertaken by those who are benefiting from a given social system, to relieve their conscience about its victims, but without actually having to do anything further to change that system – a safety-valve function.

From this cynical analysis of charity it is easy to see why the 104 participants at the Notting Hill Conference which formulated PCR preferred the concept of solidarity. At that gathering, there was also a frank awareness of guilt, as reflected in Pauline Webb's report:

> The voice of God happened to us... We became aware of the voice of God's judgment on the evil of white racism allied with political and economic and military power.[2]

Looking at the report of the proceedings, one can see that solidarity via humanitarian grants was a compromise between reparations (as demanded by the intruding radicals) and charity which, as Kenneth Slack later pointed out, could have been undertaken by Inter-Church Aid refugee schemes.

The reactions against the solidarity aspect of PCR seem to fall into three main categories:

1. Those who mistrust unmonitored projects.
2. Those who protest that solidarity implies support for violence.
3. Those who think that this solidarity is allied to the wrong side, because that side is Communist, anti-Christian, etc.

I shall be analysing the third reaction in the next chapter. Meanwhile, an example of the second reaction is expressed in a 1983 letter to the *Methodist Recorder*:

> I write about the recent car bomb crime in Pretoria committed by the African National Congress, a body supported by the World Council of Churches. Without arguing the rights and wrongs of WCC support for any given liberation movement, why does it not say to such an organization, loudly so that the world can hear: 'We support your political aspirations, but in no way can we approve of your practice of crude terrorism, involving the murder and maiming of non-military persons, as an instrument of policy.' Our charge against the World Council of Churches is that it has signally failed to do this, and that

by this failure it is setting the principles of political expediency above respect for human life. That cannot be reconciled with the Gospel.[3]

This writer seems to assert that support for political aspirations can be expressed, presumably by verbal means, without entering into the complexities of the moral choices to be faced in pursuing those aspirations. Where both sides are already using violence, the respect for human life has already been cast aside in the quest of political considerations. The correspondent appears to ignore the lack of respect for human life that the Pretoria regime shows, as evidenced in the chronic hardships and killings that have been reported over decades, caused by excessively violent government.

The mistrust of unmonitored grants has not been argued out in detail in the papers I have seen. Fears are expressed rather than specific allegations being made. While in Botswana I witnessed at close quarters the distribution of some small part of the money allocated for the refugees in Botswana. The screening process was fairly rigorous and the staff involved were under constant pressure from the refugees themselves. An obvious point to make about the Western anxiety over unmonitored grants is the lurking racism it might imply. Would these same critics trust only those projects implemented by whites? The PCR gesture of unmonitored grants can thus be seen as an anti-racist act. It also expresses something about the nature of giving. If giving is carefully directed and limited by conditions, it creates a power-situation between giver and recipient. It implies the absence of a trusting relationship. It becomes a bribe or reward for measurable behaviour. But if the giving is intended to express a different type of relationship, of equals, of friends, of fellow-Christians, then the attitude of trust becomes essential.

An interesting argument connected with solidarity emerged in the 1970 BCC Working Party Report:

> If there is in some quarters today a readiness to rethink Christian attitudes in the light of the needs of man and of the demands of the Gospel there is also some readiness for Christians to jump on currently popular secular bandwagons. It could even be argued, on the grounds of prudence, that the church's best chance of survival in Latin America, and indeed in Southern Africa, is as an advocate of revolution. But such self-interest is unworthy of the Gospel.[4]

This prediction was to some extent borne out in Mozambique, where the Burgos Fathers exposed the Wiriyamu massacres in the last years of

Portuguese rule and then withdrew from the country, but were invited
back with honour by the incoming 'Marxist' government.[5]

Another extremely important idea hit upon by the same Working
Party was that by being in solidarity with the liberation movements, in
the days of their struggles, Christians can then be in a position to offer
criticism from within:

> Usually revolution has led to dictatorship, the establishment of a new
> tyranny. It seems likely that only a church within the revolution can
> help to humanize it. A church that is trapped into deifying revolution
> and making gods of its heroes has merely updated the pagan worship
> of war. To be within a revolution, and from there to speak prophetically
> to it, may be both illogical and terrifying. It is at this point that it may
> simply be necessary to be foolish for Christ's sake. If the Church is
> simply part of the revolutionary establishment, nothing would have
> been learnt.[6]

Moral choices within the option of violence

If solidarity is to be more than a slogan it must also involve understanding.
The previous section has made it clear that one of the important areas
where understanding is necessary is that of moral choices. And these
still have to be made after the option of violence has been chosen. Even
not considering options is a moral choice, as Sartre pointed out:

> If I go to war it is because I choose to go to war. I am responsible for
> the war because I could desert or kill myself. It is as if I myself had
> declared the war. Refusing to perform certain actions is choosing, is
> being free. In the last analysis we cannot choose, for even our non-
> choosing is choosing not to choose.[7]

However, supposing that the initial choice has been made, and violent
methods have been decided upon, as a reluctant necessity, the leaders
of that body of people who are prepared to use violence still face many
choices about the degree of violence that may be necessary. In other
words, moral awareness can help in a strategy of minimum violence.
This applies as much to the maintainers of law and order as to those
fighting for liberation. It would be interesting to see what guidelines the
South African government lays down for minimum violence by its armed
servants: for minimum killings of civilians in Namibia, crowd control
without shooting, arrests without torture. What exacerbates the conflict

in South Africa, as the news increasingly reveals, is that the government forces appear to act violently without restraints.

In contrast, the opponents of the apartheid government, the ANC, have produced several statements and documents which set out explicitly their long-held policy of minimum violence. In a crucial interview reported in *The Guardian* on 6 August 1983 Oliver Tambo traced the chronology of the escalation of violent methods:

> For decades we did not think that violence had a role to play in the ANC's struggle: not until the National party came into power in 1948 and was physically violent. The obvious thing was to respond with violence, but then we thought that perhaps that was what they wanted – that they would use our violence to rally whites behind them. We decided that we would not be provoked into violence, although we knew that the National party, having taken power from the United party – from the English-speaking whites – had singled us out as the next ones to be put in our place. But as the peace went by violence increased. We saw more armed police – with pistols at first, then with guns. Then the tanks came. Women's demonstrations were put down with tanks. As we approched the 1960s our people asked: where do we go from here? ...In 1960, when the ANC leadership were still insisting on non-violence, on discipline, that we must get the support of the white electorate – the white electorate continued to support the regime. Then we had the Sharpeville shooting (67 blacks killed, 187 wounded). Even after that we decided to continue with non-violence...
>
> In 1961 we called a general strike to protest against the formation of a republic in South Africa because the government had failed to respond to our call for a national convention. But the army was mobilized on a scale not seen since the Second World War – against a peaceful strike. We knew then that the army had left the barracks and that we had reached the end of the road of non-violence. Once the army was involved, we could not take it any further than that. The police were no longer sufficient. It was a new situation.
>
> We decided then to embrace violence as a method of struggle. But we were still cautious. The strict rule was that sabotage should involve no injury to life... In 1980 we signed the Geneva protocols and said that if we captured any enemy soldiers we would treat them as prisoners of war. The fact is that we are not against civilians. We do not include them in our definition of the enemy... We do not kill civilians. But some will be hit, quite accidentally and regrettably. I am

sure that we are going to lose many civilians and many innocent people, as happens in any violent situation. The situation of heightened conflict is going to destroy human life as well as property. I'm afraid this is coming. Bombs will explode, and one or two people who were not intended to be there will be killed. We will not boast about it the way the South African regime boasts about its killings...

But surely someone is going to say: Why are you keeping the South African régime in office? Get rid of the system and everybody will be safe. I think that South Africa is going to be a very happy country one day, and we will avoid avoidable loss of life, but although this sounds harsh, we cannot allow the system to persist for the sake of saving a few lives. It is not so harsh when one considers how many lives apartheid has destroyed. The Zimbabweans lost about 30,000 people to get their independence.[8]

In this statement, the steps into escalating violence are described. The first choice was for sabotage of property, without loss of life. Then the killing of soldiers only, not civilians if possible. Tambo's words do not fit the popular scary notion of 'terrorists' as people who kill civilians and wreck property indiscriminately. It is true that in 1978, when the PCR debate was at its height, the news from Rhodesia/Zimbabwe about the killings of missionaries and airline passengers did suggest that sort of terrorism. But the balance must be kept by noting that the atrocities of the other side could mostly be kept out of the way of the world's media by the Rhodesia Information Service (see Chapter 10). The same distinction as is made by the American government in the nuclear debate, between proactive and reactive strategy, can also be applied in Southern Africa. As far as Tambo's words disclose, the violent tactics of the ANC have so far been reactive, in response to the increasingly violent methods used by the government.

Tambo's statement seems to assume a war situation. The signing, by the ANC, of the Geneva Convention in 1980 indicates the movement's willingness to abide by the humanitarian restrictions in war, as laid down by European nations from their experience of war. The *Rand Daily Mail* reported on the signing:

Although the South African Government is a signatory to the Geneva Conventions, it has not signed the latest addition, called Protocol One. According to legal experts attached to the International Red Cross, a complication is that usually a liberation group such as the ANC would only follow the protocol if South Africa was also party to it. But a spokesman for the Red Cross said that if the ANC's intentions in signing is 'For truly humanitarian reasons', it would be welcomed by the international community.[9]

From this it is evident that the ANC are showing willingness to do more than the South African Government to exercise moral restraints within the option of violence.

European attitudes to war and revolution

It could be argued that the main factor preventing European Christians, and especially English Christians, from seeing the whole issue of violence in this light is their long tradition, going back over centuries, of hostility to any kind of rebellion, conditioned by the existence of a national church in a nation state. In other political areas, most recently in the Falklands war, the same church quarters did not show themselves opposed to violence as such. This can be seen from discussions of PCR in the English press.

On 4 September 1970, the day the first PCR grants were announced, *The Daily Telegraph* editorial set the tone for much subsequent criticism of PCR:

> The fallacy about race has now led us into a position where Christians are asked to contribute to the destruction of the Christian creed in Africa, to the removal of all hopes of evolution in favour of revolution. Once it was missionaries who received our funds for dispensaries and schools. Now it is obscure many-lettered organizations in Zambia and Tanzania, who plant explosives by night and are the enemies, conscious or unconscious, of all peace and prosperity.[10]

A spate of letters in favour of PCR grants followed. Several of them pointed out the hypocrisy of the PCR critics. For example on 18 September the Bishop of Manchester wrote to *The Times*:

> If it is true that (as you state) no British money is involved in the awards made, what exactly is our standing in the matter? Do those who put nothing into the kitty automatically earn the right to be consulted? Might it not be more seemly, in the circumstances, for some of our indignant voices to pipe down? They speak, after all, from a country whose Government has proposed to send not a few thousand pounds with an ambiguous address but *arms* to another Government widely recognized to be oppressive to its non-white subjects – and

there are quite a few British Christians ready to acquiesce in such an action, if not to applaud it.[11]

This letter is a reminder that in the very month that the Arnoldshaim grants were announced, the controversy about British arms sales to South Africa also flared up. This fact compels us to question the sincerity or the moral consistency of those who could simultaneously condemn the PCR support for violent movements and approve the sales of arms to the South African government. The two issues were linked in the statements from the BCC autumn conference of that year, as reported in *The Guardian*:

The British Council of Churches, in a performance of measured ecclesiastical politics, gave general support yesterday to the decision of the World Council of Churches to help anti-racist groups. It was a moral victory for those who sought a clear, unequivocal commitment by the Council to stand beside the oppressed of Africa and Asia against unjust domination. The critics of the World Council decision, who fear that some of the money might be used to buy arms, have their consolation in the Council's failure to be specific. The detailed merits of the controversial handout – £83,000 to eighteen groups – can still be argued. But by a clear vote – fifty-nine for, five against, five abstentions – the World Council had British backing. At the same time, the British Council, which represents the major denominations in Britain except the Roman Catholics, expressed total opposition to any resumption of the sale of arms to South Africa.[12]

At the same meeting there were also the PCR critics, such as the Revd A.R.Shillinglaw of the Church of Scotland, who,

sought to dissociate the Council from the WCC's help because the money might be used for violence...it could be used to buy bullets and bombs. Member churches should have been asked their view first. The distribution of such money was a betrayal of the faith of love. Violence could only breed violence.[13]

Where such an anti-violence line comes from consistent pacifists, it would not fit the argument about selective morality. For example, Lord Soper also wrote to *The Times* on 18 September 1970, arguing:

The business of the World Council of Churches is not to pander to the heresy of 'sanctified violence' however desperate the issues which seem to demand it.[14]

However, some pacifists even wrote in favour of the PCR grants, including David Harding, General Secretary of the Fellowship of Reconciliation:

> Christian pacifists are against violence but not against justice. Therefore they are likely to support the World Council of Churches' gift to liberation movements, explicitly given for non-violent means of realizing their just objectives.[15]

One letter to *The Guardian* on 6 October 1970 pointed out the hypocrisy of classifying the actions of the freedom fighters as violent, while ignoring the violence of apartheid, especially evident in malnutrition among children:

> If these children were annually put against the wall and shot – i.e. killed by violence – what a world outcry there would be. But instead they suffer their malnutrition and disease in silence, and usually die in a coma. They are just as dead. Their parents grieve just as much. But there was no 'violence' involved, so everything is all right. Our consciences are clear, and we can denounce the WCC for supporting African guerrilla 'violence'.

A similar point had been made on 17 September:

> While I agree with your leading article of today that Christian authorities have no business to support organizations which are engaged in the use of terror, I draw a different conclusion. I have a photograph from Mozambique of Portuguese troops triumphantly holding a wooden stake on which is impaled the head of an African man. In South Africa the record of violence from Sharpeville to those methods of imprisonment and interrogation you rehearse in your other leading article hardly needs repetition. The organizations practising violence are the white authorities. Can a similar record be ascribed to the Zimbabwe National Union or FRELIMO? If not, are they not more suitable recipients of Christian Aid than those who uphold the 'terrorists'?

In 1978, when the furore about the grants to the Patriotic Front erupted, this argument would have looked a bit one-sided, for it was not then a matter of government atrocities against freedom movements which had hardly begun to use violence. During the 1978 civil war in Zimbabwe/Rhodesia, both sides were comitting atrocities. Opponents of PCR grants like Bernard Smith (another figure not all he seemed, see Chapter 10), were keen to enumerate the terrorist acts of the movements awarded grants.

Recently, SWAPO abducted 109 children at gun point from the Anglican Mission and took them over the border into Angola for training as terrorists. Another recent act of SWAPO's was the murder of Chief Clemens Kapuo, one of its political rivals. No doubt Dr Slack will say that the grants to SWAPO are for 'welfare' purposes. This is the same defence that the WCC uses. But unless such grants are accompanied by a demand that the terrorist acts cease, then both the WCC and Christian Aid must be held guilty of condoning terrorism.[16]

What these quotations show is that the arguments depend on the selection of facts, which may be conditioned by the side the writer is on.

8

Communism

As I have already pointed out, many critics of PCR from churches in the West, especially fom Britain, objected that the PCR grants were going to 'Communist' organizations. For example, in *The Daily Telegraph* of 26 March 1979 under the heading 'Aid for Marxists Threat to Churches Council Survival' Canon D.W.Gundry, a member of the General Synod of the Church of England, was quoted as saying:

Despite the doubts of some members, the programme (i.e. PCR) adopted Marxist language and seemed bent on changing society by revolution.[1]

He lists the various organizations in receipt of PCR funds but crucially omits to mention the conditions under which the allocations were made. This seems to imply that he disbelieves the 'humanitarian' claims because these are overridden by the 'Marxist' language. Gundry comments crossly:

It is no exaggeration to say that the Council has appeared to treat the criticism of the grants with undisguised contempt.[2]

The debate seems to reach a stalemate in a duel of vituperation. If the PCR objectors cry 'Communist' the PCR supporters dismiss them as racists; if PCR supporters use the language of solidarity to overturn racism, the PCR objectors dub them 'Communist'. The problems of communication between the two sides appear to derive from different value-systems as well as from different perceptions about the actual South African situation. There are also problems of media projection, which we shall be considering later. At this point we need to look more closely at the terms 'Marxist' and 'Communist', and particularly at the nature of Communism in South Africa.

Communism in South Africa

Communism in South Africa did not just materialize out of nothing. It was one option which emerged in a situation of increasing frustration at the intransigence of the South African government and the failure of the Christian conscience, in Britain, to respond politically to the pleas of the black delegations which went there in 1914 and 1919, financed by African contributions, in search of help for their people in the face of repressive legislation, like the Land Acts, which accelerated the breakdown of the subsistence economy of many black people. The birth of the Communist Party of South Africa in 1921 was not long after the Bolshevik revolution in Russia and closely connected with the failure of the 1919 delegation, which caused colossal frustration manifested in disturbances throughout the country,

In 1927 the ANC President, Joshua Gumede, went with James la Guma of the South African Communist Party to a Communist sponsored Conference of Oppressed Nationalities in Brussels, which adopted their motion endorsing:

> the right of self-determination through the complete overthrow of capitalism and imperialist domination... the principle of Africa for the Africans.[3]

This motion, put forward by the two black leaders, confirms that Communism in South Africa was not a European-made import, as is often suggested. Communication was two-way. The two delegates were not told by the Conference what they were to do in South Africa. They themselves presented the motion, in the same way as any other delegates representing the views of the people that sent them, in the light of the problems facing them, in their situation.

Back in South Africa the Communist Party then adopted the notion that change in that country would be in stages. First, there would be a nationalist revolution, which would bring about a native republic. Then this would in turn bring about a socialist transformation of society. For eighteen months, while Gumede led the ANC, the Communist Party and the ANC converged in their activities, as with the League of African Rights. In the 1930s they diverged again, the ANC towards the interests of the small black bourgeoisie and the Communist Party into the struggle against Fascism, which meant wooing the racist white working class, with corresponding decline in its African membership. By 1939, Communist Party membership was down to 280. However, by 1945 there were

67,000 subscribers to the Communist Party newspaper. In the 1940s the ANC also revived and began to be once again associated with the struggles of the urban proletariat. In 1945 there were three Communist Party members on the ANC executive. From this account, it seems that the ANC inspanned those people who had the qualities necessary in the struggle against racism and oppression. In other words, the movement was eclectic. Any Communist influence was one among several other influences that inspired the ANC leadership of those times. In the early 1950s tensions arose within the ANC between the Africanists and the non-racial democrats, the particular problem being whether or not to work with Indian activists. Where both the ANC and the Communist Party were active on labour matters they attracted similar individuals. In the Eastern Cape in the late 1940s the same people held office both in the local ANC and the local Communist Party.

In 1950, the South African Government passed the Suppression of Communism Act. The wording of the Act shows that it was aimed not only at card-carrying members of the Communist Party, but also at any forms of organized African resistance, as *The Oxford History of South Africa* explains:

> The Suppression of Communism Act included... a definition of Communism which was wide enough to enable action to be taken against well-nigh anyone who thought radically, and was in fact used to immobilize and in some instances deprive of their livelihoods trade union officials and others active in workers' organizations or in politics in general [a footnote states that by the end of 1955 no fewer than fifty-six key officials had been removed from office in this way]. The Act defines Marxist Socialism as the doctrine of Marxist Socialists, as expounded by Lenin or Trotsky, the Comintern or Cominform or 'any related form of that doctrine expounded or advocated in the Union for the promotion of fundamental principles of that doctrine... or a doctrine which aims at bringing about any political, industrial, social or economic change within the Union by promotion of disturbance or disorder, or such acts or omissions or threats'.[4]

The wording of this Act indicates the white government's perception of 'Communism'. The first part of it seems to support a view of Communism as emanating from European theories and organizations, Lenin, the Comintern, etc., but then the wording widens to include anyone advocating changes in the system. In other words, the Act implicitly recognizes that there are homegrown doctrines. It should also be pointed out that the words 'by promotion of disturbance or disorder' appears to define Communists or their South African equivalents as people determined to use violent means. The relevant question to ask at this stage is to what extent the eventual adoption of violent tactics by the liberation movements was 'Communist' inspired. The question must be asked because of the impression given by PCR critics that Marxists cause violent revolution. It is true that the Marxist analysis of social change explains why revolutions happen. It is also true that Communists tend to get involved in organizations trying to change society. But to what extent does Communism *cause* revolution? This can be treated as a general question, in which it is necessary to refer to the actual doctrines of Marx and Lenin. It can also be treated as an empirical question, asking for a set of facts about the people actually engaged in revolutionary politics in South Africa.

The alliance of identity of interest between Communists and African organizations has not been constant. At times, as in the 1930s, they diverged, but they came together again in the 1940s. However, the alliance might be interpreted in different ways. On the one hand it might be interpreted in the crude South African government view of 'agitators' infiltrating among contented 'natives' as outside influences upsetting a basically peaceful society. On the other hand there is the view that the society is basically oppressive and that the oppressed seek allies among any group ready to be committed to their cause. Hence the involvement of men like Gumede in international Communism as well as in the local party.

It is still questionable whether all revolutionary politics should be regarded as part of a Russian Soviet conspiracy. This displays the offensive paternalist assumption that black leaders have to have their politics thought out for them. It was partly to avoid this kind of attitude that the PAC was founded, with its blacks-only membership. On the whole question of Soviet influence on African politicians, Colin Legum has written:

Perhaps a majority of African leaders endorse the view that only the Communist powers (the Soviet Union, China and Cuba) can be counted upon to provide military support for the liberation movements in Rhodesia, Namibia and South Africa. They therefore give their approval to Communist military involvement in the 'liberation struggle' (especially in Southern Africa) subject to the qualifications made by Nigeria's head of state, General Olusegum Obasanjo, in his speech to the Khartoum summit of the OAU in July 1978. He declared:

'To the Soviets and their friends I should like to say that, having been invited to Africa in order to assist in the liberation struggle and the consolidation of national independence, they should not overstay their welcome. Africa is not about to throw off one colonial yoke for another. Rather, they should hasten the political and military capacity of their African friends to stand on their own.'[5]

With regard to South African liberation, an interview which Oliver Tambo gave in 1983 refutes the accusation that Communists have excessive influence in the ANC:

Stanley Uys: 'The accusation is often made that the ANC is under the influence of white Communists.'

Tambo: 'I don't know where these white communists are. When I say "Mention them" they reply "Joe Slovo". When I ask "Who else?" they are silent. It's extraordinary how white communists are credited with so much power and supremacy and superiority. Why are we not being influenced by black communists? And why can't the influence go the other way? Individual members of the Communist Party are like any member of the ANC.'

Uys: 'Does the fact that Russia gives the ANC military aid put Joe Slovo in a specially strong position?'

Tambo: 'No. We have direct access to the countries that support us. We meet presidents, prime ministers, foreign ministers. This is done by ANC delegations, sometimes led by me, sometimes by others. Why should we need Joe Slovo to convince Bulgaria or Hungary to support us? Why do people think the ANC cannot be run without the help of white South Africans? How can a whole movement like the ANC depend on one person? People who belong to the Communist Party accept that the ANC must lead. They take direction from it. If Joe Slovo comes to me and I say no, he accepts it. They have come to accept our course because it is the correct one. There is no question of the ANC being controlled, directed or influenced by the communists.'[6]

Thus the argument put forward by E.R.Norman that the Third World simply apes radical politics in the Western world and that the Third World churches are dictated to by the World Council of Churches with a Marxist theology is pretty threadbare. Rather, oppressed as we have been, since the days the whites conquered and destroyed our independent kingdoms, our leaders have sought help from whomsoever would give a useful commitment to the liberation struggle. That among white South Africans these happen to be mainly Communists is an indictment of the white Christian conscience.

'Free world' perceptions of Communism

When the PCR controversy was at its height, it was argued that to aid the Patriotic Front of Rhodesia/Zimbabwe was to aid Communists who were anti-Christian. For example, this argument was reported in *The Daily Telegraph* under the heading: RHODESIA FRONT 'NOT CHRIST-IAN' SAYS BISHOP. The bishop was Paul Burrough of Mashonaland, who wrote a letter to the General Synod of the Church of England which stated:

> In practice the Patriotic Front groups of insurgents are completely opposed to the preaching of the Christian faith, though not of vague African monotheism. They have forced the church in rural areas to go underground.[7]

It is revealing to look back with hindsight at such statements made in the confusions and pressures of war. The post-war situation has shown that the Patriotic Front, at least that part of it which formed the new government, is not completely opposed to the proclamation of the Christian faith. Thus the Bishop's letter gives the impression of reactive panic, imputing to the feared group a long-term hostility to religion which, after the confusions of war cleared, has not materialized. Wherever the church may be, it is my view that the people of God, Jesus-motivated and Jesus-taught as we are, should not fear the processes of social change. Where the people with Christian conscience have failed in their task of declaring the truth, especially if it meant sacrificial confrontation with the *status quo*, there is no need to panic or be ashamed of admitting those mistakes when they are being rectified.

The war in Zimbabwe generated many terrible actions, on and off the battlefield. But even in the midst of them, some reporters admitted that these incidents were probably not part of some long-term anti-religious plan. As *The Economist* of 1 July 1978 put it:

> Altogether thirty-one missionaries have died in the six years of bush warfare; many have been threatened. They represent easy targets for the guerrillas, and it is more likely that they have been attacked for this reason than for any ideological purpose.

In order to indicate how complex the interpretation of such atrocities is, we note that at the same time as these reports were being made in the Western press, scare stories about the endangered churches were being circulated in Southern Africa. Such stories fit in very well with the South African government image of South Africa as the bastion of Christian civilization. The implied story line is that without the whites in charge, a country lapses into barbarism and kills the missionaries. Furthermore, the story runs, the Communists are out to abolish the churches. Reports were emerging from Mozambique in particular which appeared to confirm Western fears that Communist regimes must inevitably be opposed to Christianity. The Department of Mission of the CPSA ran Lent appeals for the dioceses of Mozambique. In the publicity material there were descriptions of church buildings destroyed in the war, and clergy returning for the task of reconstruction. There were also rumours of how the Communist authorities tried to restrict the teaching of confirmation classes. However, when we heard the bishop from one of the dioceses concerned speak on the matter, he told us that once the people showed their determination to come to classes, and once he as a citizen and leader of the church had taken up the matter with the authorities, the restrictions were eased. It is difficult to assess the situation through the barriers of language and preconceptions arising from propaganda. But without wanting to deprecate a Lent effort that was motivated by a spirit of Christian brotherhood, I would want to point out that there was nevertheless the risk that such a rescue attempt for Christians in Communist countries can be merged with anti-Communist sentiments which may, or may not, be based on what is actually happening in the countries concerned. However hard it may be to admit this in the European or American churches, there are presuppositions about the plight of Christians in Communist countries, whether this is in the USSR, in Poland, in China or in Mozambique.

This view about persecuted Christians continues to be generalized, often paying scant attention to the difference between Communist countries, churches and the different changing relations and responses in those countries. Thus on 23 November 1978 Michael Bourdeaux wrote to *The Times* to correct Dr Norman's 'slander' against the All Russian Social Christians. As the work of Keston shows, the task of keeping open lines of communication with Christians in the various countries is difficult enough. But over-simplification of the publicity stories about these church groups, which feeds on the popular appetite for tales of Christian martyrdom, can make life more difficult for the churches concerned. Sometimes, at the request of the Christians in those countries, the organizations in the Western churches that are in touch with them have to be discreet in their use of information. Thus the WCC, through several of its departments, is active with regard to East European Christians, but it is in the nature of the problem that not much publicity can be given to this work.

In contrast, PCR gains maximum publicity in the Western press, and it befits its function of challenging Western racism that this should be so. The media picture of the WCC is like a lop-sided stereo, tending to be too quiet on the Eastern front and very loud on Southern African issues.

In democratic countries the media perform a valuable function of presenting in public debate important topics of the day, even religious ones. But in Communist countries the tasks and trials that face Christians have for the most part to be carried out beyond the attention of the media. The question to ask the critics of PCR is whether they want their objections to be seen in 'Cold War' terms or in ways that suggest that Christianity is incompatible with communism. And in addition, whether this assumption is helpful or unhelpful to the Christians actually living in the Communist countries.

Finally, it must be noted that because of the popular notion of the WCC as a Communist-favouring institution some have even gone so far as to suggest that clerics from Communist countries wield undue influence at the Geneva offices, a suggestion that was well refuted by Ian Mathers in *The Observer*, 27 August 1978:

> If the Council is run by a coterie of Communists, as had been claimed, the reds under the bed are very well hidden. In fact, there is hardly a Marxist in the building. The accounts show that the churches in Communist countries contribute 13% of the Council's budget, but it is nonsense to talk of a Communist bloc since there are many cross-allegiances to different churches. Some of the East German Protestants have a reputation for political radicalism. Not so, however, the Orthodox members from Moscow, whose thinking tends to be on a time-scale only short of the eternal.

Non-Marxist victims and Marxist oppressors

In order to expose the supposed bias of the WCC, some objectors to PCR draw attention to Marxist oppression. Thus *The Daily Telegraph*:

Several grants have been given to Marxist movements but none, we note, to anti-Marxist movements, though some Marxist states discriminate against Jews and racial minorities.[8]

One answer to this is to point out that when PCR was set up the special status of South Africa was acknowledged because so many Christians are involved there. Other parts of this book have shown how the present situation has its ideological roots in Christian theology. There is frequent communication between church leaders in South Africa who are in the forefront of anti-apartheid resistance and the World Council of Churches. The same line of communication as that between the WCC and the Christian Councils of various countries is not possible with groups of persecuted Moslems or Jews who have their own lines of support through international Islamic and Jewish networks. I am not trying to suggest that the WCC should ignore non-Christian victims of racial persecution. I am simply drawing attention to the facts of international Christian communication during the 1970s. It is nonetheless interesting to note that as the WCC has strengthened its links with the Pacific and with indigenous people in Australia and Canada, so the scope of PCR has broadened to include their land rights stuggle. Some, of course, may regard this broadening as an attempt to deflect anti-Marxist criticism, until it is realized that the concerns of the land rights movement are often just as critical of Western capital interests as the South African orientated PCR was.

Nonetheless, although the WCC is now found to be supporting some non-Marxist victims, the PCR is still likely to be urged continually to take a tougher line on Marxist oppressors. This, if used as a defence against blame, can be reduced to the schoolboy plea of, 'Don't blame me, sir, he did it too, sir.' Some of the letters about PCR advising the WCC to be more active about Poland, or Afghanistan, seem to be of this defensive type. Jesus' injunction about motes in the eye seems applicable in such cases. I am not trying to say that oppression by Communists is negligible, or should not be resisted, by international solidarity if necessary. Ideally the oppressors in such Communist situations should be criticized according to their own Marxist or Leninist criteria, but this does not always happen in a society which is fearful of public debates. In contrast, Christian criticism of Christian persecution is possible, and is being done by PCR and elsewhere. The main thrust of my argument is that PCR's choice of Southern Africa, rather than Afghanistan, is to be seen as a choice of an area where Western interests, in particular

British interests, loom large. Thus the defensive British reaction in the Press is hardly surprising. But if the aims of PCR are heeded, it may recall that a vital Christian teaching about conscience is to look first at one's own sins. Sins committed by the self and one's own society should be taken into account first before embarking on judgments about distant lands, about others 'out there', far away from us and our sins! After all, the West has run the world for so long that now, when the interests of exploited countries are being thrust forward for attention, there is a panic defensive reaction, often a barely disguised political anxiety that the Soviets are taking over Western global interests.

At several points in this book I have argued that the assumptions of society can shape, or even bend, theology. So at this point it is fair to assert that some PCR critics were seeing the grants through a framework of Western political assumptions. They were not concerned about the actual doctrines of Marx or of Christ, nor were they motivated primarily by compassion for the most afflicted. Rather, what appears to motivate some of them is the fear of Soviet hegemony in Africa. For example, Samuel Gifford wrote anxiously in *The Daily Telegraph*:

> Before it is too late to stem the rising tide of Marxism in Africa, the British Government should break the deadlock and lift sanctions...[9]

Lord Ventry wrote:

> Would not Dr Ramsey and his fellow bishops be better employed in attacking the Communist Powers which are anti-Christian and anti-God? If it were not for the menace of the Soviet navy, there would be no need for us to worry about our sea communications.[10]

The assumption here is that the Soviet navy is keen to move in on Africa, and that Marxist revolution would be a bad thing (for whom is not clear). Thus there are political assumptions underlying the religious guise.

By laying bare the political undercurrents of the debate, one can demonstrate that fear of Communism has two aspects: first the fear of Soviet aggrandizement and secondly fear of the threat posed to Western economic interests by the anti-Western 'Communists', often alias the local alien nationalists. It has been the argument of this chapter that often these political considerations have a stronger influence on the debate than strictly moral or religious criteria, even when the debate is taken up by church people, and the language of non-violence is evoked. One effect of seeing South Africa through this framework of Western political perceptions is a false polarity, thus:

Freedom and democracy v. Soviet tyranny
Freedom and democracy v. Communists
Freedom and democracy v. African Nationalists
White South Africa v. Marxist guerrillas
Legitimate government v. terrorists
Peace v. violence
Christian v. Communist

The kith and kin empathy operates strongly to sustain the left-hand list. From a black perspective the conflation on the left is false, because we perceive the present South African government as neither legitimate nor peaceful, nor even Christian if the Calvinist heresies on which apartheid is based are exposed to scrutiny. I have also raised some questions about the conflation on the right, for instance about the extent of Communist or of Soviet influence on African Nationalists. The question as to how far Africans find that Christianity or Communism meets our needs is one that we are still working through. PCR, set up as it was by an international gathering of Chrstians, is one body which is showing us that Christianity need not be confined to Western political interests. It is one body which is refuting Marx's argument that religion represents the ruling class rather than that of the oppressed.

9

The Disinvestment Debate

What is involved in the idea of economic boycotts? Many people are aware of the campaign to refuse to buy Outspan oranges or South African sherry. Those particular campaigns were started in Britain by the Anti-apartheid movement as an educational ploy, to get people talking and taking a stand against apartheid. But in themselves they have never been campaigns which have threatened to bring down the South African economy. In contrast, the ban on oil sales is regarded by the South African government as much more threatening, and millions of rands have been spent on SASOL, oil from coal plants, to counter this threat. Similarly the ban on arms trading has had direct economic results, as the government in South Africa has got local firms to undertake manufacture for defence contracts, and resorts to subterfuge to import the high-technology items. Whatever the economic results of these different trade boycotts, it should be noted that their scope and purposes differ: the Outspan campaign is a consciousness-raising exercise; the arms ban looks like an attempt to curtail South Africa's militarism; only the oil embargo is seriously regarded as an attempt to bring down apartheid by economic means.

However, other forms of economic pressure are being advocated as well. There has been growing pressure, via well-researched campaigns, to stop financing apartheid. In Britain, the campaign against Barclays Bank has been the best known example of this type of campaign. At first it was undertaken in the same spirit as the Outspan campaign, as a way of making more people aware of apartheid, with a High Street bank as a convenient target. But more research made the anti-apartheid activists more aware of the web of banking consortia that underwrite the state-run enterprises of South Africa, many of them strategic, like SASOL. Another form of economic campaign is therefore arguments for disinvestment, whether this be to get companies to pull out of South Africa or to stop new investments in South Africa by those companies, or to get individual shareholders to pull out in protest at those companies' collaboration with apartheid.

Before examining the details of the debate under each type of campaign, it is worth looking at the broad intentions of this type of activism.

First, there are those who reject sanctions on pragmatic grounds. They say that they do not achieve their purpose, and point to the example of the failure of the Rhodesian oil sanctions. This example is dubious because it was South Africa's connivance that enabled the oil boycott to be circumvented, and South Africa does not have a contiguous friendly country on which to depend in similar circumstances. Furthermore, the argument about feasibility looks increasingly hypocritical in view of the fact that in 1986 President Reagan reiterated calls for sanctions against Nicaragua and that earlier the USA had succeeded in bringing down Allende in Chile using mainly economic pressures.

Secondly, there are those who, like Archbishop Tutu, advocate disinvestment as an alternative to violence. There have always been opponents of economic boycotts who say that these will hit the blacks hardest. But black spokesmen like Tutu, and Chief Luthuli before him, have said publicly that the black people of South Africa would prefer this to the hardships that they already suffer or to possible worse violence to come.

Thirdly, there are those who see the calls for disinvestment as part of the pro-Communist and anti-capitalist tendencies of anti-apartheid activists. We have already considered the extent to which anti-apartheid movements are motivated (or not) by Communism. Here it is appropriate to examine to what extent capitalism and apartheid are linked. Racism can pervert any system, communist or capitalist. Furthermore some features of South Africa, for instance the treatment of farm labourers and domestic servants, predate the capitalist economy of South Africa. But the anti-capitalist arguments of the disinvestment debate draw attention to the specific features of the South African economy that are closely linked to (or caused by?) apartheid. Francis Wilson got to the nub of this by asking:

If capitalism is to be our model for the future, how are we to deal with the basic fact that it, and not Afrikaner Nationalism (if I may make the distinction in this context), is primarily responsible for the migrant labour system, not only in our past but also in our present? And lest people question that, let me ask: If the mines were free to stabilize their entire black labour tomorrow, would they wish to do so?[1]

He prefaced that remark by quoting Niebuhr:

Economic power is the most basic power. Political power is derived from it to such a degree that the just political order is not possible without a reconstruction of the economic order. Specifically this means the reconstruction of the property system.[2]

and then asked:

Is Niebuhr correct? If so, can a capitalist South Africa accommodate the necessary reconstruction?[3]

That quotation underlines what is at stake between those who argue for disinvestment and those who argue for constructive engagement. The latter argue that a more humane form of capitalist development is possible in South Africa, and that migrant labour and squatter camps are abuses caused by apartheid rather than capitalism. Others argue that capitalism itself will sweep away apartheid, because of, among other things, its need for settled skilled labour. Others, of a more radical, or a Communist, persuasion, argue that capitalism itself is the problem, that little reforms will not work and that it is better to work for a radical redistribution of the country's wealth and power structures.

However, in order to understand how these various arguments apply it is necessary to look at the actual structure of the South African economy.

The South African economy

(a) *The colonialist sector* (the sub-heading comes from a description by Vella Pillay):

The South African economy can be viewed as a dualistic one, a carefully managed conjunction of two broad sectors, one highly colonialist in character and the other a modernizing sector based on imported advanced technology with the South African State and the two thousand or so TNCs [trans-national corporations] playing a crucial unifying role in sustaining the profitability of the latter through the most intense exploitation of black labour in the former. The colonialist sector encompasses the substantial industries concerned with mining and agriculture in which cheap labour forms the dominant input. This too characterizes those allied industries which provide an infrastructure for mining and agriculture. Here the labour force is primarily organized on migratory lines, or as in agriculture by a peasant labour force subject to special conditions of employment. In both these sectors, wage payments are partially in cash employment, while in agriculture the complex set of master and servant regulations impose a kind of 'bonded relationship' between the worker and his master. In these important senses, all competition for labour is excluded in this colonial-type sector and this provides for the extraordinarily high rate of black labour exploitation here and in the allied industries... the overall rate of return on capital investments... in high technology industries tends in general to be lower than in the colonialist sector.

This suggests that the latter has to be exploited that much more intensively, to ensure a regular average rate of return on all capital investments in the South African economy at between 18% and 20% per annum.[4]

One of the main reasons why such intense labour exploitation is possible is migratory labour. Historically this was initiated by colonial methods. As the livelihood by farming for themselves became increasingly difficult for families after white settlement decreased the availability of land for blacks, so more blacks had to seek work on white farms. When the mines began, recruiting agents were sent out to the black villages to recruit unskilled workers. When there appeared to be reluctance, some assistance was rendered to the mining companies by the authorities to ensure that black families had to engage in the money economy, and some members would be likely to seek paid work, especially in the mines. The rationale behind the system, in nineteenth-century terms, was the white man's attempt to save the black man from 'idleness':

> Rhodes, himself a large-scale employer and sympathetic to the needs of the employers, devised a system of land-tenure for the Glen Grey district which was designed to force a portion of the men to work as migrant labourers. The intention was to locate the resident natives on these surveyed allotments, and to make no provision for the surplus to find work elsewhere: so that.. during the coming generation a number will be agriculturists, i.e. native farmers – and the rest will have to go out and work. The argument that land should be limited,

so that African men might not 'live in idleness' but go out to work for the Europeans, has been repeated again and again in the history of Southern Africa: Rhodesians were using it as late as 1951. Peasant production was 'idleness' to the white man in need of labour.[5]

Francis Wilson gives an account of migrant labour in this century, and in so doing shows that it now prevails not only in the old colonialist sector of mining, but increasingly in manufacturing jobs as well.

In South Africa we have a long history of migrant labour, starting primarily if not exclusively with the mines; first diamond mines and then from 1886 gold. A huge compound system developed so that today you have 99% of the 350,000 workers in the gold mines housed on a single basis, in huge hostels of about 7,000 workers. There is also migrant labour in agriculture... maize, sugar and deciduous fruit – and this is one of the most important points to note, also a rapid growth of oscillating migrancy in manufacturing. This has occurred in the last five or six years, with the massive growth in hostel accommodation in Durban, Pretoria-Johannesburg, Cape Town, Port Elizabeth and elsewhere (with the exception of East London). Every second African man legally working in the urban areas is housed as a 'single' migrant, without his family. The proportion varies from 20% in Port Elizabeth to 86% in Cape Town.

The main sources of migrant labour are: Transkei (192,000), Kwa Zulu and Bophutatswana (roughly the same as the Transkei), Lesotho (192,000), Mocambique (130,000), Malawi (100,000). Over time there has been a change in the resources of labour. The mines used to recruit nobody from tropical areas north of 22 degrees, whereas today, one third of the mine's labour force... comes from these areas. This is not because emigrants from earlier sources are no longer migrating. Rather, they are moving into manufacturing, where wages are about twice what they are in mining.[6]

Wilson is asking whether apartheid causes these aspects of the economy or whether it is the economic requirements that sustain the pass laws and labour regulations of apartheid. He explains the economic forces by a diagram:[7]

RURAL SUPPLY   push 2 → → pull 1   URBAN DEMAND
                pull 3 ← ← push 4.

Labour needs to attract people from rural areas to seek work in towns (pull 1). Poverty and lack of farming prospects push people from rural areas into the urban economy (push 2). Family and social security needs keep black workers attached to the family in the home village (pull 3). Labour laws, nine month contracts and so on, push workers out of the urban areas again (push 4). In other words, you go to the city because you need a job and money. You need money to support your wife, children and extended family. From time to time, both by stipulation of the law, for example to renew your contract, or because you have no urban residence rights, you have to go home. Since your family is not allowed to live with you in the urban area, you simply have to go home to attend to the needs of the family, emotionally and practically. While you are at home the money runs out, so you have to renew your contract and return to the mines or a factory job in the town. Wilson makes it clear that pull 1 is the primary economic force:

> It is urban immigration which is important. Hence force 1 is the pull of the urban areas as a result of economic growth: for example the growth of labour needs on the Witwatersrand from nothing in 1886 to 100,000 fourteen years later. Anywhere in the world the process of economic growth leads to an increase in the jobs in the urban areas at a rate greater than the natural population increase. Force 2 is the push from the rural areas, which may take many forms. It may be the result of the political machinations for those who run society. There may also be the push from rural areas as a result of the mechanization of agriculture: combine harvesters, tractors or weedkillers, which do away with many skoffeling [hoeing and weeding] jobs.[8]

But the point to notice about the diagram above is that push 4 is not economic in essence, but legal. Blacks need to go home to their families because their families are *not allowed* to live with them in the urban areas:

> The migrant labour system remains the cornerstone of the South African labour economy. The system is based on the assertion that the Africans are 'temporary sojourners' in the 'white' areas of South Africa. Consequently, the government has pursued a policy of making the homelands the permanent homes for Africans, dismantling estab-lished African communities in the urban areas, sending dependants back to their assigned homelands, and replacing family residences with vast single-sex hostels, such as Johannesburg's Alexandra Township. The main instrument for enforcing the migratory labour system is the pass laws. All Africans must constantly carry with them reference or

pass books properly updated with any special permissions they have received, such as leave to visit an urban area longer than 72 hours, permission to leave their homeland to take up work in an urban area, or permission to be outside their homeland after curfew. Nearly eighteen hundred people are prosecuted every day of the year for technical offences under the pass laws. Africans live in terror of police raids, which often happen at night and with dogs. Arrest can mean the loss of a job, prison, and ultimately deportation to some remote poverty-stricken rural area where there may be no jobs and no houses. The human costs of the system are enormous...[9]

This system of punishment for pass-law offence produces forced labour for the farms of this colonialist economy, as Nkosi explained:

In Johannesburg alone hundreds of Africans are rounded up every year for committing minor offences like the failure to produce a 'pass' on demand by an accredited officer of the law. If you leave your pass book in your jacket in the office and cross a street to buy a cold drink you run the risk of being shanghaied to jail without any means of communicating with those outside. The result may be imprisonment for a period of up to six months. In South Africa prisoners provide an inexhaustible supply of cheap labour for white farmers. They come to Johannesburg for truckloads almost every week... In these farms treatment is often so brutal that deaths have resulted from severe beatings. This is not hearsay, because from *Drum* and *Post* we decided to send a reporter to these farms, disguised as a common labourer, to investigate the conditions, and his exposé shook even the government. Sometimes farmers conveniently 'forget' to tell relatives about someone who has died on these farms until months after burial. Exhumations of bodies after burial on these farms have, therefore, become common affairs.[10]

Thus both the mines and the farms of the colonialist sector make profits by the cheapening of black labour. Economic forces, stimulated by white capital and enterprise, may have caused the demand for such black labour, but it is the authorities, from colonial times until the present régime, that ensure the supply of such labour by legislation that sustains the push-pull oscillation between urban and rural areas. We have already seen Francis Wilson's assertion (pp. 129ff.) that it is the state, rather than market forces, that is largely responsible for the peculiar features of the South African economy. His point is an important one.[11] When it is claimed that the economic development will put pressures on apartheid it is not always realized how many whites get their livelihood from the apparatus of apartheid. It must also be remembered that the people who get the jobs within this state system tend to be the Afrikaners, the voters for the present regime. Thus the colonialist system of controlling the black labour supply needs the policing and clerking functions that are performed by the government supporters.

(*b*) *The modern sector.* Sometimes South African businessmen operating in the modern sector, with manufacturing firms, criticize apartheid by pointing out how it restricts economic forces. For instance, under a headline '*Black Education must be Upgraded*' *says VWSA's Chief*, an article in the *Rand Daily Mail* quoted this comment from a major South African manufacturing firm:

> The education of blacks is one of the most important of several major matters of concern clouding the generally extremely favourable long-term outlook for South Africa, according to Mr Peter Searle, the managing director of Volkswagen of South Africa. It was inevitable that blacks would be drawn into the country's economic system more and more, he said a few days ago. They should and would hold top positions within the system, but the present educational standard was generally not good enough to provide the base for the advanced training needed to fill the demand for management and skilled workers. It is essential for the future stability of South Africa that blacks are not only encouraged to participate in our free enterprise capitalist system, but must be seen to succeed and to benefit. For this to happen a considerable improvement in their basic education, in content and scope, is essential – otherwise they will not be able to cope.[12]

This point about the need for better basic education for blacks links back to the previous point I made about the role of the state in shaping, or even suppressing, economic forces. Improved basic schooling is something which should be a major state investment, but there is a great disparity between the amount spent on white education and that spent on schools for blacks. The present system is not designed to produce future managers for VWSA; it was instituted by missionaries, helped along by imperial educational administrators, and then drastically pruned by the Bantu Education Laws of the Nationalists. They wanted a system which suited apartheid and the demand for *unskilled* black labourers in plenty. A plausible case can now be made for better training for blacks because the capital-intensive enterprises of the modern sector have a different job structure from the previous more labour-intensive ways of working. With more machines there is a need for more mechanics who can diagnose problems of breakdown. With changes of technology, a better educated work force is more versatile when manufacturing methods change. During the 1970s there was some recognition of this in that the Government belatedly set up two industrial training centres, with courses more technical than anything that black people had been allowed to do before. But the problems still go back to basic schooling. The student intake into such centres is hampered by poor educational groundwork. The South African state, it seems, is very slow to respond to the demands of the modern sector by adequate changes to further black advancement. Hence it is not surprising that the black revolt of the 1970s, that in Soweto in 1976, was triggered by dissatisfaction in the schools.

One reason why South African firms have not had to press very hard for black advancement is that they have been able to rely on recruiting abroad the technically qualified white workers they need, especially in the job-hungry depressed towns of Britain. The WCC made a statement about white migration to South Africa in 1972:

> The policies of the white-minority régimes in Southern Africa in encouraging white migration to these countries are aimed at perpetuating and strengthening the existing racist structures. For instance, in South Africa, the large influx of skilled personnel results in unemployment and also in keeping the black population at the lower end of the job scale... The Central Committee therefore requests all member churches and the staff of Unit 11 to mount campaigns to discourage white migration to South Africa, Namibia, Zimbabwe, Angola, Mozambique and Guinea-Bissao, which perpetuates and aggravates racial discrimination in the labour market.[13]

Why should labour migration be such an issue? Why should individuals and groups of workers not be free to sell their labour and their skills wherever there is a demand for them? In relation to South Africa it has to be stressed that the labour market is not free: blacks are not allowed to compete with whites, and their advancement is blocked. White migration therefore undercuts black opportunities, and removes the pressures for a better-trained black labour force.

South African business leaders, such as Harry Oppenheimer, often make public pronouncements against apartheid on the grounds that it retards industrial progress. But this line of argument does not seem to demand any imperative political action, as economic forces are seen to be paramount. As South Africa's economy expands and as industrial investment grows in modern technological enterprises, then (the argument runs) apartheid will crumble away. This is an argument that goes well with South Africa's need for foreign investment: continue to expand investments in South Africa, and apartheid will disappear. One problem with such arguments for increasing the modern industrial sector in South Africa is that the assertions and the evidence have often had to come from the business community itself, from management reporting to shareholders rather than from other sources.

However, in 1973 Adam Raphael wrote a series of articles in *The Guardian* about the British-owned firms in South Africa, which revealed the inequalities of pay between whites and blacks, the work segregation, lack of promotion prospects and lack of training for blacks. The public protest in response to revelations like this, adding weight to the pressure groups, resulted in some governmental action in the UK. A reporting system was set up whereby UK firms with sizeable South African subsidiaries had to inform the Select Committee annually about the pay and conditions of their workers in South Africa. In 1977 the EEC set up a code of conduct for EEC firms in South Africa. In the USA, similar pressure groups caused the setting up of the Sullivan code for US firms in South Africa.

The BCC propositions

Against that picture of the South African economy, we can now look at the main points put forward in the disinvestment debate. In 1973, a year that started with the publication of the WCC booklet *Time to Withdraw*, and then the increased public debate over the Raphael articles, the British Council of Churches published *Investment in Southern Africa*, which sets out four options for people and institutions concerned in the matter:

> We believe that there are four propositions which need to be examined and valuated. In each instance there are arguments in favour and against. We have tried to summarize these and to suggest what is, in our opinion, a sound and wise judgment to make. They are as follows:
> 1. Economic growth will, in all probability, lead to social and political

change which will bring weakening of racial discrimination and an end to the oppressive system of government. Investment may therefore be encouraged.

2. The most useful and hopeful action for the churches, institutions and individuals is to maintain investments, and possibly widen them, in order to exercise stockholder pressure to secure better labour and social policies from those firms operating in Southern Africa.

3. Churches, institutions and individuals should sell existing holdings and make no further investments in firms involved in investment and trade with South Africa.

4. Pressure should be exercised upon firms and banks in Britain to withdraw capital investment from Southern Africa and to cease trading with those countries. Such pressure can only be exercised by an energetic policy by churches and institutions upon corporations, whether stock is held or not.[14]

A decade has now passed since those propositions were published. So it is now possible to evaluate them not only according to the ideals they express, but also empirically, in the light of what has been happening in South Africa during the decade.

1. Inevitable economic progress

This argument suggests that if more money is put into firms the result is progress for the work-force. More money = more jobs. There is evidence that this is not the case. During the 1970s in the Johannesburg region when there was less money for the building industry there was less money for mechanization, so the work was done by employing more sub-contractors with black labour, like my brother. This situation can be contrasted with that of Cleveland in the north of England which is an area of chemical industry that attracted a good deal of investment via government concessions, incentives and regional aid during the 1970s.[15] Such a flood of investment actually resulted in a sharp decline in jobs: capital-intensive technology had replaced the jobs.

Obviously arguments in this area are complex and depend on which industry and region is under scrutiny. One important factor is who is making the more advanced machinery, as presumably some jobs are being created in that machine-manufacture. More investment, though, does not necessarily mean more jobs, especially if the profits from the greater mechanization are not being spent in the same region. Some proportion of the investment might get to the people of the region via the taxes levied on the firm, but that depends on how the tax system operates in the region in question.

In South Africa, foreign investment in the 1970s was sought for big projects like the Richard's Bay Port complex (located in the Kwazulu homeland of Natal), SASOL (the oil from coal plants project) and ESCOM (the Electricity Supply Comission). These projects strengthen the white economy, and some of them, like SASOL, are strategic. Indeed there is evidence that the fastest-growing section of the South African economy is the military, and the ancillary industries to back up the militarization of South Africa.[16] This does not benefit the black population (though there are clear cases, like the Richard's Bay Port complex, where the development is in homeland territory), nor does it provide as many jobs as would, for instance, a housing renewal programme. Where money has been spent for the black community, it has been for political purposes, such as setting up government-controlled black television services instead of providing improved roads and street lighting for Soweto.

Those who advocate more investment say that it would make the homelands viable. But it is unlikely that big investment will be attracted to areas like the Transkei with scant infrastructure unless there is a big incentive of newly-discovered minerals. Bophuthatswana has the best chance of economic viability because of its minerals (though there have been attempts to draw its boundaries so as to exclude the areas with white-owned extractive industry) and its proximity to the Val industrial areas. It is significant that the area of the Richards Bay development was specifically excluded from Zululand, and that the taxes from it will primarily benefit the white community. The story is the same with border industries. These have been set up on the periphery of some homelands, and draw labour from the dormitory settlements in those areas. But again the taxes and profits are drawn back into the white community. The so-called 'aid' which the Pretoria government gives to the homelands should be assessed in the light of such a tax system.[17] Even if a greater proportion of the wealth of border industries were to be clawed back by homeland governments, there would still need to be questions about the way that money would be spent, whether for the benefit of the ruling and administrative elites or in a distributive fashion that ensured that the prosperity 'trickled down' to village level. 'Trickle down' arguments are out of favour with aid experts who have considered the data from other parts of Africa. This first proposition is really a version of 'trickle down' applied to South Africa.

The argument that more investment will create better promotion prospects for blacks is difficult to investigate empirically at this stage. The firms might be willing to open up more jobs, but many blacks, as we have seen, cannot take advantage of them, and white immigration and a cunning process of job-fragmentation have also blocked their advancement in many industries.

However, against these pessimistic indications, in the mid-1980s there has been a little evidence that economic change is altering the South African political scene. First, the white Afrikaner electorate no longer consists primarily of white farmers or of erstwhile 'poor whites' struggling for a foothold in the modern economy. Afrikaners are now firmly established in the modern sector and some of them are beginning to see the arguments for the liberalization of apartheid on business grounds. It is hard to guess at the internal arguments of the Afrikaner community, but it is manifestly plain that Mr Botha is now facing a split party. However, it should be noted that an argument based on Afrikaner self-interest cuts both ways: there are probably at least as many Afrikaners getting their livelihood from the administration of the apartheid system as there are engaged in wealth-getting enterprises in the modern urban economy.

Secondly, it could be argued that the increased strength of the black trade unions is a result of economic progress. Where a stable labour force is more important to a technically advanced firm than a 'colonial-type' enterprise that needs only unskilled labourers, it is likely that the management of the advanced firm will have to negotiate more carefully with the labour force it hopes to retain, and even to train. Thus in the 1980s the validity of the 'economic progress' proposition can be measured partly by the success or otherwise of the black trade unions. However, as far as can be gauged fom current labour disputes, the inevitability of economic forces does not seem to have been proved. Political and governmental action are clearly influential in the situation, as evidenced in the arrests of labour leaders. At what point will the economic forces overwhelm the political hurdles? Another problem with this proposition is that it appears to allow for a long wait without taking into account political factors. What is emerging in the news nowadays is that many people involved in the situations, above all the blacks, are not prepared to wait as long as this line of argument presupposes. The businessmen who went to Lusaka in August 1986 to have discussions with the ANC are presumably those who are disillusioned with their former beliefs in inevitable economic progress, in that they are now ready to take political factors into account.

2. Constructive engagement

This was formulated in Britain in 1973 as a lenient alternative to disinvestment. But if it is not to be mere diversionary talk, it has to be carefully monitored. A small organization, Christian Concern for Southern Africa (CCSA), backed mainly by money from the Quaker trusts, set about collating the figures that the companies gave to the Select Committee on employment. It continued to do this year by year, and published a series of reports on UK business links with South Africa. Although BCC was involved in formulating the terms of the debate and church funds are tied up in South Africa-linked firms, it is regrettable that BCC member churches never gave CCSA full backing, so that it has had to continue as a fringe organization.

Whether pressure for reform through continued investment works or not is essentially an empirical question, which should be assessed by monitoring the results. But the flaw in the procedure set up by the Select Committee was that it relied on facts supplied by the companies involved, as CCSA pointed out as early as 1976:

In 1976, our report *Poverty Wages in South Africa* reviewed the effectiveness of voluntary disclosure by companies on their labour practices in South Africa at that time. In concluding then that company response had been unsatisfactory, it was observed that:

'The inability to obtain reliable information on company perform-ance not only demonstrates that the government's current reliance on voluntary disclosure is not working but also makes the case for constructive engagement much more difficult to sustain. Without adequate information we lack the quantitative basis upon which a policy of engagement can be assessed, criticized or defended.'[18]

Another investigation commissioned by the anti-apartheid movement scrutinized the reaction of South African firms to *The Guardian* disclos-ures of 1973:

South Africa's thirty years of economic development and the emerg-ence of its manufacturing economy have taken place in conditions where the *per capita* incomes of Africans have improved, if at all, only marginally... Moreover, the average black wage, even in the most advanced sectors of manufacturing industry, has tended to be below the poverty datum, that is, the calculated absolute minimum (based on expenditure only on food, rent and fuel) at which a family with three children can exist. Finally, while real wages in manufacturing industry may have risen for Africans during the 1960s, as inflation began to bite in the early 1970s the real wages of Africans fell dramatically. This undoubtedly was a major factor in the strikes of 1973 and after. *The strikes did produce a tendency among South African companies to increase black wage levels in money terms. British companies, whose wage policies have never shown any difference from wholly South African owned companies, tended to follow suit.* A few of the increases were quite dramatic, then, and in the following months: but these were specifically companies that had been subjected to very unfavourable publicity in *The Guardian.* Some of them were in respect of forestry/plantation activities (where the wage had been at prevailing agricultural rather than manufacturing wage levels) and were accompanied by substantial redundancies in the work force. The timing of wage increases in British companies was also related to *The Guardian* exposures and the establishment of a Parliamentary enquiry...[19]

Thus although the constructive engagement lobby seemed at first to produce some improvements on the labour scene in South Africa in 1973, if scrutinized the increases turn out to be illusory. It is doubtful if the increases were introduced mainly as a result of the constructive lobby, as internal pressure from the black work force since the strikes of 1973 seems to have been a factor compelling many companies to raise wage levels in that year.

In subsequent years CCSA continued to monitor the company returns, but the 1982 Anglican publication *Facing the Facts* had to acknowledge:

> The organization Christian Concern for Southern Africa (CCSA), after years of careful research, said that they found it difficult to establish accurately what companies were really doing in South Africa.[20]

When Barbara Rogers introduced the CCSA study of the EEC code in 1980, she commented:

> One of the fundamental problems of any attempt to protect black workers in South Africa from outside is the difficulty of obtaining corroboration of the companies' reports on their own activities... Academic observers are also unable to provide corroboration of

company reports on a broad basis, because of an atmosphere of official discouragement of any research in this field that could be useful to the opponents of apartheid. Moreover, the South African subsidiaries of companies themselves are subject to the Second General Law Amendment Acts 1974 and the Companies Amendment Act 1978, which severely restrict their freedom to make information available to other parties. Some actually submit their draft reports for the Department of Trade to Pretoria for clearance beforehand.[21]

After the survey she concludes that the criteria used by the Code, i.e. the minimum wages levels and the fringe benefits, are so elastic as to be useless. The Code also stresses recognition of trade unions, but according to a comment from the Federation of South African Trade Unions (FOSATU), the reports were riddled with 'untrue statements'. The question of black advancement still faces legal barriers. The Code does not tackle redundancies, or hiring and firing practices.

In conclusion, Barbara Rogers states:

> The British Government has effectively abdicated any responsibility even for the minimal pressure of public exposure: the effort it is putting into the monitoring of the Code has also been reduced. The major structural problems of the Code – omission of vital data, lack of corroboration, the retreat from the principle of a standard minimum wage, and the lack of enforcement machinery – are unlikely to be rectified. Many observers see the Code of conduct as a policy which was never really intended to work, being introduced as a means of deflecting pressure for a withdrawal from South Africa...[22]

The constructive engagement movement was essentially linked to the managing board of firms. But increasingly it is being realized that the black workers themselves have views on the matter:

> It is a fundamental weakness of the Code that those affected, the black workers, were not consulted in drawing it up and are not consulted in monitoring it. This perpetuates the paternalistic attitude that is an essential part of the ideology of apartheid, that one does not talk with blacks, one talks about them.[23]

A different approach was used by a German group which commissioned secret interviews with black workers in South Africa that were subsequently published. These shed some light on the ambiguities of black advancement:

Question: 'Does the firm classify jobs differently, according to whether a white or a black is doing it?'

Answer: 'In my case – I work in quality control - there are whites as well. We do exactly the same job, have the same title, only the wage isn't the same. The whites get salaries and get a higher monthly salary. I get a weekly wage.'

Q: 'Do you think there are equal job opportunities for blacks and whites here?'

A: 'No – I believe there's no chance for a black to get a job until the moment when the whites regard a certain job as uninteresting for them. And then there is the point when we work together with whites and coloured with whom we don't always (if ever) have equal rights.'

Q: 'Tell me more precisely. In what way don't you have equal rights?'

A: 'With respect to our opportunities – we don't have equal opportunities. Although the whites often have lower qualifications than we blacks, they have the better jobs.'[24]

In another set of questions the black worker expresses a view on the unwillingness of companies to do anything extra even when there are no legal barriers:

'If the management wants to, it can abolish segregation inside the factory on its own without asking anyone. We're all employees, after all. And if the management wants to do something, then of course it can. Believe me, a company can do anything it really wants to. Anyone else who says otherwise is lying. They just don't try enough. Precisely because it happens to suit them all.'

Q: 'Could management for example see to houses for the workers, so they don't have to live separated from their families?'

A: 'They probably couldn't get them houses, but they could give them loans so that they could build houses themselves.'

Q: 'Do they do that?'

A: 'No they don't. But they could. They've got so much money. The awful thing about apartheid isn't only that the Afrikaners exploit us. No, the Germans do it, the English do it, the Americans do it. There they all sit, miles away from South Africa, and they're all crying out for equality. That's awful. They could force a change in things here. They could impose a trade embargo if they really honestly meant it about changing things. They could stop investing in South Africa.'[25]

The interview just quoted indicates that black workers are very much aware of their disadvantaged situation. Furthermore, during the 1970s in some industries, they were increasingly organized to bargain with management. The same report pointed out:

> In spite of the repression by the government and managements, the independent trade union movement has become a major political force in South Africa. In 1980 there were 207 strikes by black workers involving 175,000 black workers involving 175,000 working days lost. Membership was increasing rapidly, and reached 184,000 by the end of the year.[26]

3. *Withdrawal and embargo*
Because the churches play an institutional role as investors, it seems appropriate to merge discussion of the third and fourth BCC options.

(*a*) *Sanctions*
There had been talk about economic sanctions long before the WCC took it up. It was being discussed in South Africa in the late 1950s. From the beginning it was realized that sanctions would hurt the blacks. Albert Luthuli declared in 1959:

> The economic boycott of South Africa will entail undoubted hardship for Africans. We do not doubt that. But if it is a method which shortens the day of bloodshed, the suffering to us will be a price we are willing to pay.[27]

It is important to note that Luthuli, a declared pacifist, saw sanctions as an alternative to violent confrontation. Archbishop Tutu, also a Nobel Peace Prize winner, is another advocate of sanctions on the same grounds. Similarly, pacifists in other countries, such as the Friends, see the campaign to use economic leverage on South Africa as a non-violent option, hence the Quaker funding of CCSA in Britain.

Historically, the idea of trade sanctions was initiated by the ANC. Tennyson Makiwane left South Africa in 1959 to activate an economic boycott by overseas countries. The boycott campaign was among the first activities of the Anti-Apartheid Movement in the early 1960s. Within South Africa boycotts of various kinds have featured in the resistance campaigns organized by blacks, the most memorable being the bus strikes. An example of a consumer boycott against a manufacturing firm was the boycott of Fattis and Monis (makers of pasta foods) in solidarity with strikers at their factory. Such an alliance between workers and consumers is an interesting precedent for localized action. This type of consumer action is increasingly being used in the 1980s, as the black community flexes economic muscle, realizing that white businesses in the towns are dependent on their black customers. For instance at Christmas 1985 the young radicals picketed the supermarkets and forced black customers to throw away their purchases. In one case a woman was forced to drink all the cooking oil she had bought. One of the most determined of boycott campaigns is that of the rent strikes which are bankrupting township administrations. Thus within South Africa, boycott strategists have clear targets to pick on.

But disengagement is complex when internationalized, because the profit-takers and the consumer are then remote from the scene of actual labour exploitaiton. It requires much diligence to dig out of Economic Yearbooks and company reports the facts and figures of who is investing, who is trading, who is profiting out of apartheid. In 1972 Counter Information Services produced a series of reports on major companies such as Rio Tinto Zinc and Consolidated Goldfields. The latter not only reported profit takings and wage levels, but also tabulated the major shareholders, which included church bodies, local councils, pension funds and MPs. This helped to focus concern, as it exposed the fact that the churches in particular were giving institutional support to apartheid. After the Adam Raphael articles of March 1973 it was realized that British companies in South Africa would have to be carefully monitored by concerned activists. Thus Christian Concern for Southern Africa emerged out of some work done at CIIR. Researchers in other countries were also gathering data: in the Netherlands, the anti-apartheid groups began their campaign on Royal Dutch Shell, and in the United States the Corporate Data Exchange and the Interfaith Center for Corporate Responsibility began to compile records which have been used in the disinvestment movement.

(b) Trade boycotts

In order to see the feasibility of trade boycotts in the British context, CCSA analysed UK trade links with South Africa. Figures for the decade 1976-77 seemed to show that Britain was more important to South Africa than vice versa. For instance in 1976 the UK was the country receiving the greatest proportion of South African exports, 22% of them, totalling £879m. This amounted to 2.4% of total imports into the UK. Although the total volume of trade rose in the decade, in percentage South Africa declined as a source of imports for the UK by 1%. An analysis of these South Africa imports to the UK by categories of products is illuminating:[28]

Product category	Value £m	% of UK total imports from South Africa
Non-metallic minerals	420.8	19.9
Fruit and vegetables	96.1	8.6
Metalliferrous ores	81.8	11.8
Non-ferrous metals	53.4	4.7
Hides and skins	25.1	11.9

These are only the important categories from a much larger table. Fruit and vegetables are second in the table for value, and South African produce is conspicuous on the British market, but it only amounts to 8.6%. The valuable first category consists mainly of diamonds. An even more vital export from South Africa is gold, which is excluded from the table. In 1970 gold accounted for 53% of South Africa's total mineral production and was the largest export item.[29] South Africa's monetary position depends on the international gold price. In addition to other sources, South Africa gets valuable foreign exchange by selling gold Krugerrands internationally.

Apart from gold and diamonds, South Africa exports eight other rare minerals: platinum, vanadium, vermiculite, chromium, antimony, manganese, asbestos and uranium. During the 1970s South African apologists used to argue that these metals had 'strategic value' to the West, and could not be got from elsewhere. That argument is increasingly questionable. The steel industry, which uses vanadium, chromium and manganese, is being cut back because of over-production. Zimbabwe can also supply chrome, and there are alternatives for vermiculite and asbestos. Uranium, of course, is used for nuclear processes. The UK had a contract to buy much of the output of mines in Namibia, but has now stockpiled so much that the termination of the contract has been announced.

The CCSA document discusses the feasibility of a ban on South African imports. There are alternative sources of supply for all the bioproducts, but it would be impossible to disengage unilaterally from gold, as there would be indirect importation while gold is the *de facto* anchor of the world monetary system. Diamonds constitute one half of the visible UK imports from South Africa, but most of these are re-exported.

In 1977 the balance of trade was against the UK, but in preceding years it had been in surplus. In 1977, the value of UK visible exports to South Africa had been £581m. Table 5 of the CCSA document estimates that about 19,500 UK jobs would go if these exports were cut, 'although it is extremely difficult to make meaningful statistical predictions'. In 1967 South Africa was the third most important country to receive UK imports; by 1977 it had dropped to sixteenth place, receiving only 1.8% of UK imports, representing 17.6% of total South African exports (USA and West Germany exported more to the Republic of South Africa). It is difficult to gauge what impact on the UK economy an embargo on trade with South Africa would have. On the basis of a 1970 Treasury model which calculated the impact of an externally induced change in UK trading patterns of £400m (equivalent to £1bn in 1977 money values), CCSA concluded that 'a loss of exports to South Africa would have only a very small percentage impact overall on unemployment in the UK'. An interesting comparison might be the effect of the Iran revolution[30], which caused comparable disruption of trade. In 1977 UK trade with Iran stood at about 2% of UK exports, i.e. slightly more than with South Africa.

It is sometimes suggested that government cannot do very much about trade. But CCSA points out that the British government does have direct influence over the volume of trade by means of the Export Credit Guarantee Department. In 1976, around 39% of exports to South Africa were supported by ECGD. Stopping ECGD support for contracts with South African enterprises would not halt trade with South Africa, but it might reduce it a little by making exports dearer. Free trade is a key concept in the ideology of Western capitalist nations. But in practice some Western nations are prone to use trade sanctions for political purposes. During the Falklands crisis Britain imposed an embargo on trade with Argentina. The USA imposed trade sanctions against Poland in 1981 in support of Solidarity and it has recently imposed economic embargos on Nicaragua. So Western governments do see the possible effectiveness of economic leverage when their national interests are at stake. Selective morality is apparent among the very people who sometimes try to insist that economic matters are morally neutral, and should be left to the workings of the market free of political intervention.

(c) Disinvestment

Britain is by far the largest single investor in the South African economy. In 1976 the total EEC investment in South Africa was £7,660m, of which 63% was from the UK, which represents 36% of all foreign investment in South Africa. In 1974 UK investment in South Africa (excluding oil, banking and insurance) amounted to 9.9% of equivalent UK investment in all foreign countries. In 1974, the rate of return on these South African investments averaged 20.9% as compared to 14.2% from all the other countries.

The CCSA report discussed what might happen if the UK tried to disinvest. If this were done by legislation, requiring British investors to sell off their assets in South Africa, these assets would merely be bought up by other investors, unless there was multilateral action throughout the world. A requirement by the UK that all dividends and profits be repatriated to the UK could be blocked by South African legislation. Direct investors in South Africa, especially the big transnationals, would not be much affected, as in any case their expansion is often financed out of unrepatriated profits in South Africa. If a freeze on investments were to include indirect investment, i.e. loans and the purchase of South African shares in the United Kingdom, then this might affect the business climate, as people would begin to want to disinvest, especially if it looked as if the South African government was about to ban withdrawal of capital from the country.

The whole matter would clearly be extremely complex, and the complexity of the matter is often given as a reason for inaction. For example, it took until 1982 for the General Synod of the Church of England to be convinced of the disinvestment argument, and even then the Church Commissioners, who hold the purse-strings, did not concur. They argued that as most of the major British companies have some South African operations it would be impossible to disinvest from all of them, or even from the minor ones, because they could not then have a balanced portfolio.

Like the argument over constructive engagement, the excuse of the 'complexity' of disengagement calls for patient investigation and detailed research. For this purpose a new body, the Ethical Investment Research and Information Service (EIRIS) was established in April 1983 and launched in November 1983, with the aim of providing information on a variety of issues connected with investment and especially of helping investors to apply positive or negative ethical criteria for investement as well as social ones. It tabulated the practices of UK companies over a whole range of ethical concerns, including armaments, pollutions and drugs as well as links with South Africa. Its aim was not to make ethical judgments for investors, but to set out the facts in such a way that those with ethical criteria could rearrange their investment portfolios accordingly. In his comments to me, Richard Pond, who is doing the research, pointed out that there is no untainted investment: it is a matter of choosing better or worse on a relative scale. The creation of EIRIS seems to me to be a significant advance within Western culture, in that it acknowledges the applicability of ethical principles to the complexity of economics. This enhanced ethical awareness would seem to be not least a result of PCR.

It could be argued that the churches are being made more 'political' by being influenced by secular movements. So it must be asked whether the churches are in fact in the forefront of the disinvestment campaigns or whether they are active in withdrawing their funds because they have been targeted by secular groups as large corporate investors, along with local councils, pension funds and so on. The tactic used by activists in the disinvestment campaigns is to buy up small numbers of shares, enough to give the right to go to the Annual General Meeting and ask some awkward questions, to embarrass the Board of Directors in public and to exert moral pressure. Such a disinvestment move has no hope of securing disinvestment by a majority vote among shareholders. Even if all corporate bodies open to moral argument were to back a motion, such moves would rarely result in securing more than four per cent of the total shareholding. Still, the numbers of influential bodies prepared to vote for a moral proposal is a significant factor in the campaign, and every effort is made to identify the corporate shareholders and influence them, especially where they are susceptible to democratic pressures, as are local authorities, colleges, and to some extent the churches. But I think that it would be a misreading of the campaigns to assume that the churches who have backed disinvestment campaigns have done so because they are influenced by 'Marxists' or secular concerns. On the contrary, Christians have been in the forefront of the debate, as evidenced in CCSA and ELTSA, even if some of the actual church institutions, notably the Church of England, have been tardy in following through the arguments.

And it is important that they should be. At a time when the prime consideration has come to be whether or not an investment makes a good financial return or not, and the most important job for portfolio managers and trustees is profit maximization, social and theological issues must not be forgotten:

> When at the birth of our modern world, economics came to be regarded as no longer part of ethics but as an autonomous science

governed by immanent laws to be discovered by analysis and induction, and when this new faith was embodied in the myth of the 'invisible hand' which would ensure that the sum total of individual self-seeking would add up to general welfare, good Christians, contemplating the appalling cruelties of the 'dark Satanic mills', believed that it was impossible to interfere with the workings of 'economic laws', that the writ of Christ's kingship did not run in the autonomous kingdom of economics, and that the best one could do was to offer charity to the victims. Blake was correctly interpreting the biblical teaching when he used the word 'Satanic' at this point. Any sphere of human life which is withdrawn from the kingship of Christ does not remain under ours; it falls under another rule.[31]

This seems to me a powerful reason for keeping the disinvestment issue on the agenda of church meetings.

(d) The arms trade

Many of the arguments used in the disinvestment debate are applicable to the armaments industry, too. In addition, the fact that British firms have assisted the militarization of South Africa can be a point at issue in the debate about violence. At the very start of the PCR debate, in 1970, the Bishop of Manchester pointed out (see pp. 113f. above) that it was hypocritical of Western Christians to condemn aid for the liberation movements when their industries were still supplying arms to the South African government.

Throughout the 1970s the militarization of South Africa continued apace, aided by the investment and technological exchanges of the big Western transnational companies, as reported to a 1978 UN seminar:

South Africa's military build-up played an important role in stimulating the growth of transnational corporate investment in the South African manufacturing industry in the 1960s and 1970s. Transnational corporations with investments in South Africa benefited both directly in the form of contracts to provide parts and materials for the military and indirectly in terms of the expanded market. In the 1960s, South Africa's military expenditure multiplied over six times, from $65m to $405m a year. By 1977/78 it had more than tripled once again to R1,645m.[32]

The South African munitions industry has become almost self-sufficient because of the aid and technological cooperation given by the

Western firms. The British registered firm ICI is one of the companies which, through its South African subsidiary AECI, has assisted militarization, as a CCSA report explains:

> Whilst ICI's involvement in South Africa does not constitute a major part of its worldwide operations, it does represent a substantial and historically lucrative investment. More importantly, however, the technical and financial support given by ICI to its associates, and especially to AECI, during the last fifty years has changed them from merely serving South Africa's mining industry into pillars of an increasingly diversified and self-sufficient economy...
>
> ICI's major role in the foundation of the South African munitions industry and its reported continued involvement (through its associate AECI) in the production of tear gas for the South African security forces raises commercial questions for the company and serious questions for the shareholders. Similarly, the company's past involvement in the South African uranium industry and the increasing strategic importance that the industry is assuming, make it imperative that the shareholders should seek assurance that the ICI group's expertise in these areas is not being placed at the disposal of the South African government.[33]

There have been varied attempts to halt this trade in arms and military technology by official *fiat*. In 1963, the UN called for voluntary embargoes on the arms trade with South Africa, but Britain continued to supply arms under the Simonstown Agreement. It is for this reason that the South African govenment is very keen to fan fears about Russian naval plans for the Indian Ocean and the Cape sea-routes, because South Africa can then be seen as a bastion against Communism in the southern hemisphere, which justifies continued supplies for the military. In theory the goods supplied are supposed to be for external use only. But the Labour Government allowed a contract for four Wasp helicopters and for Vauxhall armoured cars to go through, presumably under the Simonstown deal. The attempts at official control of the British arms trade with South Africa contained 'glaring loopholes', as CCSA pointed out in *Arms for Apartheid*:

> The British Export of Goods (Control) Order 1970... used to enforce the embargo between 1970 and 1978...contained a list of prohibited orders, known as Schedule 1, covering several hundred items. A number of the most obviously military items were marked with an 'A',

prohibiting their export anywhere without a special licence. All not-'A' items were prohibited for export without licence, except to any 'port or destination in the Commonwealth, the Republic of Ireland and the Republic of South Africa, or to the United States of America'. Thus South Africa was able to obtain, without special licence, inter alia: radio direction finding equipment, airborne radar, sophisticated and high powered ground and marine radar, computers, nuclear decay powered sources, advanced military communications equipment (tropospheric scatter equipment), primary explosives, minerals and metals appropriate for military use, engineering products and more. Britain's NATO allies were not given this special status... The Order seemed to have been drawn up to circumvent the embargo in every way short of the provision of ready-made direct combat weapons. British industry could not actually arm South Africa, but was free to provide most of what was necessary for South Africa to arm itself.[34]

The British Government's ambiguous position with regard to this military trade with South Africa is shown up in the Honours lists. Shortly after an ICI deal supplied the South African police with advanced computers, the South African director, John Starkey, rceived a CBE for 'Service to British Commercial interests in South Africa'. Mr Starkey had earlier commented:

No pressure at all has been brought on us to curtail this business. The Foreign Office is happy and we've had no problems with the EEC.[35]

What can concerned people do about this? The campaign against the arms trade is wider in scope than just the arms trade with South Africa. However, during the 1970s the anti-apartheid activists can be credited with drawing attention to the complexity of Western commercial networks, and the difficulty of targeting arms deal in particular. More-over, in the early 1970s the disinvestment campaigns had the problem that they were asking people to exercise ethical judgments before the facts about various firms had been researched enough for comparisons and choices to be made. But since then a number of significant reports have been produced, and it is to be hoped that EIRIS will go on supplying detailed tabulated facts from which church and private investors can make their investment choices on ethical criteria.

(e) Bank loans
The campaign for withdrawal from banks assisting South Africa followed

a similar course to other disengagement campaigns, in that it began with rather vague directives, which were then sharpened up as more research indicated the precise degree of involvement in South Africa. We have already seen the role of the WCC in the campaign against banks. It actually financed further investigation, for instance subsidizing Counter Information Services to produce the 1974 report *Business as Usual*. Such investigative activity, together with shareholder lobbying, has resulted in what Prexy Nesbitt termed 'enhanced visibility'[36] of corporate collaboration with apartheid.

In the early years of the banking campaigns in Britain, Barclays was chosen because it is obviously involved in South Africa, with its many branches there, and it has many High Street branches in Britain which were the focus of local demonstrations. However, the campaigners were increasingly able to point to instances of specific collaboration, such as Barclay's militaristic advertisements in South African newspapers which endeavoured to capture the accounts of soldiers fighting in the 'operational zone', and also Barclay's purchase of Defence Bonds, with blatant publicity about this in South Africa to attract loyalist customers.

However, by the end of the 1970s the culpability of other British banks had been exposed, through their involvement in banking consortia which financed big contracts, largely to state-owned corporations of South Africa like ESCOM and SASOL. This obviously represents a big expansion of the state-owned sector of the economy, and also assistance to 'strategic' enterprises. For instance, SASOL, the oil from coal programme, was undertaken to beat the possible effects of the oil embargo.

The Centre against Apartheid at the UN produced a comprehensive document in 1979 listing all the major loans made to South Africa. Such documentation should make ethical choices possible. However, it might well be asked whether all types of loans to South Africa are equally reprehensible. The hard-liners insist that their demand for withdrawal of aid involves all types of financial aid, but some of the loans listed by CCSA are for apparently humanitarian purposes, like the five-year loan of $30m to the Medical University of Southern Africa.[37] However, when it is realized that most of South Africa's educational resources for medicine are geared up towards providing white doctors for the affluent white minority, the usefulness of the loan as far as the black majority is concerned can be questioned. It is because the cash ends up by being used according to the priorities of a racist government that the anti-apartheid campaigners say that any loan can be seen as bolstering up apartheid.

British banks and finance houses have provided more money for South Africa than any other country. For instance in the three-year period 1979-1982, British banks provided $1068m of loans. Switzerland came next with $998m, followed by Germany and the USA. In spite of the formidable task of tracking these movements of high finance, the activists have succeeded in making an impact on the banking community. Groups like ELTSA work by attending AGMs and asking questions. They also produce a 'Shadow' annual report on Barclays. Although cynics have said that the main visible effect is that banks have learnt to be more careful about their public image and in the editing of paragraphs about their South African activities in annual reports, the 1986 withdrawal of Barclays from South Africa indicated that the cynicism was uncalled for.

High financiers in the West appear to be insulated from moral arguments by the persistent Western tradition of amoral economics and money-making – of 'following the market movements', with no initiatives or judgments involved. In fact, when there was a panic flight of capital from South Africa in 1960 after the Sharpeville shootings, the big transnationals, backed by the banks, were determined to staunch the flow by fresh transfusions of capital, which they carried out then and in the succeeding years, even during the next crisis, Soweto in 1976.[38] The strong gold price also added to confidence in the South African economy.

It is only in the 1980s that the withdrawal of financial backing is becoming a serious political factor in South Africa. How much of this is due to the growing strength and publicity of the ethical campaigns overseas is hard to assess. As the instability of South African society under apartheid becomes more apparent, the reactions of Western investors are influenced by fears for their money. But it would be sad to conclude that the growing violence in South Africa has had a greater impact on the foreign investors than all the moral arguments initiated by the WCC against the banks. However, for the historical record it is noteworthy that the ethical campaigns began in the years when the South African economy seemed stable and thriving. Whatever might be imputed to those who have continued to make profits from apartheid, at least it must be fairly recognized that there was sufficient Christian concern in the West to spotlight the issues and develop increasingly effective campaigns against the financing of apartheid.

(f) Oil embargo

Like the campaigns against the bank loans, the oil embargo is politically motivated and can be seen as a strategy aimed at bringing about the downfall of the South African regime. A modern economy can grind to a halt without oil. This is why Prime Minister Harold Wilson predicted that Ian Smith's regime in Rhodesia would topple 'within weeks'. He was assuming that the country's oil stocks would run dry and would not be replenished because of the embargo. The failure of this embargo enabled the Smith regime to continue. Thus the oil companies which broke the embargo should be held partially responsible for the deaths of 20,000 people who were victims of the long-drawn-out guerrilla war. The 1978 Bingham Report revealed how most of Rhodesia's oil needs were met through Shell Mozambique, a subsidiary of a British registered company. After the war, church leaders from Britain, the US, Holland and France wrote to companies:

> It has been persuasively argued that the war was prolonged, and the destruction considerably increased, by the continued supply of your companies' products. There is therefore a clear moral case for a form of reparation to be made by your companies for the devastation which has occurred.[39]

The ability of the oil firms to circumvent an oil embargo is now evident with regard to South Africa. Although all members of OPEC now ban the supply of oil to South Africa, oil still arrives at the Durban terminals. A CCSA report[40] revealed that this oil comes from four possible sources: Britain via a third country; Brunei (through British connivance, as Britain guides that country's foreign policy); the Netherlands Antilles (through Dutch connivance, similarly): or Oman, through the Shell offices in contravention of Oman's ban. This suggests that commercial firms as powerful as the oil countries can outwit government controls. It also suggests that some Western governments, those of Britain and the Netherlands in particular, are not prepared to make strong efforts to enforce the oil embargo strictly.

We have already seen the importance of monitoring by non-governmental organizations, like Anti-Apartheid and CCSA; in the Netherlands, a similar organization called KAIROS took the initiative after the 1972 WCC call for disinvestment, deciding to concentrate on the oil issue because Shell is a dominant company in the Netherlands. Their work is perhaps the clearest example of church activism in the economic area, inspired by PCR.

What... would a dozen volunteers ever achieve in a campaign against such a huge concern, but strengthened with the idea that once Goliath had seemed undefeatable?[41]

They made a start. They aroused support in the churches, which included financial pledges, signing of appeals, letter campaigns and talks:

without the active support of a number of churches the oil campaign... would not have been possible.[42]

The campaign grew to such strength that it nearly brought down the Dutch government in 1980. What the government spokesman said at that time gives the impression that the government's dilemma was that the oil companies were too powerful for national legislation to deal with effectively. The activists continually harrassed the company at shareholders meetings. In response to such pressure, the company changed its voting procedures so that the moral vote would have less impact. As a Shell executive confided in a letter:

Dear old clergymen, who kick up a fuss at shareholders meetings, cause more concern within Shell than they can possibly know about.[43]

A glowing tribute!

The KAIROS report also emphasized that these Dutch Christians were inspired by the calls that came from African Christians:

Contacts with the South African Churches have changed the minds of many Dutch people. Not much is left of the traditional bonds with the white Dutch Reformed Church. The views of Bishop Desmond Tutu, Dr Allan Boesak and the Broederkring (Brother Circle) have taught Dutch Christians to see South Africa through black eyes. The courageous statement by Bishop Tutu about the necessity of economic pressures on Pretoria have made a favourable impression. It took quite some time for Dutch Christians to realize that one should listen to what cannot be said in South Africa.

From time to time the voice of the African churches can also be heard in Holland. Particularly the appeal of the All African Council of Churches, in which more than 115 churches and councils of churches from thirty-three African countries co-operate, was given attention. In this appeal an urgent request was made to the Dutch parliament to implement an oil embargo and to listen to the prophetic call of the Dutch Council of Churches and Anti-Apartheid movements in which Shell was asked to stop oil supplies to South Africa.[44]

Furthermore, the disinvestment campaign had an invigorating effect on church thinking in Europe:

> Another important effect of the oil campaign has been that many local churches take their responsibility for church investment seriously.[45]

This has a bearing on the point made by Adler that talk about general principles was uncontroversial but that PCR, because it recommended particular actions, became controversial. In the case of the oil campaign in the Netherlands the conscientization occurred because particular actions were being demanded, not just vague pity for the plight of the blacks. But KAIROS does not expect instant political effect:

> This conscientizing process can hardly be stopped. Only in the long term will the eventual results of this campaign become perceptible.[46]

The pressure for sanctions, fuelled by outrage at growing violence in South Africa, is now bearing fruit. In the US, because of the increasing power of the black caucus, the anti-apartheid sanctions movement has more political clout than in the UK. The pressure on the UK has been mainly from the Commonwealth. The 1985 Nassau meeting of Commonwealth leaders failed to agree on sanctions, mainly because of Britain's reluctance, but agreed to set up an Eminent Persons' Group instead. Some people always regarded this as a delaying tactic; however, the group gained in credibility as it set about its task. It drew up a set of demands to the Pretoria government, including the release of Nelson Mandela, and the suspension of violence. The response from Pretoria was yet more specious promises about 'reforms', like the abolition of pass laws and influx control. Then when South Africa made night raids on neighbouring states, the EPG decided that the time had come to discontinue negotiations. It subsequently published its findings, *Mission to South Africa. The Commonwealth Report.*[47]

Following the collapse of the EPG effort, the EEC also tried to delay decisions on sanctions by sending Geoffrey Howe, the British foreign minister, on a mission. There was much reluctance on the part of South African black leaders even to meet him. The question was what he could hope to achieve that the EPG had not tried to do. When his mission failed, the EEC was forced to consider sanctions. Again Mrs Thatcher refused to impose significant sanctions. When the black majority of

South Africa achieve their aims, Britain's betrayal in this matter in 1986 will not be forgotten.

However, despite the political obstructions, the commercial firms were looking into the future and have begun to pull out anyway. In 1985 Barclays bank had reduced its holding in its South African operation to 40%. This was noted at the time, but the Barclays spokesman claimed that it had no significance and was for commercial reasons. As we have seen, the sale, at a loss of more than £40m, of the whole South African branch, with local South African money buying up most of the shares, was heralded as a victory for the anti-apartheid movement. However, the activists say that the campaign against Barclays will not stop until Barclays cease all forms of help to South Africa, including help with technical personnel and loans. At the same time as this Barclays withdrawal the news came through of the withdrawal of some big American firms, like General Motors, which also sold out to local management. This represents success for the disengagement movement. But it is too early yet to assess what the political effects will be in South Africa, especially whether it will increase the pressures that the white South African owners can put on the government, or how it will affect the power of the black workers. The latter question is particularly interesting in the case of General Motors, as the car-workers in Port Elizabeth are militant, with growing experience of trade union action.

Mokhethi Motlhabi wrote:

> It may be worth while for Black South Africans to begin concentrating on what they can accomplish by themselves, without placing too much reliance on what help they can receive from those who appear to sympathize with them.[48]

The car workers of Port Elizabeth are among the first who are likely to suffer from economic sanctions, and they are also the ones most likely to share this view. I do not mean by this to dismiss the sanctions movement as irrelevant – it is undoubtedly having a growing effect, and most importantly it has injected some moral clarification into Western ideas about economics – but this other dimension must not be forgotten.

10

The Communication of PCR

In 1979, following the row over the 1978 grants to the Patriotic
Front, the WCC was admitting that there were some problems with
communications over PCR. At the 1979 Jamaica Central Council
meeting Philip Potter acknowledged that 'an information gap' was
apparent. When the deputation from the Church of England visited the
WCC in March 1979, the Director of PCR admitted that 'mistakes were
made'[1] in the way in which the grants were publicized. Such frank
admissions raise the question whether the WCC was prepared for the
communication task entailed in its most radical actions.

A realization that communication is a problem goes back a long way
in WCC circles. At the time of the Uppsala assembly in 1968 Visser
t'Hooft pointed out that the WCC 'believed too much in persuasion by
declarations and was not sufficiently aware of the irrational factors in
the situation', and nowhere was there more irrationality around than in
connection with the subject of racism. Education about racism was also
high on the agenda of the Notting Hill consultation.

The question is, was there a particular ineptness about communicating
PCR over and above the problem of racism which is always in the
background? We might begin by asking how the accusations that the
WCC has been communicating badly are to be understood. One way
would be to see PCR and its sympathizers as being bad at media
packaging. In other words, PCR had a task to fulfil, namely giving money
to liberation movements, but failed to explain clearly the intentions
behind the grant, through whatever communication networks were
available to it, so as to reach its constituent churches in an acceptable
manner. But there is a hidden assumption here, a carry-over concept
derived from Western-style consumer advertising, that a product is

made acceptable, desirable or more commendable, by the skill of the advertisements that promote it.

What we need to ask is whether this was really a problem of inept media packaging, or whether the problem was not a more fundamental one of an unpalatable, or unpackageable, anti-racist message. Perhaps the consumer resistance was too great, a resistance that derived strength from prejudice and the irrational factors that the first consultations so trustfully acknowledged. Another way of putting it would be to say that the aim of expressing solidarity with the victims of racism involved challenging racism via the media and the educative programmes of the churches. Mere declarations about universal goodwill and human dignity would not stir people into thought and action about racism: but the symbolic action of the grants undoubtedly did.

An extreme form of this view would be to say that though the grants undoubtedly did go some way towards alleviating the plight of refugees in war-torn zones in Southern Africa, the actual amount involved (50p per refugee, as we have seen) was hardly important in terms of the struggle for material support, and especially for armaments, the liberation movements and other sources of supply. What was of the greatest value about the token PCR grants was precisely the impact they made on Western awareness of the problems. Thus this extreme line of argument asserts that the educative process mattered more than the money. Along this line of thinking, the controversy which the grants stirred up was not a sign of failure to communicate, but a sign of the beginning of the educative process.

Now if this educative process is examined more closely, it can be seen that there have been a variety of 'boxing rings' for the debate. The Western newspapers have been most vociferous, via editorials and their readers' letters. The church press in particular has given frequent coverage. The national councils of churches have issued various pamphlets and arranged consultations. The debate has also been held at formal denominational gatherings, either at the local or the national level. The underlying divergence of interest between these different circuits should give pause for thought. In particular, the church-based organizations have a different frame of reference from the secular newspapers, i.e. a Christian one. This provokes another line of inquiry, namely whether the communication 'failure' of PCR is primarily with the secular media or with the church networks. Obviously there is a connection, because Christians also read the secular newspapers. If they get the wrong idea of PCR is it because the Western press is an unsuitable vehicle for conveying radical Christian ideas? Should the apologists for PCR have tried harder to get the message across via the Press, or would it have been better to put the main effort into communicating via internal church links? A hypothesis well worth testing is that there is a significant divergence of interests and assumptions between the churches and the secular media, and that this was a powerful factor in widening the communications gap.

The announcement of the 1970 grants

When the 1970 Arnoldshaim grants had been decided on, on 3 September the WCC sent out a press release. *The Times* published the information from the release on 4 September. There was a major difference in the headlines: for the WCC original:

> ## WCC EXECUTIVE ALLOCATES FUNDS TO GROUPS
> ## TO COMBAT RACISM

The Times had:

> ## CHURCHES TO AID AFRICAN RESISTERS

The Times can be congratulated on avoiding the more blatantly biassed terms 'terrorist' or 'revolutionary'. Given the decision to emphasize the African implications of the announcement, 'resister' at least suggests the two points of view on the violence and that the violence implied was secondary or defensive against prior aggression. However, praise for the careful choice of this word should not obscure the fact that the total impact of the headline together with the following article entirely eliminated the emphasis which the PCR director placed in paragraphs 3 and 4 on the fact that these grants were part of a wider effort to combat racism. The insertion of the word 'aid' in the headline, though neat and handy for the layout, made the grants seem a type of hand-out, closer to the 'charity' concept, with its connotations of paternalism, non-political do-gooding and guilt money within the *status quo*. The headline as it stands has the shock effect of a paradox: 'churches' (i.e. non-political, peaceful, charitable people) 'to aid resisters' (political, determined, possibly violent people). It should be noted that the WCC original 'allocates funds' has different connotations, belonging to the world of budgeting, of communal money that must be shared out according to agreed criteria. Too clumsy for a headline, of course, but close to the ideas of sharing and solidarity.

The changes in the headline emphasis were also continued in the body of the article. *The Times* looked at the list of nineteen organizations and realized that PCR was concentrating on African liberation movements. The wider purposes of the Programme were omitted from the article. In the original, the fact that the grants would not be monitored was placed in the same paragraph as 'strengthening the organizational capability of racially oppressed people', indicating that the WCC was trying to establish a relationship of trust with such groups. But *The Times* used it as a final punch line in a paragraph built around the possible military aims of such groups.

In addition, *The Times* made enquiries and told its readers which churches were actually giving money to the Special Fund, as well as repeating the point that some money had come from the WCC general reserves. The Bishop of Manchester was quick to write in to point out that British churches were not putting anything into the kitty. But it is interesting to note that which churches were or were not giving never became an issue. People wanted to express their opinions on the idea of churches aiding such movements, whether or not they themselves, through their churches, were actually committing anything at all.

The Times has a high reputation among all newspapers of the Western media for thoughtful, 'balanced' reporting, so it seemed fairest to select it rather than a paper more to the right or left, or the more popular press. But even in such a short article it can be seen how selectivity can work. And sure enough, the British public responded to what they were told in newspapers by keeping to those very points: the possible military use of charity money; Christians funding violence, and terrorists misusing unmonitored grants. And there the debate has remained ever since, with varying degrees of intensity, depending on events in South Africa.

The outcry following the announcement of the first grants meant that the report of the BCC working party *Violence in Southern Africa*, due to be received by the BCC assembly in September, was in for a rough time. In the circumstances it was not endorsed by the BCC but published under the names of the Working Party only: evidently a compromise after a hard wrangle. BCC files seem to indicate that the main criticism of the report was the argument about violence in it: here the BCC reacted in the same way as the general public writing to their newspapers, i.e. 'churches to aid guerrillas'.

The outcry was an occasion for close scrutiny of the way in which the BCC dealt with the Press, and new procedures were devised and put into practice. Particularly close attention was paid to the reception of the 1978 BCC report *Rhodesia Now: The Liberation of Zimbabwe,* which was published at the height of the furore following the Elim massacres and the shooting down of an airliner, which coincided with the publication of grants to the Patriotic Front. Great care was taken over the press release, and the follow-up by the media and correspondence received were both analysed. There was no question of ineptitude at this level. So why was it that church members still felt so aggrieved about the grants, and were inclined to accuse the BCC of acting beyond its authority? Where was the comunications gap between PCR and the person in the pew?

One major factor seems to be a failure on the part of the churches and church newspapers to present these issues to Christians. The receptivity of new ideas within the churches depends on the reaction to them by church leaders, beginning at the diocesan level or its equivalent and working down to the parishes. It would have been encouraging to be able to argue that the internal church communication network served as an alternative to the bias of the secular media and its influence on readers and viewers. But the analysis made of the 1978 controversy suggests that the secular press has the strongest influence on church people. The attempts to communicate by the BCC were inevitably restricted by conditions; few church leaders were informed and gave public guidance, and the coverage in the church press was delayed because the controversy blew up in the holiday season. Yet Christians would feel confident to debate the issues in local synods and parish meetings on the basis of what they had picked up from the secular press.

The BCC examination of the affair suggests that those who wrote about the Zimbabwe report seemed to have made up their minds from what they read in the secular newspapers. As far as could be ascertained, only one writer of a hostile letter had read the report in detail. People seemed unaware of the divergence of values between commercially motivated newspapers and Christian proclamation, with the result that British newspapers (along with other media) were regarded as sources of value-forming authority rather than the churches and the theology found in those churches. In other words, the weight of opinion comes down from secular debate rather than from the processes of inter-church communication.

But why should it be asserted that there is such a divergence between the secular press and the church's task of proclamation? To answer this question we must look in more detail at the workings of the secular press.

Secular press sources

The public trust the news agencies to get reporters to the places where noteworthy events are happening. But who judges what is noteworthy and why? It is a truism that a lot of good news is happening all the time all over the world – unnoticed. But a disaster in an accessible place gets planeloads of reporters to the spot. Nevertheless, a lot of agency news comes across from staff stationed in the country concerned: 'Our man in...'. The choice to pay for a man on the spot seems determined by several factors extraneous to noteworthy news. First, most journalists prefer to live in a metropolis, with facilities for their family and other benefits of urban life. They also need to be near rapid lines of communication. This means that in many cases the news they gather is what comes into that metropolis. They only go out 'on location' if the newspaper head office thinks the trip worth paying for. The quip about hotel bar journalism may be all too true in some situations, especially during some of the more confusing current events in Africa.

For instance, during the last days of the Ian Smith régime in Rhodesia, the movements of journalists out of Salisbury were severely restricted. They were allowed to follow up stories only if the Rhodesia Information Department wanted them released to the rest of the world, as in the case of the Elim massacre. Some astute British readers realized this and commented on the resulting bias:

> The Press believes without question what an illegal régime chooses to have known to the world at a stage of a war that it knows it is losing, and whose only hope is to gain Western support for the interim régime and for the subsequent lifting of sanctions. The Sunday papers, however, gave no coverage, let alone front-page treatment, to the Rhodesian security forces' fresh incursion last week into Mozambique, and the murder of nineteen people.[2]

Since the end of the Zimbabwe war, a thorough examination of Rhodesia's manipulation of the news-images has been compiled by Julie Frederikse.[3] Her book reveals which stories the Rhodesia government withheld from world exposure, and what efforts they made, by special press conferences, government transport to the scene, etc., to get publicity for events like Elim that would swing sympathy behind the white population. Such special efforts inevitably fuel rumours and suspicion among us, in Africa, that some of the atrocities which provide advantageous propaganda for the white régime are carried out, instigated or urged on by some 'dirty tricks' department or other of the white régimes such as the Selous Scouts within the Rhodesian security forces and their equivalent the Koevoet of the SADF.

Whatever the truth behind this, it is undeniably the case that most of the stories about Southern Africa reaching the Western press come from reporters stationed in Cape Town, Johannesburg or Salisbury/Harare. For example, it is noticeable that most of the stories about the war in Angola come via Cape Town, presumably being whatever scenes the SADF invites the Press to come and see, like the press conferences of Jonas Savimbi 'in the bush'. Thus the logistics of getting reporters to these remote and difficult-to-reach areas (hundreds of miles from major cities and good roads) can be overcome if the authorities concerned deem it important to arrange the whole show. Reports from the same war zone, but from the other side, are extremely rare: for example, there is no article about what the Angolans are doing about Savimbi. For a British news agency, the language barrier of Portuguese and the preference among journalists for being stationed in white South Africa is good reason for feeling that it is sufficient to get the main stories via Cape Town. But ideological bias also has a major influence. One might compare the number of reporters dodging around with the gunners in the valleys of Afghanistan with the dearth of stories from the remote battle zones of Southern Africa.

By comparison the church networks may well provide a more authentic source of information than most journalists obtain, especially about events happening in rural areas. Governments find it easier to restrict journalists, especially foreign ones, than to suppress the communications networks of the churches, which may be more indigenous. This argument probably applies beyond the Christian churches. For instance, before the fall of the Shah the Ayatollah had communications within Iran via the mosques which the Shah was unable to obstruct.

In Southern Africa the churches have a unique claim in witnessing to events through their local networks. For instance, the Burgos Fathers beat the news agencies and unmasked to the world the Wiriyamu massacre that the Portuguese had concealed. They did so because, unlike the journalists who jet across the world, they have a presence in the locality where the people concerned are. That presence links the churches with many a little village, obscure dorp or township. Messages can easily be conveyed to denominational headquarters or to the council of churches, and from there to international centres like Geneva or the Vatican for dissemination to the rest of the world. I was told that news of events in Soweto in 1976 was getting to the WCC directly via the telex of the SACC, providing first-hand accounts from people in the areas worst affected, before the reporters of the secular news agencies had identified the sources and relayed the stories out by their usual channels.

So there was no reason for some church newspapers to join the bandwagon of those who were against grants to 'guerrillas'. For if there is one body that has access to the sufferings of the poor and oppressed, it is the church in these affected areas. That is because of the abiding presence of the church amongst the people. Nor is this something unique to Southern Africa. It is also true of Latin America, where because of this presence among the people the church has been able to stand by them in their struggles.

In the case of Southern Africa it is certainly true that inter-church communication links provide a different view of the situation from that which can be obtained from mere newspaper reading. If the churches are witnessing in the actual scene of events, they have a special competence to judge the applicability of principles. During the Rhodesia-Zimbabwe war, when events were being revealed selectively, whenever the churches published views favourable to the black cause they were open to abuse from readers on the other side, like that from Ronald Bell MP, who complained in *The Times* about an article by James Wilde from the Africa desk of the BCC:

> There would have been no need to read the article at all for anyone who takes the view that the World Council of Churches do not see events in Africa with a clear and impartial eye.[4]

Here is someone who is clearly committed to the white régime and hostile to the BCC interpretation of events. His comment about not reading the article neatly confirms the BCC dossier impression that the more prejudiced critics were not bothering to read! It is not at all clear what Mr Bell means by 'impartial', when he is so clearly prejudiced. If the important criterion for valid opinion is a clear view of what was happening, then it can be proved that the BCC had access to a good deal of authentic information from first-hand witness which was not reaching the newspapers – nor, apparently, Mr Bell. My perusal of the 1978 BCC files turned up a good many letters from missionaries and others in the churches in Zimbabwe at that time which had arrived on James Wilde's desk.

The press and ethnic slant

News stories are selected and relayed according to the tastes of the mass readership of the Western world. That is likely to involve racial slanting, as with the reporting of the 1978 Elim massacre. Many violent incidents were going on in Zimbabwe at the time, but it was the massacre of whites which made the headlines. At least one African was able to point out the racist slant of this in the *Methodist Recorder* of 16 November:

> White missionaries have been among the innocent victims of massacre in war among thousands of nameless African victims... What is surprising and even alarming to us is that many, even most, British white Christians seem to regard a few white lives as being of more value in the sight of God than thousands of black lives. The Christian Gospel does not support this point of view.[5]

The problem is that in times of war and violence 'we/they' instincts tend to overwhelm other feelings arising from Christian beliefs about commmon humanity. This has been evidenced abundantly during two World Wars in which Christian leaders have often had attitudes far in advance of those whom they lead. Where the ordinary church member reacts with instincts fuelled by the Press, the church leaders have to call to mind that we are all God's children. Regrettably, far too many Christians submit to the prejudices of the racial/national/social group of which they are part.

This was obviously true, as the letter pointed out, in the response to the Elim massacre. The problem is that the reporters were constricted first by the sources of news controlled by the Rhodesian régime and secondly by the racial preferences of the majority of their readers.

The manipulation of the news

If news can be distorted by racial or nationalistic feelings, it can also be distorted by calculating individuals to feed those feelings. The WCC realized that the adverse publicity over PCR was orchestrated:

> The Unit report on PCR was well received. In the ensuing discussion there was unanimous agreement that well-financed propaganda

agencies in the media, hostile to PCR and the WCC in general, were distorting the member churches' understanding of PCR's work. Mention was made in particular of the recent scandal in South Africa, which exposed the clandestine efforts of the South African Government to influence the news agencies in the Western world.[6]

The clandestine efforts referred to are the by now well-known 'Muldergate' scandal. Through the efforts of investigative journalists in South Africa it was eventually disclosed that taxpayers' money had been used for secret projects, notably the 1978 international propaganda offensive, the inner workings of which have been traced by Derrick Knight. In the preface to his book *Beyond the Pale*, he writes:

The South African Department of Information's secret projects list... included initiatives aimed at discrediting the authority of the major Protestant denominations, in Britain and elsewhere, by exploiting the fears and doubts of their members. By doing so it was hoped to neutralize the stubborn Christian opposition to racist policies of the Republic of South Africa to defuse the campaign of disinvestment launched by many church bodies to stop world-wide support for the South African Council of Churches... to discredit the growing mission of the World Council of Churches... to combat the evils of racism and to speak of racial justice for the poor and opppressed – as unChristian, and to deny the Church's right to engage in any 'political activity'.[7]

The book contains some useful information about the right-wing groupings in various countries that were used in this campaign. Derrick Knight comments:

Very often a list of grandiose-sounding organizations are the facets of just one individual who can use bogus organizations as leverage on behalf of a non-existent pressure group.[8]

He also gives a list of connections between the different organizations and individuals, like Fred Shaw and Bernard Smith, who were used and assisted by the Muldergate fund. The campaign resulted in this sort of article, from *The Daily Telegraph*:

CHURCH AID MAY GO TO TERRORISTS

Fears that British churchgoers may be misled into making donations for the terrorist causes were expressed yesterday by a leading member of the newly-formed International Christian Network set up to oppose

Marxist infiltration (*sic*: and the article continues in this vein for most of the column)... Mr Shaw reiterated the views expressed by Mr Smart of the Christian Affirmation Campaign. Mr Shaw, who is setting up the headquarters of the INCC organization in London, said yesterday:

'We fear that unless something is done soon to counter these anti-Christian tendencies it will be too late. There is a new language now, a new meaning for biblical terms. Salvation means political liberation. God is equivalent to fellow-man. Jesus Christ is the same as Che Guevara, Mao and Castro. There is a keenness to equate heaven with a Socialist state.'[9]

This is enough to give the flavour of such propaganda. Here both the two organizations which confer and concur together were probably financed from Muldergate. The Christian Affirmation Campaign distributed its founder's book, *The Fraudulent Gospel*, which is the source text of most of these ideas, at below cost price, so it was being subsidized from somewhere. Bernard Smith, the author, had 'a self-confessed interest in the overlay between religion and politics'. He was a member of the Monday Club, too, and wrote a number of other pamphlets along the same lines. The evidence in Derrick Knight's book suggests that much of the publicity given to the idea that churches should have nothing to do with politics is actually instigated by right-wing political groupings. Much of the bad press for PCR at this time was actually being paid for by the South African government.

The concept of balanced reporting

The concept of balance is supposed to be the lodestar of British reporting in such respected institutions as the BBC. But its position is queried by Philip Schlesinger, who argues that the notion of impartiality is 'latter-day Mannheimianism – a response to social cleavages which attempts to gain some measure of epistemological privilege for those who survey and report on it'. Mannheim had argued, fifty years earlier, for the impartial rule of intellectuals. Schlesinger writes:

It is this claimed detachment from any particular view of society, therefore, which is the linchpin of the comparison between the Mannheimian intellectual and the BBC's official corporate role in British society. In keeping with this, the BBC says it reports 'unadorned fact' and 'untainted information'. This flow of 'pure fact' to the public, allegedly unhampered by the intervention of values, is officially linked to the BBC's social purpose, that of informing 'a mature democracy'.[10]

By way of a case study in how this is actually done, Schlesinger found out how the BBC chose to present the news story of the Wiryamu massacre in Mozambique in 1973. The story reached the international media from Fr Adrian Hastings, who got it from local Roman Catholic priests (this is the grass-roots network functioning in the way described earlier). In the television newsroom, decisions had to be made over what coverage to give the massacre. There was a feeling that it was left-wing, and timed to cause the government embarrassment during the imminent visit of the Portuguese Prime Minister, Dr Caetano. So attempts were made to check the political affiliations of Adrian Hastings. The TV team were also keen to check the authenticity of the story, but it was difficult to locate as Wiryamu did not feature on any maps. A reporter was also dispatched to Portugal to get the Portuguese version of the incident. By mid-morning the location was identified as the village of Wiliamo. On the lunch-time news the story was screened together with the Portuguese ambassador denying the massacre. BBC staff were still balanced between belief and scepticism. They were especially worried about the domestic politial implications, because the Opposition was taking up pressure-group hostility to the Caetano visit. Hastings then offered BBC2 some films showing Portuguese troops burning down villages. It was rejected on two grounds: it was four years old, and it contained no pictures of dead bodies, so had no bearing on the question as to whether killing was the sort of thing the Portuguese were doing. Schlesinger comments that the rejection of this film is highly significant in that it shows a failure to grasp the importance of contextual knowledge. The BBC wanted only evidence for that particular Wiryamu story, and did not see that the earlier film corroborated it. Schlesinger calls this 'the ahistorical tendency of going for immediate news value to the exclusion of relevant historical background'.

So news of Southern Africa as it is packaged for Western media is limited by Western ways of doing things. The treatment of the Wiryamu news shows that the BBC concept of balance is influenced not so much by evidence about the content of the event as by the political pressures in the news-receiving countries.

11

Types of Disagreement

In the debate about apartheid and about PCR, both within South Africa and abroad, certain types of disagreement recur. In this chapter I propose to analyse them in detail.

Most arguments about apartheid or PCR are based on the statement of a moral premise. There are four ways of contradicting such a premise:
1. To challenge the point at which the premise is applied.
2. To challenge the description of phenomenon to which it is applied.
3. To deny the existence of the phenomenon to which it is applied.
4. To challenge the value system of the premise itself.

The first three approaches would seem to be related to facts and open to some objective criteria; the fourth to require a clear view of which value system is taken as a basis of discussion. However, even the apparently objective criteria for the first three run into trouble because, as we have seen, facts come to us filtered through a set of social assumptions.

How does it apply?

(a) *All of them including this one.* Some people subscribe to generalized morality but baulk at applied instances, where their values could involve them in hard choices. In connection with the PCR debate Elisabeth Adler remarked:

There has been a general consensus on a theological level about the equality of all races: all men, black, white, yellow, whatever were created in God's image; Christ died for men of all races; the Christian community just expresses the brotherhood of all men across racial and ethnic barriers. There had been general agreement that racism is one of the worst heresies, that it is contrary to the gospel, and a denial of the Christian faith and the nature of Christ's Church. However, when conclusions were drawn from this theological agreement, it was revealed how far theory was removed from practice. When PCR tried to move from words to action... the church was divided.[1]

In short, some people indulge in generalized morality but object to its application. A major accusation from the Third World is that Western churches, whilst having a long tradition of philosophy and theology based on 'universal' principles, lack the will to apply these principles. Hence a theology of commitment has been propounded to provide a counter-balance.

(*b*) *This one or that one?* When discussion about South Africa gets too hot, a diversionary question tends to be raised: 'What about Afghanistan?' This can imply that some people in the debate do not want to discuss the topic on the agenda. When discussion is pointing to one place, they want to shift it elsewhere. Of course, we all realize what underlies the Afghanistan question (it might be Poland or Czechoslovakia, depending on the year, but never Chile or El Salvador) is the East/West confrontation, which to many in the West is a more urgent topic than South Africa. A neat letter to *The Guardian* expressed this under the heading 'Parallel Bars':

> Sir, Why all this fuss to release Sharansky? That is because he is in the Soviet Union. Why is there no similar move being made to release Mandela? That is because he is in South Africa. Thereby hangs a tale.[2]

Thus human rights agitation in the West seems to be selective rather than of universal application. In the minds of many it is East/West in orientation rather than North/South. South African government propagandists are very keen on this particular diversionary manoeuvre. In putting South Africa's case in the West, they keep the effects of apartheid under wraps, and play up the fear of Communism. For instance in 1980 the South African government funded FARI, Foreign Affairs Research Institute, with at least £96,000 and in 1981 in Britain with £68,000.[3] FARI is a right-wing publishing house, which distributes such books as *The Communist Challenge* and *The Extent of Soviet Support for African Liberation Movements*, both by Ian Grieg. FARI was also a Monday

Club enterprise. Thus when we analyse the reactions of Western churches to apartheid, we have to consider not only how far they are under the influence of the East/West debate, but also the extent to which their reactions have been fuelled by South African propaganda messages about Communism.

(c) *The part instead of the whole.* In some South African debates, a fact is put forward which is true and looks good in isolation, but when considered as part of the total picture looks rather different. For example, in debates about education published in the South African newspapers during 1980, the government spokesman quoted the total increase of pupils and total expenditure on black education, whereas the more telling statistics would have been the pupil-teacher ratios, the *per capita* expenditure and the teachers' qualifications. *The Sunday Post* pointed out the omitted facts:

> Mr Rousseau paints a very rosy picture of black education: but he fails to compare the lot of black children with that of whites... (and so on with a list of the more revealing statistics).[4]

Another way of confusing the issues by putting forward the part instead of the whole is by giving the views of a prominent black person as if those views were representative of all black people, whereas in fact the views have not been allowed to be tested in open elections. Thus in his book *Progress Through Separate Development* Mr Botha quotes Mr Matanzima:

> Separate development was never imposed on us; we asked for it because it is the only realistic way of bringing about equality among all races in South Africa.[5]

Given the lack of interest among urban blacks in applying for homeland passports or voting in homeland 'elections', that 'we' should not be taken to refer to all blacks in South Africa, nor to all AmaXhosa. Bearing in mind that the opposition candidates were all put into custody before the 'election' in the Transkei, the statement quoted by Mr Botha should be read as referring to the view of Mr Matanzima himself.

One way of sustaining apartheid is to select a small class of black people who would act as a buffer to them in the masses. In the Homelands, this class consists mainly of officials directly paid by the administration. In the urban areas, there are some blacks who have managed to get rich despite the odds against them. The facilities enjoyed by this elite can then be presented as 'proving' that apartheid is of benefit to black people. This is what happens when tourists in Johannesburg are taken to those streets in Soweto where the 'millionaires' live. Duly impressed by these houses, the tourists are supposed to conclude that apartheid is not all that bad after all. It is not surprising that recently such tourist buses have been stoned in the townships.

The same technique, of putting forward the part instead of the whole, can be used to advantage in photography, as in the glossy publications of the South African propaganda departments. For instance, on the pages of *Informa* black people are depicted as dressed up in tribal attire with beads around their heads. The cumulative effect on someone who has never been to South Africa is that of assuming that black people are still at the tribal stage of living and hence rather backward. The intention seems to be to show that blacks are proud of their culture and hence prefer apartheid and life in their 'own' areas. But anyone who ponders the role of the picturesque in today's tourist culture will realize that such pictures do not give a true idea of the political and economic situation of the people, any more than does a photograph of a Scots piper in a tartan kilt. It could also be asked why it is that our African ceremonial costume and functions appear to have these associations with the tribal and primitive, to a greater degree than European ceremonial and folk occasions. These pictues of smiling 'tribal' blacks seem to have some derogatory intent.

Other pictures in *Informa* are markedly different. Some show graduates receiving degrees, some show school laboratories, agricultural assistants at works, factories, and so on. But we are not given the statistics which would show up the selectivity of these pictures. Those graduates are the few who were allowed to stay on, following student strikes at a homeland university in which hundreds were not allowed to return to their studies. Those school laboratories are showpieces in a country where very few schools for blacks have adequate equipment for science teaching. Those factory farms are run by the South African Defence Force – *Informa* tells us that much, without revelaing what else SADF is doing in the same region. Thus in all these examples it can be seen how facts which are true in part can be used to conceal, or divert attention from, the fuller picture of the whole social context.

Description of the phenomenon

Another type of argument is to shift the terminology of the premise, for instance to claim that the issue is not racism but something else, such as freedom to develop in your 'own' way. Such persuasive redefinition of terms is very common in South African propaganda:

> It is of paramount importance to know that the real issues in South Africa are the existence of different nations and different nationalisms, confused coincidentally with race and colour. The objectives of the policy are not old-style segregation or white supremacy but separate freedoms and territorial separation. It is not based on notions of racial superiority; it merely accepts and respects the fact that peoples and nations are different. Finally, if the South African acts differently... it is because he has fundamentally different circumstances to deal with.[6]

The word 'different' appears no less than five times in the above statement as the writer, J.S.F.Botha, struggles to use a neutral term that does not arouse the moral indignation associated with discrimination or racism. The neutral Afrikaans word for separateness, apartheid, rapidly gained an evil connotation once it became apparent exactly what social coercion went with it. Many other examples of such newspeak could be listed. As soon as a word has gathered too much opprobrium, the South African propagandists try another one. Unfortunately words cannot replace reality in any situation. When it was announced that the Department of Bantu Affairs was to be renamed the Department of Plural Affairs, it was obviously the same department under a new name.

The existence of the phenomenon

Another type of confusion enters the debate when one of the parties denies that the phenomenon, event, fact under discussion really exists or really happened. So what does it need to prove that the facts of apartheid, as outlined at the beginning of this book, really exist?

(a) *Experiential evidence.* There are plenty of testimonies from the victims of apartheid. I myself can describe how apartheid has affected me. Many testimonies are on record at the United Nations, Amnesty International, International Defence and Aid and other such bodies that have recorded first-hand accounts.

One way of denying the validity of such experiential evidence is to disparage the one who testifies. This is reported to be what happens in the Soviet Union, where mental health provisions are used to restrain political dissidents. South Africa disparages opponents by attaching to all of them the label 'Communist' or 'agitator', which thereby puts their view beyond the consideration of most white people.

Another way of dismissing an experiential proof is by not allowing an opportunity for it to arise. This is exactly what the South African way of life does, as it does not give rise to occasions when blacks would be likely to tell the truths that would make many white people feel guilty. I have heard a version of this avoidance of experiential evidence from English people who return from trips to South Afrca where they have visited their relatives. 'The family loves their servant,' they say; 'she is very happy with them. She has been with them ten years.' In the circumstances of the mistress/servant relationship the black woman is hardly likely to speak her mind about apartheid, There is scarcely any opportunity in South Africa for a conversation between blacks and whites as equals that is free from the power relationship which binds the black person under the white's domination. Even within the churches, this is so where the hierarchy is mainly controlled by the whites. Even whites who are apparently on the same level as blacks – for instance, two ordained priests at a diocesan synod, can inhibit the frankness of the conversation, as the blacks are aware that the whites move in the same gossip-circles as the white power-figures, so a black person is unlikely to speak out if he fears for his job.

So it must be realized that the value of black testimony is contextual and situational. If black and white South Africans meet abroad, the habits of mistrust still continue. Their first topic of conversation is not usually the current political situation but a searching for clues about personal circumstances that will give some information about where the other stands, about whether the other can be trusted. Those who cannot go back to South Africa are likely to be more outspoken, while those who are going back are guarded, knowing the surveillance that the South African system has organized overseas.

Furthermore there have been atrocities such as letter bombs that have killed outspoken exiles, as a deterrent to others who might be tempted to emulate them. Truthful black testimony does reach the outside world, but it is costly.

(*b*) *The personal story*. Some people recoil from depersonalized reporting on social trends, statistics etc., but they do pay attention to a heart-rending personal story. One such story which made the headlines in the Afrikaans press was that of Sandra Laing. Sandra was born at Amersfoort in 1956 at a hospital reserved for whites. She was from a well-known, well-established family, of indisputably white parents. She was registered as white at birth, and baptized in the NG Kerk. Although she was rather dark and had crinkly hair, for the first eight years of her life it made no difference. She was accepted by her playmates and in her school as white. Then in 1965 the authorities told her parents that there had been objections to her presence at a school reserved for whites. The parents told an Afrikaans newspaper that when they first heard of these objections they thought death had come to them. When the plight of the family was publicized, there were letters in the Afrikaans press like this:

> I refer to the tragedies which took place in the case of little Sandra Laing, also the case of the Mullers of Berkley West, of the Crags school at Knysna. Towards these things the great majority of our ostensibly Christian Afrikaner people maintained a deathly silence. We watch the suffering of parents, but especially that of children, allowing all this to pass without protest. Where, Christian Afrikaner, is your justice? Is this coldness which you exhibit the answer to the command that you should 'love your neighbour as yourself'?[7]

de Klerk comments that there is sufficient evidence in such press debate that Afrikaners who had once shared the vision of South Africa reconstructed according to the great design of apartheid were now being shaken by the frequency of such heart-rending cases as that of Sandra Laing.

In this way the personal story follows the same methods as denial of experiential truth, i.e. to disparage the teller of the story, to cast doubt upon its sources in such a way as to make it likely that the reader will dismiss it without serious consideration.

(c) *Newspaper truth.* An English teacher was once travelling in a train from Botswana to Cape Town. She was in a crowded carriage reserved for whites: the other five passengers were all white Afrikaner women. The one who spoke English most easily, a university secretary, asked the foreigner what she thought of South Africa. After mentioning the ostriches, the farmlands and the climate, this teacher boldly got on to the social and political aspects, starting from the educational facts such as the amount of money spent per child in black schools. The figures were all from the recently published 1972 SPROCAS reports on education. After a few minutes of listening in to these unpalatable facts, presented, I guess, in a tone of indignation, the Afrikaner university secretary exclaimed: 'This is not true. Our newspapers do not tell us this.' By this remark she revealed the effectiveness of the government control over the press, especially the Afrikaans newspapers. It reveals an astonishing belief that what is reported in newspapers is true, and what is not in the newspapers is to be disbelieved as if it never happened or does not exist.

We have already seen those factors which constrain or distort the truth of newspaper reporting. Press censorship laws have been constantly strengthened in South Africa, the censorship coming to a climax in December 1986 when publishing realistic news seemed to have become almost impossible. Newspaper ownership is another important factor, and there has been much wheeling and dealing to force out of business newspapers critical of the government.

The actual process of journalism may involve distortions too, especially in South Africa, with its language barriers and social divisions. The social origins and linguistic ability of a journalist may be crucial in determining how much of a story he can grasp. Black reporters may be used to gathering in the stories from the townships, but one wants to know more about how a journalist is regarded in the black community, and what his status is within the newspaper hierarchy. Once again we see the inevitably contextual nature of 'facts' about South Africa.

(*d*) *Social research*. In contrast to newspaper reporters, social researchers are supposed to gather data by systematic methods, such as question-naires. A good deal of data which are eventually tabulated into the depersonalized statistics of social reports originate in interviews and questionnaires. But as social researchers know, no matter how sophisti-cated the statistical methods used, the final survey is only as valid as its raw data. So if the interview is set up wrongly, for example by using the wrong people or ignoring language problems, the results will be falsified. Some idea of the difficulties of interviewing for research purposes can be gained from the German project to assess the position of black workers in German firms in South Africa. One of the interviewers was frank about the difficulties he encountered:

Naturally I did have some special problems with the work, when I had to make contact with a worker I did not know at all, or even when I wanted to talk to a worker I knew well. The problem is that people here are dreadfully intimidated because whether we like it or not, South Africa is quite simply a police state. They know very well that we are preventing an enormous number of people from expressing their opinion... they can only hold on to power because they give the world an entirely false picture of what is going on.[8]

This worker was harrassed by the police:

If I'd had a slow car they'd have got me long ago, because in many cases you just have to run away.[9]

The police also tried to bribe him into becoming an informer for them. It is not surprising that he had to build up a relationship of trust with each person interviewed:

You must go there, sit and chat a bit with a worker, and try to create a certain level of trust, a feeling of brotherhood. You have to try and convince him that you're only interested in getting information about the work situation, without having solutions to offer. Then when he is ready to give information, everything's all right. But then, again you always come across people who aren't prepared to part with any information: they just don't trust you and you can't hold that against them. Sometimes they don't even trust each other – that's what the constant spying by the secret police and informers does.[10]

In spite of such difficulties in gathering data about apartheid within South Africa there have been courageous enterprises engaged in research throughout the 1970s, such as SPROCAS, Black Sash and labour researchers sympathetic to the unionization of black workers. However, as soon as such research programmes begin to get a cutting edge in the apartheid debate the government acts to ban the leaders. Peter Randall, the editor of the SPROCAS series, was banned in 1976, as were a group of Durban labour researchers.

(e) *It was, but it isn't now.* Another method of fending off criticism of apartheid is to claim that changes are taking place, or are about to take place. Mr Botha's government has over-used this tactic. In 1979 he promised changes. Mrs Thatcher believed him and said:

There is now a real prospect that conflicts in South Africa's borders, in Rhodesia and Namibia, will shortly be ended. This, combined with welcome initiatives in South Africa's domestic policies, offers a chance to defuse a regional crisis... and to make progress towards an ending of the isolation of South Africa in world affairs.[11]

Mr Duffield, who dissented from the report by the Board of Social Responsibility of the Church of England, also swallowed the bait:

The report strikes me as seriously out of date already, and ignoring or minimizing many of the staggering changes within South Africa in recent months.[12]

This type of argument has the effect of postponing any conclusions or effective action until the result of the claimed changes can be apparent. It is a clever delaying tactic. The changes about which Mrs Thatcher and Mr Duffield were ostensibly so optimistic were the new labour laws and influx control recommended by P.G.Rierkert. About these, Black Sash commented in November 1980:

Until this year people have been able to find illegal work and so have survived. Now for the first time in all our experience we have no hope and no comfort to offer to the unregistered and the endorsed out...all hope has now been removed and when you take away hope all that is left is rage and anger, bitterness and hatred.[13]

Thus in the 1980s South Africa is seeing the rage which breaks out as a result of a policy of unfulfilled expectation, a policy of improvements that do not materialize.

The tricameral parliament is another example of raising expectations that are unfulfilled. The Indians and the Coloureds who were supposed to vote representatives to this body mostly boycotted elections: there was only a 30% turnout of voters, and only a 10% turnout in Cape Town, where the majority of Coloureds live. Blacks were totally excluded from the whole arrangment, so it is hardly surprising that the townships erupted into violence in 1985. Now even those who supported these constitutional arrangements to the extent of agreeing to be elected representatives are finding that they are thwarted in their attempts to change the things that matter to Coloureds – for instance in the hoped-for, and half-promised, change to the Group Areas laws. Other changes to the Immorality or Marriage Laws make little difference if mixed families cannot then legally reside together.

The promise to end relocations is another example of government insincerity. After some well-publicized examples of forced removals, and forthright statements by church bodies, such as the SACC's report on relocations, the government announced amid a fanfare that forced removals would cease. But at the end of 1986 the stories were still coming out, in spite of the censorship, of continued forced removals.

Values

(a) *Natural law.* Some discussions about South Africa, most notably over conscientious objection, use natural law arguments, especially about the notion of a just war. Although they grew out of mediaeval theology, ideas in this area passed via Spanish jurists to the European Enlightenment, ending in general, non-theological discussions of human rights and international law.

However, most Afrikaners believe that theology should form a basis for society. In social reconstruction they go back, as we have seen, to neo-Calvinist theology, but in theological disputes they tend to take refuge in biblical texts rather than trust in theologians. With regard to international law, the government of South Africa was aggrieved when the International Court in the Hague ruled against South Africa's occupation of Namibia. They have shown little inclination to obey this forum of conscience and move out of the territory they occupy with military might.

(b) *Human rights.* In its charter the United Nations draws upon the universalist tradition of the Enlightenment. Anti-apartheid literature frequently points out how the apartheid system infringes human rights.

Simon Gqubule has made a systematic comparison between the articles of the UN Universal Declaration of Human Rights and the apartheid system. Article 2 of that Declaration states:

(i) Everyone has the right to take part in the government of his country, directly or through freely chosen representatives.

(ii) Everyone has the right of equal access to the public service of his country.

(iii) The will of the people shall be the basis of the authority of government; this will shall be by universal and equal suffrage and shall be held by secret vote or by equivalent free voting procedures.

Gqubule commented:

This article advocates that all men should have a share in the government of their country and this is denied to the blacks in

South Africa. We would like to have the right to vote for our own representatives in the central Parliament and in provincial, regional and municipal bodies, as well as the right to be voted into these bodies.

In South Africa, however, the ruling white minority government imposes on all others their own will and rules without the consent of the voteless and the voiceless majority. Therefore the rulers have on their own imposed from above a system of homeland governments. These governments are not of our own choice. Those who accept them do so as second best or as stepping stones towards something better. The distribution of land is something that is determined by the rulers and is out of all proportion to the numbers of people concerned. Even in the homelands themselves, certain parts are carved up for white occupation. The millions of blacks in the city are damned to be migrants and temporary visitors in the towns, even if they have been in the towns for more than a century, Here they eke out a kind of twilight existence where they live without rights. Coloureds and Indians, with no prospect of a homeland of their own, are also in a kind of life and death in the middle of nowhere. Even educational institutions which are styled our own are rigidly controlled by the nationalist government. Those who desire to serve their own people in the public service of the country are restricted to serving only people of their own racial group.[14]

And so Gqubule argues on, point by point, to show how South African blacks are deprived of basic human rights.

The problem with proposals for dialogue is that the two sides do not use the same value system. The Nationalists resist all arguments that stem from the Enlightenment tradition of universal human rights. They did not accept the Freedom Charter of 1956, nor did they enter into discussions about the proposed Bill of Rights in 1974. Nor is South Africa a signatory of the UN Universal Declaration of Human Rights. In the same book on the Bill of Rights Brian Johnson lists a few articles written by Afrikaners on the UN Declaration during the 1950s, including what the NHK church said of it in 1951.[15] The depressing conclusion appears to be that NHK thinkers are impervious to human rights ideas. Some cynics have observed that the Afrikaners left Europe before the Enlightenment and so never carried around its ideas in their intellectual inheritance.

Nevertheless, in a recent case before the South African Appeal court, the judges were compelled to consider a human rights plea. This legal history was reported as follows:

> South Africa's Appeal Court has indirectly but unmistakably ruled that the Terrorism Act and the Internal Security Bill, now before parliament, are in conflict with accepted Western principles of justice, legal experts said yesterday.
>
> The appeal court had upheld the appeal against conviction under the Terrorism Act on the grounds that the Act is inconsistent with the Declaration of Fundamental Rights under the constitution of Bophutatswana... The appellant, Mr Wilfred Morewane, was found guilty under the Terrorism Act in 1979 and sentenced to fifteen years imprisonment in Bophutatswana's Supreme Court. He appealed against his conviction, arguing that the Terrorism Act was inconsistent with Bophutatswana's Declaration of Fundamental Human Rights. Bophutatswana inherited the act when it attained 'independence' from Pretoria in 1977. Bophutatswana's Declaration of Fundamental Human Rights is based on the European Convention on Human Rights. Professor Marius Wiechers, of the University of South Africa, said: '... the implication of the judgment is that South Africa's Terrorism Act cannot stand the test of measurement against the European Convention. Inasmuch as the Terrorism Act continues to exist in the internal security bill, the Appeal Court judgment applies equally to it in a moral, though not legally enforceable, sense.'[16]

This piece of legal history reveals a twist in the policy of separate development which must be galling to the political thinkers of Pretoria, who do not accept human rights arguments. Here the Appeal Court was compelled to give a judgment because of the political need to show the constitutional independence of a homeland government, and their right to make a law which contradicts a previous law. So a supposed terrorist had to be acquitted on a human rights plea!

(*c*) *Legalism*. We have seen how Sobukwe contended that he had no obligation to obey the laws made by the white minority. The value system he was using as a basis for his plea is that laws should be the result of participatory politics. However, a lawyer who bases his arguments strictly within the bounds of what in fact is the law would argue from different premises. The process that goes into the making of that law is irrelevant. The law is made by Parliament, and it is not the job of the lawyer to question the legality of the legislating power. If every individual member of society were to be allowed to use such a plea, there is no way law could be enforced, for each time an individual was charged with breaking the law, the trial would have to decide whether or not such an individual was party to the formulation of the law. The fact is that in the Western legal tradition, it is taken for granted that the legislature derives its powers from the majority consent and that it therefore overrides the wishes of individuals. But anyone who compares the English scene with the South African will rapidly realize that the South African Parliament is not representative of most of the people of South Africa, though the laws that it makes are supposed to apply to those voteless people – which is exactly the point to which Sobukwe was drawing attention.

The majority-minority tension underlies the political trouble in South Africa. The Afrikaners hang on so ruthlessly to power precisely because they fear being put in the minority position. It is for this reason that they have constructed the whole apartheid dream of each having 'their own', rather than a political system in which they could be outvoted.

Academics of jurisprudence have attempted to argue that laws could be constructed to transcend the politics of majority-minority. R.E.Goldblatt, for instance, explores the model of 'non-sovereign legislatures',[17] by which he means a system somewhat similar to that in the United States, where the Supreme Court has the power to quash laws made by Congress if they are at variance with the Constitution. This brings us back to Enlightenment ideas, as the Constitution would then have to be of the Enlightenment type, enshrining in its make-up some ideas of fundamental rights.

One obvious disadvantage is that the final arbiters would be the judges, and they are fallible:

As long as the judicial function is entrusted to men, not automatons, sub-conscious prejudices and preferences will never be completely removed from the judicial process. They will only be concealed.[18]

In support of this assertion Goldblatt cites a number of studies made both in South Africa and in other countries of different types of judges. The most striking statement he quotes comes from Mr Justice F.N.Broome, Judge President of Natal from 1951 to 1960:

The judge's mental make-up must necessarily influence his judgment, and the influence is, of course, nearly always sub-conscious. Nearly every judge who has anything of a judicial personality... may be placed in one or the other of two categories which are difficult to describe precisely, but which may broadly be called the conservative and the liberal, the right and the left, the category of those who lean towards the rights of the state and the category of those who lean towards the rights of the individual. I have no doubt that I belong to the former category.[19]

So the search for moral validity bestowed by legal sanction appears to lead us back to discussion of the type of social consensus that underlies the law and the process of law-making. The judges do not act independently of the society that appoints them; social ideas influence their arbitration. Goldblatt concludes pessimistically that even the search for a better constitution would not be worthwhile, unless some kind of social consensus were arrived at first:

> The answer surely lies in the creation of the 'right' social conditions, in so far as this is possible, and truly democratic political institutions: constitutional enactments of one type or another might be necessary to achieve those ends, but they are certainly not nearly sufficient.[20]

This seems to be confirming what Sobukwe implied: that the solution must lie in political rearrangements rather than in a purely legal approach.

(*d*) *Functional morality*. During the same discussion about the Bill of Rights in 1974, C.J.Alant put forward a relativistic view of moral values:

> 'Universal' values rather tend to become *post-factum* legitimations of the divergent wants and aspirations of society. Fundamentalist apartheid-men as well as fervent SASO exponents refer to the same 'eternal' values when they stake contradictory claims! They quote the same texts, the same Bible! Values thus seem to be idealized conceptions which the 'mind' of society constructs in order to bridge the gulf between its metaphysical and situational realities. What does it actually mean if A or B or C accept the 'same' Bill of Rights? Does it make sense to look at any code of action 'outside' its function for a specific society?[21]

Such a realistic view of the social context of moral assumptions is valuable, but this argument leads in the direction of every group to its own, and so back to Bantustans and the subtle rationalization of apartheid. This aspect of the argument emerges in Alant's attack on the proposal for the Bill of Rights as 'cultural imperialism'. On close examination, this turns out to be another version of avoidance of

Enlightenment universalism. What Alant is basically saying is that South Africa is so unique that it cannot be equated with any other situation in the world, an argument often heard by foreign visitors to South Africa.

Moreover the notion of different value systems for each different group exaggerates the difficulty of finding some moral premises on which some of the differing parties can agree. In a plural society universal values can be seen as a *standard by which* any excesses, contradictions and abuses of the law can be measured. If there is no such corrective standard, greater divergences are more likely.

However, it would be unfair to Alant to present him as being totally antagonistic to a Bill of Rights. At one point he asks:

> What are the communicative (reconciliatory) qualities of a universal bill for our South African situation? As it is, it does not seem as if the application of consensus principles has solved the problem of inter-subjectivity.[22]

This interest in communicative qualities but not communication about 'consensus' echoes the usual white avoidance of either human rights arguments based on Enlightenment consensus or Sobukwe's plea for the majority to take part in the legislature. Nevertheless Alant continues to advocate dialogue:

> Conflicting societies can only be reconciled in creative (reflexive) communication, i.e. that creative communication is a pre-requisite for reconciliation.[23]

The word 'creative' seems to redeem his argument from sociological determinism, for it seems to suggest that communication achieves a value-forming function, and that this can even lead to new social groupings. In other words, the argument comes back to a need for consensus, in spite of Alant's avowed pessimism about it.

Complicated as this argument is, it is useful to follow it through because it highlights the problems of finding a basis on which to begin creative discussion between the different parties in South Africa. Dialogue is what is needed, and the blacks have been asking for it for a very long time. The problem is that we cannot find a common premise, of shared aspirations and moral visions, on which to base such a discussion between the rulers and the ruled.

(*e*) *Pragmatism.* Another type of moral cleavage is between the idealists and the realists. Some of Alant's arguments fall into the latter category.

Pragmatism is an argument increasingly to the fore in defence of apartheid, for instance:

> It (separate development) is neither a doctrine nor a dogma, it is simply a practical policy to deal with a complex existing situation... In any event South Africans do not presume to know all the answers and being human they are bound to make mistakes. Their daily exposure to the realities of life and the magnitude of their task where history provides no adequate guide cannot but inject a certain humility.[24]

This is an unctuous mixture of all too familiar arguments: the white man's burden, the uniqueness of South Africa and pragmatism. To counter such specious pragmatism it is important to recall that the programme of the Afrikaners is basically idealistic:

> The formal declaration by the National party of its policy was also the confirmation that the politics of Afrikanerdom had been finally accepted as more than just a working programme for the running of the country. It was now the logical expression of a volk beweging, a people's movement. The goal towards which they were now striving with such disarming confidence, *doelrigtigheid*, dedication to an ideal and energy, was that of the 'permanent solution'. This meant the final securing of the future and the definitive vindication of all that Afrikaners in their 300 years of history on the continent of Africa had worked, hoped, prayed and suffered for. They were a people who had articulated for themselves a political theology and secular creed, with a view to establishing their identity and survival.[25]

Thus the Nationalists are idealists, not pragmatists. But their idealism does not run to universalism as well. Their political theology is a highly particular, almost tribal one arising out of their distinctive historical experiences. We have noted several times the plea for uniqueness put forward by apartheid apologists.

(*f*) *Self-interest*. Finally, it is important to note that some observers do not consider that any type of moral persuasion will change the mind of the white electorate in South Africa. They are pessimistic about human nature, and see apartheid as being sustained by the self-interest of the whites. First there is the fear of losing group identity. The whites fear being swamped by the blacks, so they make the many laws that check the advance of black people, which is seen as threatening the well-being of whites in South Africa.

Much is made of cultural, educational and other social differences between the races, of their level of civilization compared with that of most blacks, and of what they see as a natural tendency for people to stick to their own kind. These perceptions are sincerely held, but, seen objectively, operate to legitimate and justify continuing white supremacy.[26]

Most white people in South Africa simply accept the way things are as perfectly normal and natural, and are unable to see anything wrong with the position of black people:

As nice, ordinary conforming people acting in ways prescribed by the norm of the situation, they genuinely see the active critics of the situation as trouble-makers and agitators. The enforced surface calm among blacks also encourages this view. Accusations of selfishness, cruelty, unfeelingness etc. directed at whites make little sense to most of them. Within the norms of the situation they behave as perfectly decent and ordinary people. To appeal to the conscience of most white people is, therefore, a waste of time.[27]

On this argument, white supremacy is such that even when the logic of the system is called into question, the whites retreat under a legal umbrella, claiming that their opponents are just agitators and law-breakers. But they also go out and buy guns to defend themselves with. Here we see the force of the argument that no moral persuasion can avail.

It is highly unlikely that the whites will share power and privilege with the blacks without a good deal of pressure being brought to bear upon them, or without it being in their interest to do so. It is understandable that any group which enjoys privilege in a basically acquisitive society will never willingly relinquish its power. In general terms, some degree of conflict, whether it takes the form of effective pressure backed by a series of threats, or of more open confrontation, is likely to precede any significant change in South Africa. such pressure could come from other countries, or from the South African blacks themselves.[28]

With such a pessimistic conclusion we have reached a point beyond hope of dialogue, beyond the serious search for a common basis for discussion, a point where coercion takes the place of moral persuasion.

12

Theology and Church

There is clearly a problem, as we have just seen, about finding a common centre of value on which to base discussion. But why should there be fundamental disagreement about values when both sides are Christian? The previous chapter traced the disagreements mainly from a logical or philosophical perspective, and did not dwell on the theological implications. We must now look more closely at the theology behind the dispute, and the nature of the church.

At Nairobi in 1975, the WCC Assembly issued this statement:

> South Africa, which highlights racism in its most blatant form, must retain high priority for the attention of member churches. Apartheid is possible only with the support of large numbers of Christians there.[1]

In other words, if all the protagonists in the Southern African debate, both within those countries and abroad, could grasp this Christian involvement in apartheid, the debate would be likely to assume a different form, because the theological dimension would be introduced. The Christian position must be that:

> We have value because we receive it from a source of value. That is what I mean, for a start, by God. We know him as giving us value.[2]

In order to arrive at moral judgments on particular values, for the Christian, these values have to be seen in relation to the source, the centre of value. And since ethics has to do with value, that too is related to this centre.

South Africa claims to be a Christian country. Furthermore, the arguments used by those outside the country, for instance in criticism of PCR, have a Christian frame of reference. PCR asserts that its declared origins, purposes and sources of support are Christian, while opponents claim that it is acting in un-Christian ways. So the argument inevitably involves theology; and if there are disagreements, they need to be measured against 'the source of value'.

However, theological discussion is further complicated by the fact that this transcendental point of reference, this 'source of value', is often used to justify strange forms of argument. Nowhere is this more evident than in the Dutch Reformed Church use of the Bible.

Eccentric biblical exegesis

As I have already said, it is important to realize that the NGK is a Bible-based Reformed church. Its church leaders on the right find enough Bible texts to justify any aspect of apartheid under criticism. Genesis 1.28 ('Be fruitful and multiply and fill the earth and subdue it; and have dominion over the fish of the sea and over the birds of the air and over every living thing that moves upon the earth') is used as a basis for the argument that ethnic diversity is in origin in accordance with the will of God for this dispensation. Acts 17.26 ('God made from one every nation of men to life on all the face of the earth, having determined allotted periods and the boundaries of their habitation') and Deuteronomy 32.8 ('When the Most High gave the nations their inheritance, when he separated the sons of men, he fixed the bounds of the peoples according to the numbers of the sons of God') are used to justify separate development and the homelands, and were used during 1980 in arguments within the NGK about mixed worship, at funerals and so on. Faced with such eccentric exegesis it is difficult for other churches to find common ground in initiating discussion starting from a common Christian understanding of scripture.

Biblical themes and historical experience

This eccentric biblical exegesis is coupled with a marked religious sense of more recent history. The Voortrekker Monument proclaims the essence of the Afrikaner self-image and his perception of black people in South Africa:

December 16: the day when, in 1838, an Afrikaner force of fewer than 500 men utterly defeated an army of 20,000 black Zulus at the battle of Blood River in Natal. They had made a covenant with Providence, and December 16 is celebrated as a day not just of military victory but of spiritual commitment – statistical procedures, we are assured by the Monument handbook, show that there was only a one per cent chance of Afrikaner success at Blood River 'supporting the belief that this victory was an Act of God'. Over the years the historic meaning of Afrikanerdom itself came to be embodied in this divinely sponsored triumph over the Powers of Darkness, visibly and symbolically expressed in the black skin of the defeated adversaries, and the Voortrekker Monument was created to perpetuate the message for posterity. The divine privilege of being white is demonstrated in the slaughter of blacks, achieved against all statistical odds by the direct intervention of God.[3]

John de Gruchy comments:

In their struggle against British imperialism, especially in the aftermath of the Anglo-Boer War, or the Second War of Independence, the Afrikaners drew immense strength from this interpretation of history. They detected a sacred thread through all the events of their past, beginning with the Great Trek into the unknown (the exodus) and including the encounter with and victory over the black nations (Philistines) especially at the Battle of the Blood River, where they entered into a sacred covenant with God, the entry into the promised land of the Transvaal and Orange Free State, and the encounter with the pursuing British.[4]

As a black man, when I look at the Voortrekker Monument I see the concrete, visible presentation of a symbol that perpetuates racism as a theological, biblical and God-ordained reality governing the Afrikaners' life and attitudes. This monument expresses the Afrikaners' self-image as 'the chosen people of God', the divine election that justifies their power over black people. The black man's black skin identifies him, not only with the biblical Philistines who fought the chosen people, but also with the powers of darkness and evil, doomed to perdition.

On this extremist viewpoint, missionary enterprise is a vain endeavour because black people can never be regarded as brothers and sisters in Christ. An example of this type of rejection of black Christians is recounted in a letter by the French missionary Collard in 1876:

As our little party was being led to Pretoria a lieutenant of police said to Onesima that they were quite mad to have been led into the delusion that they were preachers or catechists...they were neither the one or the other, they were simply kaffirs, and always would remain so. As for God, they had nothing whatever to do with Him, and if by any accident a kaffir, even one, were to be seen in Heaven when he got there, he would pick up his hat, and wish (the Almigtij) goodbye and walk straight out.[5]

Such historically acquired hatred by the Afrikaner for the blacks in South Africa, justified as it is by a selection of Bible stories from the tribal history of early Israel, is antithetical to the biblical concept of the value of love.

From this it is clear that not only is God perceived along colour lines by many Afrikaners, but he is also of the same colour group as they are – and in a similar position of mastery. The sermons of Dr Boesak, who is a theologian of the same Calvinist tradition, but is classified as Coloured, form a powerful critique of this type of justification by biblical destiny:

In South Africa God is white and he votes for the Nationalists. Just as he blessed the weapons of the Boer commandos a century and a half ago in the Battle of the Blood River on Dingaan's day, so today he blesses the weapons of the riot police. And a clergyman who became a Cabinet Minister can say without blushing: 'To be an Afrikaner is to be white and Afrikaans-speaking... on the side of right and justice, and on the side of God.'[6]

Theology and race

If the Afrikaners stress the whiteness of God, it is not surprising that their views are countered by the opposite assertion, namely that God is black.

Theology from a perspective of blackness has to begin with self-definition. As Manas Buthelezi has put it:

For many people today, blackness is a life stigma from which they continually try to escape both psychologically and intellectually.[7]

Hence,

A relevant message of the Gospel is that which not only helps the black man to regain his self-confidence and respect as a human being, but also that which focusses attention on the removal of the dehumanizing facets of modern life.

In the South African context that message will focus on a quest for justice and freedom from oppressive notions which white people have of blackness. And the assertion that blackness is an essential basis of the theologizing by black people indicates an attempt to struggle free of second-hand theology as received by white people who have coloured the Word of God with their own whiteness and encumbered it with their cultural baggage.

Within South Africa the debate about theology is heavily ringed about with the fact of race. The only way in which that debate can be taken out of the prison of racism is by relating it to the universal church. Part of the task of doing this is firmly to refuse to accept the plea that South Africa is unique in any sense which excludes South African theology from the responsibilities that Christians have anywhere. Of course, theology in South Africa will continue to be contextual, heavily coloured by the facts of history and the persistence of racism, but this does not mean that it should appeal to the type of uniqueness which exonerates injustice. The theological reason for refusing to accept the plea of uniqueness is that even in South Africa we have the 'absolute value' which is common to theology in the rest of the world, i.e. God himself, and the derivative concept of man created in God's image. It is these two values that confront even the most contextual theology. It is these values that can unlock the prison of racism that bedevils any conversation between black and white in South Africa. As Manas Buthelezi well put it:

> If the Gospel means anything at all it must save the black man from his own blackness.

Indeed one can adapt this statement to say that it must save South Africa from racism. The aims of PCR state one of the ways in which this could happen.

> Oppressed racial groups (are) encouraged to reflect theologically on their present and historical experience of oppression and... share this with the wider church.[8]

Culture conditioning in Europe

If South African theology is strongly conditioned by South African culture, precisely the same thing can be said of theology and the church in Europe and America. And this culture conditioning has been evident in reactions against PCR.

In his book *Combating Racism*, Kenneth Sansbury quotes the comments of a minister from a congregation in a prosperous London suburb:

> Where it has got through that the WCC is 'up to something' in the field of race relations, it is on the basis of its support for freedom fighters, or guerrillas, and since, in the minds of many, these movements are identified with extremist groups of the political left, the average suburbanite, be he church member or not, sees this as a threat to the established way of things, and he tends to be a supporter of 'law and order'.[9]

It is important not to underestimate his opening remark 'where it has got through', because in spite of sensational Press coverage, notably in 1970 and 1978, many congregations, being inward-looking, remain impervious to the concerns of the wider church except on the basis of limited charitable giving. As a Baptist minister from Wales put it:

> I fear that apart from some enthusiasm for Christian Aid... there is not much understanding of the wider international and racial issues.[10]

Some even saw PCR as the special concern of jet-set Christians, out of touch with grass-roots concerns. A vicar commented:

> The danger of being involved centrally either at Church House, Westminster, Eaton Gate or Geneva is that one can easily assume that the issues which cause one deep and passionate concern are equally interesting to the general public, which is patently not the case.[11]

But here, too, the point made in the previous section needs to be reiterated. At the international level or rather at inter-church level, as on the WCC agenda, the issues raised by PCR were raised precisely because they were, and are, of pressing local concern to one part of the body, South African Christians. These issues can only be tackled if they are seen in the universal perspective of the gospel. Against that, to suggest that the concerns of local congregations should dictate what programmes are carried out on a world-wide scale is extreme cultural arrogance; it shows how insulated those particular congregations are from what is causing pain to Christians elsewhere.

One of the great achievements of the PCR debate, however inadequate, has been to crack open the comfortable confines of normal theological and church subject-matter by drawing attention to situations complex and disturbing to hear about. It has exposed the racism latent in British attitudes towards churches overseas. Sansbury's book quotes two remarks (both from ecumenical officers, who had the detachment to observe local reaction from a more internationalist perspective). The first was from Dr Payne:

> We are still bemused by the loss of our Empire and the alteration in the standing of Britain and the white race. The Churches have declined in strength and the economic situation has reduced their resources.[12]

The second came from the Revd Elliott Kendall:

> Liberation movements have not got across to the British public. As an imperial power, defending its gains, we have an instinctive reaction against those who rise up against white authority. There is deep colonial race prejudice in Britain, of very interesting historic origin. The common stance is not for the liberation and equality of the black, but for humanitarian or mission help.[13]

Hence the plot-forms of Western myths, in the structuralist sense, are to be seen in the Press treatment of South African events, plot-forms which were substantially reinforced by the settler myths and the *swartgevaar* of the Afrikaners: the fear of the rebel; of massacre by savages; atrocities in the bush; the march of anti-Christ and the rolling tide of Communism. A comparison between the actual events of the Rhodesia/Zimbabwe war and the propaganda treatment of it which is now possible thanks to the work of Julie Frederikse,[14] shows how easy it was for the whites to manipulate public opinion in Britain by use of these myths.

In contrast to the stories about violence, the issues to do with investment were until recently given scant coverage in the Western press, with the exception of the 1973 *Guardian* articles by Adam Raphael. There is a paradox here. It is ironic to observe that while public fury was directed most to the grants made by PCR from 1970 on, the main impact that is now felt by people in Western countries is the disinvestment campaign, yet not much of the Special Fund Money has gone into subsidizing this.

While it has to be stressed that PCR had above all a psychological effect, it should be noted that there is some ambivalence in its declared purposes. On the one hand the declared aim of PCR was for the churches 'to become agents for the radical reconstruction of society', which suggests that the churches have power to influence political events, that is, to make an objective impact. On the other hand the grants were token: 'a symbolic gesture of solidarity'. So what really was the intention? Was PCR really supposed to be giving the liberation movements the means of achieving revolution in Southern Africa? Was it 'guns for guerrillas'? Or was it mostly a paper gesture, with a few cheques, but mainly for the purpose of proclaiming moral support for the liberation cause? Which was more important, the means of revolution or the moral support?

I suggest that if the former view is to be assumed, then PCR should be regarded as a failure. Sixteen years after the Notting Hill Consultation no radical reconstruction has taken place in South Africa. And it is doubtful whether PCR money made any strategic difference to the actual course or outcome of the wars in the ex-Portuguese colonies and Zimbabwe.

By contrast, the aim of solidarity with the victims of racism was to some extent achieved. Black people became aware through the news about the grants that at least some Christian people did not think like the Afrikaners and their white supporters. The reactions against these grants, both in Britain and elsewhere, showed up the latent racism. In the Notting Hill Assembly, the educative function of the programme was a vital matter, taking up a good deal of the agenda and occupying one of the three working parties. Thus it is fair to judge PCR on its educational effectiveness. Some people think that controversy is always negative and to be avoided, but in some cases it represents a vital and creative phase which forces rethinking and a growth in new attitudes. Thus another apologist for PCR, Pauline Webb, had this to say on its educative achievements:

> I believe the PCR has been the most significant educational programme in the Churches over the past five years. Its first achievement has been to expose the racism which is latent in our society and in the life of the Church and I think exposure is the first step towards repentance.[15]

So it is a mistake to assume that the social reconstruction envisaged by PCR applies only to Southern Africa. Such a radical social reconstruction is not to be seen as a quick coup achieved by guns and bombs, paid for out of 'grants'. Following Pauline Webb's arguments, we have to see that the radical reconstruction initiated by PCR was precisely that questioning of underlying prejudices within Western, especially British, society that I have been describing. In so far as there is much in British society, especially economic interests, that colludes with apartheid, such a questioning of underlying values has political implications for South Africa, as its government was well aware when it chose to use taxpayers' money to finance the slur campaign against PCR. However, this questioning, notably about ethics and economics and the relationship of churches to governments, along with the resurgence of interest in political theology, has an application far beyond the South African situation that gave rise to it.

The culture conditioning that is the theme of this chapter takes different forms. We have seen that in Afrikaner thinking it emerges in their peculiar use of the Bible to fit their historic experiences and their political intentions. In Britain, it emerges in the terminology of social philosophy, in terms like 'Marxist', 'revolutionary', 'human rights', 'utopian', 'law and order'. A naive reader might assume that the Afrikaner style is more theological, being more closely attached to the Bible, but the more discerning would observe that the language of British social philosophy takes on faith dimensions, dominated by unquestioned assumptions. Just as in theology there are key terms, like 'grace' and 'salvation', which have to be grasped by thorough examination of the context of faith, so too the key terms in British socio-political language have to be understood in context, preferably through history. In acquiring any language one grasps a meaning either by fitting the word to the object or, at the next degree of abstraction, by discovering its opposite and what goes with it. So it is important to keep track of the conflations and antitheses in the PCR debate. There is a kind of subliminal dialogue within it connected with Western fears and prejudices, underlying even apparently dispassionate socio-political arguments. There are pitfalls of misunderstanding for the interlocutor from another culture or country, for whom it is not obvious, for instance, that law and order go with government, or that violence which threatens is 'Marxist' rather than an activity of, say, the government.

It is no cause for reproach that the dialogue is subliminal. So is most religious inspiration. But when it is assumed that the debate can be conducted on a purely intellectual basis and that the categories of Western thought are neutral, errors and misunderstandings abound. Theology is neither neutral nor dispassionate. It involves our deepest hopes and fears, with the fiercest problems and the roughest edges of life, as well as the serene moments of peace, fulfilment and coherence. By nature it is not essentially private, but it is a corporate activity. We are trying to make sense of our lives within the society in which we live.

The hypothesis of God, the gospel kerygma and the person of Jesus seem to help Christians in this task. If there are difficulties in applying such religious ideas to the messy problems of life, this is no reason for trying to separate the two into the sacred and the secular. Religion has to do with how we actually live our lives as a result of our beliefs. So theology, in so far as it is about the beliefs that structure our lives, is bound to concern itself with politics as well, especially with the potent ideas that empower political movements.

Thus communication problems arise because people approach the debate from different belief structures, as Klauspeter Blaiser put it:

The old problem of theology and culture is obviously in need of redefinition in the sense that cultural context, including socio-political aspects, becomes primary for theological discourse and for the communication of the gospel.[16]

How then can we communicate across these culture gaps? Does the gospel break down barriers? First we have have to look critically at the nature of culture conditioning, to assess the nature of the barriers before attempting to transcend them. With that behind us, we must go on to look at the church.

The church

If the Western churches are inevitably culture-conditioned, to what extent can those churches still retain the ideal of the worldwide church and the universalist claims of the Christian gospel? M.M.Thomas has given forthright expression to this problem:

The Gospel of Jesus Christ should not be identified with any one culture, political order, social order or moral system... As a word and deed of God, transcending all cultures, the gospel is divine power for their judgment and redemption. This is an understanding which gives the church the ability to relate itself positively but critically to all creative movements of renewal of man and his world without absolutizing any of them.[17]

What is of concern to many theologians in the Third World is that this culture-conditioned theology still puts European theology in a dominant position in the churches of the Third World. But how can the church at local level transcend the limitations of culture domination and find a common ground on which churches at the local level can resonate

with the world-wide church? Where does parochialism end and true
ecumenism begin?

Of course no church anywhere can fail to be affected by the social,
cultural and other influences within which it develops. So the comments
made on conditioning so far are not meant as a criticism. However,
the crucial difference between the culture-conditioning of Western
churches and of churches elsewhere is the fact of *power*. The churches
of the UK, Europe and North America have the power to dominate us
psychologically in so far as they still retain the status of being the churches
from which the gospel first arrived in our lands. Furthermore this is not
just a nostalgic, but a real factor to be taken into account, since the
money, the institutions, the staffing of key positions are all decided by –
or until very recently were decided by – people from the richer churches.
For theological education, this means that decisions about funds for
programmes, centres and colleges, resource people, books all come
mainly from the dominant churches. The PCR debate showed that some
people in these dominant churches still expected the WCC to take
Western interests into account. It was as if the WCC was expected to
get prior clearance for such radical programmes before taking the first
steps to implement decisions taken at so truly ecumenical a gathering as
Notting Hill 1969. The PCR debate has done worthwhile service in
indicating the need for a much broader and more inclusive type of
theology than that which had been taken for granted.

If we look beyond ecumenical writers like Thomas, we discover a
growing awareness of the limitations of past theology among writers in
the West, too. One of these is Professor Charles McCoy:

> Pluralism and liberation, as cultural forces today, are disclosing the
> theological dimensions of all human action and communities.[18]

And he continues with a critical statement about the dominant
theologies of the West:

> The context of ethnic pluralism in the United States and impetus
> towards liberation around the globe, for example, appear to me to be
> more certain clues to the future shape of theology than do the
> ecclesiastically and nationally isolated theologies of Europe and North
> America.[19]

Faith must be pluralistic, but not in the sense that it relates to several
realities; rather, it relates to one reality shared by all people but capable
of being grasped and symbolized in infinite ways. Black people have to

be taken into account because we are included in the created order no less than the other races on earth. But sometimes it seems as if the white world were demanding that there be a white world only, with a resultant mono-culture determined by white language and values.

Such theology tends to give definitions and formulae about man and then regard these as authoritative norms for how theology is to be understood everywhere, by everyone. Some scholars like Professor T.Wesser have responded to this type of mono-cultural outlook by commenting that it is necessary to look at changes in the ecumenical movement to see the new approaches to theology. This change comes, he suggests, from the style of thought within the ecumenical movement, which starts from 'a particular limited experience'. He points out how this 'particular limited experience'

> challenges the Western theological tradition that seeks above all universal, absolute truth rather than a contingent truth. Black theology and the theology of liberation are the best-known types of this new style. Black theology is a theology of liberation, it was said in Bangkok, because 'Black theology tries to make sense of the particular black experience of suffering oppression from rampant racism in the light of God's revelation in Jesus Christ.[20]

In so far as I am writing from a black perspective, I must unashamedly assert, in the company of many other black theologians, that our viewpoint needs to be heard in theology. But as our way is relatively new, it does not easily find a place in the traditional theological mainstream. That is evident simply from the arrangement of libraries in the more conservative academic institutions, where material relating to it comes from many different sections. Western theology is based on centuries of scholarship and a long tradition of universalist philosophy, but now students from churches in other parts of the world are beginning to look critically at this heritage to see which parts of it are truly universal in a pluralistic world. This is not just an academic problem, but concerns the way in which churches across the world can relate to one another. As T.Wesser puts it:

> It means first of all that our churches recognize themselves for what they are, i.e. Western, and that they accept that particularity. Moreover in the ecumenical context, they are called to enter into relationship with churches in other parts of the world and must resign themselves to being relative in relation to them. They must renounce the attempt

to define the *church*, the universal faith. They must admit that they occupy a particular corner of the globe. The fact that this particular Western corner presently dominates the rest of the world makes it very difficult for these churches to assume a genuine occidental stance to become signs within their own context.[21]

If the last phrase is applied to the PCR debate it can be asked to what extent PCR was intended primarily to have effects, or evoke responses, mainly from South African Christians and to what extent it became a 'sign' within the Western context. As I have already demonstrated on several occasions, some of the PCR activities began as critiques of aspects of Western society, for example bank loans to South Africa, that collude with apartheid institutions, but the debate generated ideas, for instance about the need for social audit of investments, that could have wider application than just the South-Africa related parts of Western society. In other words, the particularity of the PCR debate produced some rethinking which has universal value.

13

Conclusion

People who have read thus far may still have some questions. What will happen in South Africa in the near future? What should the churches do about it? What can I do about it?

Prophesying about South Africa is a difficult task. It is important not to narrow the meaning of prophecy to that of predicting the future. The biblical prophets put their main energies into preaching against the injustices of their society. Their moral and spiritual insights are thus more important than the details of their predictions. I would hope that the same would apply to a book like this. The raw material for it is what is going on in South Africa, and what the churches, both in South Africa and elsewhere, are doing about the crisis. The discussion has focussed on their actions. The questions that arise are thus inevitably theological as well as political. It may be dangerous to produce utopian blueprints of the future: an Afrikaner blueprint produced apartheid; Hitler's blueprint produced the holocaust. The most we can do as Christians, aware that all fall short of the glory of God, is to ensure that however we act, it is not out of fear or self-interest, but out of motives trained in the insights of our faith.

Those who seek political predictions should direct their questions to those taking the political initiatives. Within South Africa itself, the censorship laws and the clamp-down, along with the jailing of black leaders, make it almost impossible to ask those questions of some of the key protagonists. One should also be sceptical of the pronouncements of the South African Government because it is in its interests to deceive the South African public and the outside world. There is some evidence of double-sided policy, especially with regard to the events of 1983 and the pact with Mozambique, where President Botha was signing a truce while the armed forces were continuing as before – either deliberate duplicity or evidence of a split with each faction following its own schemes. There are also increasing complaints from English-speaking politicians of a parallel power structure being set up by the National Security system, with agents appointed even on the lowest local level, as in Parent-Teacher Associations, a structure which by-passes the democratic process of the white community.

As for pressures outside South Africa, the external wing of the ANC is increasingly being listened to, as was evidenced by the visit of South African businessmen to Lusaka, by the invitation to Oliver Tambo to address British MPs in Westminster, and by his meeting with George Schulz in the USA. I abhor the tendency to perceive regional conflicts in Cold War terms. From a black perspective, talk of defence of human rights, of democracy and the free world is gross hypocrisy if it is not leading to support for the democratic rights and liberty of the majority of people in countries where Western governments have some influence. I am appalled by the selective morality that operates with regard to the use of armed force and of economic sanctions as a political weapon. If the rhetoric of 'the free world' is employed mainly in the pursuit of national interest, then it should command no more moral credence than should Marxist doctrines if used for national hegemony.

However, in the USA the growing power of black voters is likely to have some influence as election time approaches. The rest of the world, black and white South Africans included, have to recognize that what happens in the United States elections is often crucial in determining forthcoming events in one's home region. Would that more voters in the United States would realize that how they cast their votes affects the fate of many people outside the United States – in the war-zones of Central America, of Southern Angola, of Afghanistan. While the voters of the United States are apparently being exhorted to make up their minds on matters of abortion, of sex-education or other such issues related to 'family life', the cost of their decisions is likely to be felt in the lives of non-United States citizens.

The same criticism could be made of the forthcoming British election. Many British people will be voting for the government that seems best to protect their personal standard of living. Very few put South Africa on any list of election issues. Yet we, who are deprived of a vote, know that the next British government could take a decisive role in South Africa's affairs at this crucial stage.

There have been pressures for a number of years for concerted international action over apartheid. The United Nations should have been able to take the initiative over Namibia, but in spite of the decision by the International Court of Justice at the Hague that South Africa's occupation is illegal, the United Nations is powerless to take effective action because of the constant vetos by the United States, the United Kingdom and, usually, West Germany. These vetos allow the United Nations only to act as a kind of safety valve for anti-apartheid speeches by the less powerful, and as a documentation centre (which is in fact a useful source of information, particularly on the economic side). However, recently there have been more attempts at multilateral action, such as the Commonwealth Eminent Persons Group and Geoffrey Howe's visit on behalf of the EEC. The sad thing about such efforts is that they are allowed to become substitutes for effective action, so that one has the suspicion that they are set up for this cosmetic purpose.

However, regardless of the level of government action or inaction, the anti-apartheid movements overseas are determined to attack economic collusion with apartheid South Africa. The movements for sanctions are clearly going to strengthen, especially in Britain, where the Anti-Apartheid movement is going to target Shell distributors and also persuade local authorities to boycott firms associated with South Africa. The decision of Barclays to disinvest shows that once the campaigns reach the stage where the cost bites into the firm, as with Barclay's loss of student clientele, then these campaigns begin to bring in long-term results.

Although there is bravado talk of South Africa being able to go it alone, the reality is that the South African economy is tied to international forces. The most powerful of them is the price of gold. Oddly enough it is the Russians, as the only comparable gold-mining country, that have the most potential influence over that, although they do not choose to exercise it. Next to the gold price, South Africa is vulnerable to the refusal of financial loans, as the events of 1985-86 show. Governments, in particular the United States government, exercise control over the International Monetary Fund, but private banks are more open to direct public pressure. In the short term, the 1970s have shown that financial managers are not swayed by moral arguments alone, as these are raised by PCR. However, there are signs that a growing number of corporate bodies can be persuaded to consider ethical criteria, and the founding of EIRIS makes such decisions more feasible than they were when PCR initiated its economic campaign. However, there are still those who argue against sanctions both on pragmatic and on moral grounds.

From the regional perspective of Southern Africa, decisions about the morality of violence or of sanctions are not hypothetical. The countries near South Africa have been suffering from various sanctions or forms of economic pressure exerted by South Africa for a number of years. This is backed up by South African forces fighting, sometimes by proxy with forces they supply, in Angola, Namibia and Mozambique over a number of years, and sporadically striking with massacres in Lesotho and Botswana and other towns of the front-line states. The battle-zone to watch in 1987 is the Beira railway in Mozambique. Other African countries are now offering to help to defend this line from attacks instigated by South Africa because it is a crucial lifeline for exports and imports of some of the front-line states. It is no easy thing for countries to devote a large part of their budget, much needed for development, to military purposes. It has been reckoned that South Africa has cost the region more than £10bn[1] in economic damage. South Africa wants to dominate the region, and will undermine the economic union of the front-line states in the Southern African Development Coordination Conference (SADCC) by whatever means she can. The countries of the SADCC have begged for Western aid, but pledges have fallen far short of what has been hoped for. One wonders how long it will take the industrialized nations to realize that it would be more prudent to invest in the future of Black Africa than in that of apartheid South Africa. Economically there has been an interesting development in that the firms that are willing to invest have proved to be the competitors of the British, West German and American firms that invest in South Africa. The economic involvement of many institutions and individuals in the West in South Africa shows that the oppressors and exploiters of my people are not 'out there' in Afrikaner South Africa; they are also here. The main difference is that whereas South Africans see the oppression and exploitation face to face, in Europe it all takes place a long way away, as if by remote control. And many people in Europe simply cannot be bothered to find out the details or draw conclusions about the links.

It is right that the churches have been in the forefront of trying to inform people about these links, even though for reasons described in Chapter 10, on Communication, there have been many blockages in the communication.

Within South Africa, some Christians are continually speaking out prophetically. The objectors to 'political churchmen' are failing to understand the biblical tradition of prophecy. They are also failing to realize how valuable it may be for any society to have a number of leaders who can speak out on social issues without needing to enter into the political arena itself as party leaders or candidates for election. The churches give an independent platform for such social leadership. Because of their presence at grassroots level the churches have a diaconal role of serving the people where they are, for example during the evictions, the funerals and periods of violence in South Africa. The fact that clergy are in prison is a measure of their participation in the local events of the national crisis.

Within the churches, people are known by name and valued as individuals. From the Gospels, we learn that God values each of them. So it is a particular duty of the churches to ensure that none are forgotten. When people disappear, lists of missing persons should continually be revised, and the world must be told. When individual Christians face a lonely interrogation or incarceration for their pacifist principles, the churches must support them. When people face torture because they will not betray their friends, the churches must confront their torturers. All this the churches in South Africa are doing. It is up to the world-wide fellowship of Christians to support this courageous activity.

This book has tried to outline what the churches have been doing about apartheid. The reader who wants more details can turn to some of the publications listed in the Bibliography, and a number of organizations are also mentioned. The fact that some of them are Christian-sponsored is important. But the level of commitment to them varies from denomination to denomination. It should still be realized that by and large British churches have been very tardy in following the lead of PCR. Action and commitment have instead been delayed and avoided amid a welter of debate, while the oppressors strengthen their position and increase the suffering, spreading it to the neighbouring countries as well. We are not asking that every Christian becomes a politician, but we are asking each to be aware that wherever one suffers it should be the concern of all – the whole body suffers where one part suffers.

Notes

1. A Black Perspective

1. David E.Jenkins, *Ecumenical Review* XXV.4, 1973, 401.
2. *PCR Information* No.9, World Council of Churches, September 1980, 17.

2. Portrait of Apartheid

1. Robert Sobukwe, quoted in *The Sun Will Rise – Statements from the Dock by Southern African Political Prisoners*, ed.Mary Benson, International Defence and Aid 1976, 7.
2. J.S.F.Botha, 'Concepts and Objectives', in *Progress through Separate Development*, Information Service of South Africa 1973, 29.
3. Albert Luthuli, *Luthuli Speaks*, Solidarity Committee of GDR with UN Centre against Apartheid 1982, 49-50.
4. Church of England Working Party chaired by Peter Wheatley, *Facing the Facts*, CIO 1982, 11.
5. Ibid., 12.
6. Barbara Rogers, *Divide and Rule*, IDAF 1976, 30.
7. Alexander Kirby, *South Africa's Bantustans*, WCC 1976, 20.
8. Francis Wilson, Conference paper in *Towards Economic and Political Justice*, SAIRR 1980, 8.
9. *Facing the Facts*, 13.
10. Ibid., 11.
11. Ibid., 19.

3. The Programme to Combat Racism

1. Quoted in John Vincent, *The Race Race*, SCM Press 1970, 39.
2. Ibid., 40.
3. Ibid., 99f.
4. Ibid.
5. Elisabeth Adler, *A Small Beginning*, WCC 1974, 12.
6. The document is given as Appendix D in Vincent, *The Race Race*.
7. Ibid., 100-103.

8. Ibid., 105.

9. Ibid.

10. Adler, *A Small Beginning*, 15.

11. Ibid., 16f.

12. Ibid., 17.

13. *Study Encounter*, Vol.VII.3, WCC 1971, 1.

14. Ibid., 2f.

15. Ibid., 3.

16. *Ecumenical Review*, XXV.4, October 1973, 434.

17. Ibid., 437.

18. Ibid., 441, 442.

19. Ibid., 442.

20. Ibid., 442f.

21. Ibid., 446.

22. *Breaking Barriers – Nairobi 1975*, WCC 1976, 99 (NB The voting figures differ slightly from those given in Kenneth Slack, *Nairobi Narrative*, SCM Press 1975, 72).

23. Ibid.

24. *PCR Information* No.1, WCC 1979, 7.

25. Ibid., 14f.

26. Adler, *A Small Beginning*, 16.

27. *PCR Information* No.9, 73f.

28. *PCR Information* No.1, 15.

29. *Time to Withdraw*, WCC 1973, 2 (a), (b).

30. Ibid., 1.

31. Ibid., 7.

32. Ibid., 18.

33. *The World Council of Churches and Bank Loans to Apartheid*, WCC 1977.

34. *Breaking Barriers*, 118.

35. *PCR Information* No.9, 21.

36. *PCR Information* No.1, 3.

37. Ibid., 14.

38. *PCR Information* No.6, WCC 1980, 5.

39. *PCR Information* No.10, WCC 1980, 61.

40. S.Macride, 'Protection of Journalists', in *International Commission for the Study of Communication Problems*, UNESCO 1978, 21.

41. *PCR Information* No.10, 67.

4. PCR and the Churches in South Africa

1. For this table see J.W.de Gruchy, *The Church Struggle in South Africa*, SPCK 1979, 240.

2. W.A.de Klerk, *The Puritans in Africa – A Story of Afrikanerdom*, Penguin Books 1975, 313.

3. Cf. ibid., 204.

4. Ibid., 205.

5. de Gruchy, *The Church Struggle in South Africa*, 63.

6. Peter Walshe, *Church Versus State in South Africa – The Case of the Christian Institute*, Hurst and Co 1983, 11.

7. Ibid., 13.

8. Ibid., 32.

9. Trevor Huddleston, *Naught for Your Comfort*, Collins 1956, 116.

10. As quoted in *Violence in Southern Africa: A Christian Assessment*, SCM Press 1970, 86f.

11. de Gruchy, *The Church Struggle in South Africa*, 132.

12. Ernie Regehr, *Perceptions of Apartheid*, Herald Press 1979, 207.

13. de Gruchy, *The Church Struggle in South Africa*, 132.

14. Ibid.

15. Ibid., 134.

16. Adrian Hastings, *A History of African Christianity 1950-1975*, Cambridge University Press 1979, 206.

17. Walshe, *Church Versus State in South Africa*, 108.

18. Steve Biko, in 'Policy Document of the Black People's Convention of South Africa', in *The Quest for a True Humanity* as adopted by BPC, 13-16 December 1975.

19. Steve Biko, *I Write What I Like*, Bowerdean Press 1978, 23.

20. Documents obtained from W.Kistener at SACC, p.8.

21. Ibid., p.9.

22. Walshe, *Church Versus State in South Africa*, 115.

23. SACC documents (see n.20), Appendix 2.

24. Ibid.

25. Ibid., 10.

26. Hastings, *A History of African Christianity*, 207.

27. SACC documents, 12.

28. Ibid., 13.

29. Barney Pityana, 'What is Black Consciousness?', in *Essays on Black Theology*, UCM Johannesburg 1972, 4.

30. Walshe, *Church Versus State in South Africa*, 115.

31. Ibid.

32. Ibid., 115f.

33. Pityana, 'What is Black Consciousness?', 37.

34. Ibid., 38.

35. Ibid., 41.

36. As described by Regehr, *Perceptions of Apartheid*, 1979, 112.

37. Ibid., 211ff.

38. Ibid.

39. Ibid., 212.

40. Ibid.

41. SACC documents, Appendix 4.

42. Ibid., 9; also refers to *Ecunews* 32, 1979.

43. Ibid., 10.

44. *Challenge to the Church* – A Theological Comment on the Political Crisis in South Africa, CIIR and BCC 1985, 25.

45. Ibid., 28.

5. *Non-Violence*

1. Nelson Mandela, in *Statements from the Dock, 7 November 1962*, UNCAA, New York 1982, 6.

2. Sol.T.Plaatje, *Native Life in South Africa* (1913), reissued Greenwood Press 1982, vii.

3. Ibid, 17.

4. Ibid., xxvii.

5. Ibid.

6. Ibid., 96.

7. Dutch Reformed Churches of South Africa, *Statements on Race Relations*, No.1, November 1960, published by the Information Office of the DRC, 119 de Korte Street, Johannesburg, 12.

8. Walshe, *Church Versus State in South Africa*, 10.

9. Bill Burnett, as quoted in *War and Conscience in South Africa*, CIIR 1982, 20.

10. Albert Luthuli, as quoted in *The Sun Will Rise*, ed. Mary Benson, 12.

11. CIIR, *War and Conscience in South Africa*, 15.

12. Ibid., 25.

13. Ibid., 38.

14. *The Guardian*, 7 March 1983.

15. *War and Conscience in South Africa*, 39.

16. Hastings, *A History of African Christianity*, 195.

17. H.G.Alexander, *The Growth of the Peace Testimony of the Society of Friends*, The Friends Peace Committee 1939, 1.

18. Ibid., 37.

19. Anglican Pacifist Fellowship, publicity leaflet.

20. *War and Conscience in South Africa*, 20.

21. Quoted in *APF Newsletter*, Vol.xxi, no.4, 2.

22. *Seek*, January 1983.

23. *Seek*, September 1982.

24. *War and Conscience in South Africa*, Chapter 3, cf. also the reference to Namibia in the penultimate paragraph of p.15.

6. Status Quo *Theology*

1. 1979 Provincial Synod of CPSA, typescripts from CPSA office.

2. Leonard Verduin, *The Anatomy of the Hybrid*, Eerdmans 1976, 11.

3. Ibid., 34.

4. Ibid., 32.

5. Ibid., 37.

6. Ibid.

7. Weiland and Vierdag Hauf, *South Africa: Prospects of Peaceful Change*, Collins 1981.

8. Quoted in Kenneth Slack, *Nairobi Narrative*, SCM Press 1976, 72.

9. *Apartheid is Heresy*, ed. John W.de Gruchy and Charles Villa-Vicencio, Lutterworth Press 1983, 22.

10. W.Vorster, in *Apartheid is Heresy*, 22f.

11. NGK Synod Report, *Human Relations and the South African Scene in the Light of Scripture.*

12. Vorster in *Apartheid is Heresy*, 22f.

13. Beyers Naude, *The Trial of Beyers Naude*, Search Press 1975, 90.

14. Allan Boesak, *The Finger of God*, Orbis Books 1982, 12.

15. *Seek*, January 1983.

16. *War and Conscience in South Africa*, 100.

17. David Gill, 'Power, Violence, Non-Violence and Social Change', *Study Encounter*, VI.2, 1970, 70.

18. Jürgen Moltmann, 'Racism and the Right to Resist', *Study Encounter*, VIII.1, 1972, 2.

19. J.G.Davies, *Christians, Politics and Violent Revolution*, SCM Press 1976, 131.

20. *Study Encounter* VII.3, 1971, esp.4ff.

21. *The Daily Telegraph*, 13 July 1978.

22. *Methodist Recorder*, 9 November 1978.

23. Peter Hinchliff, 'Religion and Politics: The Harsh Reality', in *Christian Faith and Political Hopes. A Reply to E.R.Norman*, Epworth Press 1979, 27.

24. *The Sunday Times*, 20 August 1978.

25. *The Times*, 15 September 1970.

26. Ibid.

27. *The Times*, 28 August 1978.

28. *Methodist Recorder*, 5 October 1978.

29. *Methodist Recorder*, 19 October 1978.

30. Community and Race Relations Unit of the BCC, September 1978.

31. Kenneth Skelton, Presidential Address to the Lichfield Diocesan Synod, 5 October 1978.

32. *Methodist Recorder*, 28 October 1978.

33. *The Trial of Beyers Naude*, 92.

34. *Study Encounter* VII.3, 1971, 19.

7. Theology of Solidarity

1. Elizabeth Adler, *A Small Beginning*, 11.

2. Ibid., 12.

3. *Methodist Recorder*, 23 June 1983.

4. *Violence in Southern Africa*, 69.

5. For further details see Hastings, *A History of African Christianity*, 211ff.

6. Ibid., 73.

7. Jean-Paul Sartre, *L'être et le néant*, Gallimard 1949, 555.

8. *The Guardian*, 6 August 1983.

9. *Rand Daily Mail*, 29 November 1980.

10. *The Daily Telegraph*, 4 September 1970.

11. *The Times*, 18 September 1970.

12. *The Guardian*, 28 October 1970.

13. Ibid.

14. *The Times*, 18 September 1970.

15. Ibid.

16. *The Daily Telegraph*, 28 September 1978.

8. Communism

1. *The Daily Telegraph*, 26 March 1979.
2. Ibid.
3. Tom Lodge, *Black Politics in South Africa since 1945*, Longmans 1983, 8.
4. *The Oxford History of South Africa*, ed. Monica Wilson and Leonard Thomson, Vol.2, Oxford University Press 1971, 412.
5. Colin Legum, 'African Outlook towards the USSR', in *Africa and International Communism*, Macmillan 1980, 28.
6. *The Guardian*, 6 August 1983.
7. *The Daily Telegraph*, 10 November 1978.
8. *The Daily Telegraph*, 26 August 1978.
9. *The Daily Telegraph*, 17 July 1978.
10. *The Daily Telegraph*, 28 October 1970.

9. The Disinvestment Debate

1. Francis Wilson, 'The Politics of Rising Expectations', in *Towards Economic and Social Justice in South Africa*, SAIIR Johannesburg 1980, 32.
2. Ibid.
3. Ibid.
4. Vella Pillay, *Transnational Corporations: Allies or Instruments of Apartheid?*, UNCAA 1980, 3.
5. *The Oxford History of South Africa*, Vol.2, Oxford University Press 1975, 85.
6. Francis Wilson, 'Migrant Labour in Perspective', in *South African Labour Bulletin*, July 1974, Vol.1 No.4, 22-6.
7. Ibid., 23.
8. Ibid.
9. Ernie Regehr, *Perceptions of Apartheid*, Herald Press 1979, 32.
10. Lewis Nkosi, *Home and Exile – and Other Selection*, Longmans 1965, 27.
11. Wilson, 'The Politics of Rising Expectations', 8.
12. *Rand Daily Mail*, 18 November 1980.
13. *Emigration to South Africa*, BCC, November 1973, 1.
14. *Investment in Southern Africa*, BCC, April 1973.
15. This information comes from Canon Bill Wright of the Teesside Industrial Mission.
16. Pat Fitzsimons and Jonathan Bloch, *Arms for Apartheid. Military Collaboration with South Africa*, CCSA 1981, 63.
17. A.Tuke, as reported in *The Guardian*, 16 May 1982.
18. From *Poverty Wages in South Africa*, CCSA Report 1976, quoted in the second paragraph of Donald Black's preface to *A Code of Misconduct*, CCSA 1980.
19. David Hemson, *Foreign Investment and the Reproduction of Racial Capitalism in South Africa*, AAM 1976, 10.
20. *Facing the Facts*, CIO 1982, 40.
21. Cf. Chapter 1 n.8 above, where I draw attention to this ubiquitous nature

of state power and control in the South African employment scene with reference to Francis Wilson.

22. Barbara Rogers, *A Code of Misconduct*, CCSA 1980 31.

23. *Facing the Facts*, 38.

24. *Speaking Out – The Secret Interviews with Black Workers in South Africa*, CCSA 1982, 20.

25. Ibid., 63.

26. Ibid., 62.

27. Albert Luthuli, quoted in *Time to Withdraw*, WCC 1973, 17.

28. CCSA, *Britain's Economic Links with South Africa*, 1979, 19.

29. Ibid., 19ff.

30. Ibid.

31. Lesslie Newbigin, *The Other Side of 84*, BCC 1983, 41.

32. *International Seminar on the role of the Transnational Corporations in South Africa*, 4/79, UNCAA, 4.

33. Rodney Stares, *ICI in South Africa*, CCSA 1977, 3.

34. Fitzsimons and Bloch, *Arms for Apartheid*, 18.

35. Ibid., 29.

36. *International Seminar on the Role of Transnational Corporations in South Africa*, UNCAA, 4.

37. *Bank Loans to South Africa 1979-1982*, UNCAA, 44.

38. *Bricks in the Wall*, UNCAA 1981, 6.

39. *Oil and Apartheid. The Churches' Challenge to Shell and BP*, CCSA 1982.

40. Ibid., 13.

41. Ibid., 43, 52.

42. Ibid., 47, 49.

43. Ibid., 59.

44. Ibid., 53.

45. Ibid.

46. Ibid., 52.

47. *Mission to South Africa. The Commonwealth Report: The Findings of the Commonwealth Eminent Persons Group in South Africa*, published by Penguin Books for the Commonwealth Secretariat 1986.

48. Mokhethi Motlhabi, *The Theory and Practice of Black Resistance to Apartheid – A Social Ethical Analysis*, Skotaville Publishers, Braamfontein, South Africa, 1985, 256.

10. The Communication of PCR

1. *The Church of England and the World Council of Churches*, Bocardo Church Army Press 1979, 35.

2. *The Guardian*, 29 June 1978.

3. Julie Frederikse, *None but Ourselves. Masses versus Media in the Making of Zimbabwe*, Heinemann 1982.

4. *The Times*, 27 July 1978.

5. *Methodist Recorder*, 26 October 1978.

6. PCR: Central Committee Document no.2.

7. Derrick Knight, *Beyond the Pale*, CARAF 1982, 10.

8. Ibid., 11.
9. *The Daily Telegraph*, 13 July 1978.
10. Philip Schlesinger, *Putting Reality Together*, Constable 1978, 167.

11. Types of Disagreement

1. Adler, *A Small Beginning*, 39.
2. *The Guardian*, 12 February 1983.
3. *The Guardian*, 11 February 1983.
4. *The Sunday Post*, 19 October 1980.
5. J.S.F.Botha, *Progress through Separate Development*, Information Service of South Africa 1973, 24.
6. Ibid., 11.
7. W.A.de Klerk, *The Puritans in Africa*, Penguin Books 1975, 270.
8. *Speaking Out*, CCSA 1980, 5.
9. Ibid.
10. Ibid., 6.
11. *Facing the Facts*, 31.
12. Ibid., 21.
13. Ibid., 23.
14. Simon Gqubule, 'Black Experience', in *Human Rights in South Africa*, SACC, Johannesburg 1974, 3.
15. Ibid., and see 37, where the list of Afrikaner articles is given.
16. *The Guardian*, 21 May 1982.
17. R.E.Goldblatt, 'Legal Problems', in *Human Rights in South Africa*, 18.
18. Ibid., 22.
19. Ibid.
20. Ibid., 23.
21. C.J.Alant, 'Some Sociological Questions', in *Human Rights in South Africa*, 25.
22. Ibid., 26.
23. Ibid.
24. Botha, *Progress through Separate Development*, 29, 32.
25. de Klerk, *The Puritans in Africa*, 270.
26. Laurence Schlemmer, 'Strategies for Change', in SPROCAS 6, 1971, 159.
27. Ibid.
28. Ibid., 160.

12. Theology and the Church

1. Quoted in Kenneth Slack, *Nairobi Narrative*, SCM Press 1976, 72.
2. Dom Illtyd Trethowan, *Absolute Value*, Allen and Unwin 1970, 89.
3. Jan Morris, *Destinations*, Oxford University Press 1980, 105.
4. de Gruchy, *The Church Struggle in South Africa*, 31.
5. *The Oxford History of South Africa*, Vol.2, 111.
6. Allan Boesak, *The Finger of God*, Orbis Books 1982, 33.

7. Manas Buthelezi, 'An African Theology of Black Theology', in *Essays in Black Theology*, 8.

8. *PCR Information No.9*, 17.

9. K.Sansbury, *Combating Racism*, BCC 1975, 22.

10. Ibid., 22.

11. Ibid.

12. Ibid., 25.

13. Ibid.

14. Frederikse, *None but Ourselves* (see above).

15. Pauline Webb, as quoted in Sansbury, *Combating Racism*, 24.

16. K.Blaiser, 'Communication of the Gospel – Gospel Communication', *Study Encounter* XL.3, 1975, 8.

17. M.M.Thomas, quoted in *Farewell to Innocence*, Orbis 1977, 82.

18. Charles McCoy, *When Gods Change – Hope for Theology*, Abingdon Press 1980, 13.

19. Ibid.

20. T.Wesser, 'The Church: A Sign of Liberation and Salvation', in *Liberation Theology and the Message of Salvation*, ed. J.B.Metz, The Pickwick Press, Pittsburgh 1973, 135.

21. Ibid.

13. Conclusion

1. SADCC submitted a memorandum with this total to the OAU in 1984; cf. Joseph Hanlon, *Beggar Your Neighbours*, CIIR 1986.

Bibliography

1. Books

Alexander, H.G., *The Growth of the Peace Testimony of the Society of Friends*, Friends Peace Committee 1939

Biko, Steve, *I Write What I Like*, Bowerdean Press 1978

Boesak, A., *The Finger of God. Sermons of Faith and Responsibility*, Orbis Books, Maryknoll 1982

– , *Farewell to Innocence*, Orbis Books 1977

Bonino, José Miguez, *Doing Theology in a Revolutionary Situation*, Fortress Press, Philadelphia and SPCK 1975

Brown, R.McAfee, *Religion and Violence*, Westminster Press, Philadelphia 1973

Cone, James, *Black Theology and Black Power*, Seabury Press, New York 1969

Davies, J.G., *Christians, Politics and Violent Revolution*, SCM Press 1976

de Gruchy, J.W., *The Church Struggle in South Africa*, SPCK 1979

– and Villa-Vicencio, Charles, *Apartheid is Heresy*, Lutterworth Press 1983

de Klerk, W.A., *The Puritans in Africa – A Story of Afrikanerdom*, Penguin Books 1975

de Vittoria, F., *The Law of Nations*, ed. James Brown, Oxford University Press 1934

Derr, Thomas S., *Barriers to Ecumenism: The Holy See and the World Council on Social Questions*, Orbis Books 1983

Desmond, Cosmas, *Christians or Capitalists? Christianity and Politics in South Africa*, Bowerdean Press 1978

Dumas, André, *Political Theology and the Life of the Church*, SCM Press 1978

First, Ruth, with Gurney, C. and Steele, J., *The South African Connection*, Penguin Books 1985

Gutiérrez, Gustavo, *A Theology of Liberation. History, Politics and Salvation*, Orbis Books and SCM Press 1974

Hall, Mary, *A Quest for the Liberated Christian*, Peter Lang, Frankfurt 1978

Harries, Richard, *Should Christians Support Guerrillas?*, Lutterworth Press 1982

Hastings, Adrian, *A History of African Christianity 1950-1975*, Cambridge University Press 1979

Hauf, Weiland and Vierdag, *South Africa: Prospects of Peaceful Change*, Collins 1981

Hinchliff, Peter, *Holiness and Politics*, Darton, Longman and Todd 1982

Huddleston, Trevor, *Naught for your Comfort*, Collins 1956

Jenkins, David E., *The Contradiction of Christianity*, SCM Press 1976

Knight, Derrick, *Beyond the Pale*, CARAF 1982

Kirk, Andrew J., *Theology Encounters Revolution*, Inter-Varsity Press 1980

Lehmann, Paul, *The Transfiguration of Politics*, Harper and Row and SCM Press 1974

Lodge, Tom, *Black Politics in South Africa since 1945*, Longman 1983

McCoy, Charles, *When Gods Change – Hope for Theology*, Abingdon Press, Nashville 1980

Marx, Karl, *Selected Works of Marx and Engels*, Moscow 1966

Miranda, José, *Marx against the Marxists. The Christian Humanism of Karl Marx*, Orbis Books and SCM Press 1980

Morris, Jan, *Destinations*, Oxford University Press 1980

Naude, Beyers, *The Trial of Beyers Naude*, Search Press 1975

Nkosi, Lewis, *Home and Exile – and Other Selections*, Longman 1965

Norman, E.R., *Christianity and World Order*, Oxford University Press 1978

Peires, J.B., *The House of Phalo. A History of the Xhosa People in the Days of their Independence*, Ravan 1981

Pérez-Esclarín, A., *Atheism and Liberation*, Orbis Books 1978 and SCM Press 1980

Plaatje, Sol.T., *Native Life in South Africa* (1913), reissued Greenwood Press 1982

Regehr, E., *Perceptions of Apartheid*, Herald 1979

Schlesinger, P., *Putting Reality Together*, Constable 1978

Trethowan, Dom Illtyd, *Absolute Value*, Allen and Unwin 1970

Tutu, Desmond, *On Trial*, The Preacher's Press 1982

Verduin, Leonard, *The Anatomy of a Hybrid*, Eerdmans 1976

Walshe, Peter, *Church versus State in South Africa. The Case of the Christian Institute*, Hurst and Co 1983

Wilson, M. and Thompson, L. (eds.), *The Oxford History of South Africa*, Vol.2, Oxford University Press 1972

2. *Articles*

Alant, C.J., 'Some Sociological Questions', in *Human Rights in South Africa*, ed. Brian Johanson, SACC 1974

Blaiser, Klauspeter, 'The Communicating of the Gospel – Gospel of Communication', *Study Encounter*, XVI.3, 1975

Botha, J.S.F., 'Concepts and Objectives', in *Progress through Separate Development*, Information Department of South Africa 1973

Buthulezi, Manas, 'An African Theology or Black Theology?', in *Essays on Black Theology*, UCM 1972

Gill, David, 'Power, Violence, Non-Violence and Social Change', *Study Encounter* VI.2, 1970

Goldblatt, R.E., 'Legal Problems', in *Human Rights in South Africa*

Gqubule, Simon, 'Black Experience', in *Human Rights in South Africa*

Hinchliff, P., 'Religion and Politics: The Harsh Reality', in *Christian Faith and Political Hopes. A Reply to E.R.Norman*, Epworth Press 1979

Jenkins, D.E. 'On the Humanum', *Ecumenical Review* XXV.1, January 1973

Legum, Colin, 'African Outlook towards the USSR', in *Africa and International Communism*, Macmillan 1980

Mandela, N., *Statements from the Dock, 7 November 1962*, UNCAA 1982

Moltmann, J., 'Racism and the Right to Resist', *Study Encounter* VIII.1, 1972

Pityana, Barney, 'What is Black Consciousness?', in *Essays on Black Theology*, UCM Johannesburg 1972

Schlemmer, L., 'Strategies for Change', in SPROCAS 6

Small, Adam, 'Blackness versus Nihilism', in *Essays in Black Theology*

Swift, A., 'Leaving the Laager', *New Internationalist* 145, March 1985

Torres, Sergio, 'Opening Address', in *African Theology en Route*, ed. K.Appiah-Kubi and S.Torres, Orbis Books 1979

Wesser, T., 'The Church: A Sign of Liberation and Salvation', in *Liberation Theology and the Message of Salvation* ed. J.B.Metz, The Pickwick Press, Pittsburgh 1973

Wilson, F., 'The Politics of Rising Expectations', in *Towards Economic and Political Justice in South Africa*, SAIRR 1980

– , 'Migrant Labour in Perspective', *South African Labour Bulletin*, 1.4, July 1974

3. Reports and documents published by corporate organizations

1. International

UN Centre against Apartheid (UNCAA: in date order)

Martin Bailey and Bernard Rivers, *Oil Sanctions against South Africa*, 12/78

Ann Seidman and Neva Makgetla, *Transnational Corporate Involvement in South Africa's Military Build-up*, 35/78

Corporate Data Exchange, *Bank Loans to South Africa 1972-78*, 5/79

Greg Lanning, *Role of Transnational Mining Corporations in the Plunder of South Africa's Mineral Resources*, SEM 3/79

Simon Clarke, *The Role of Transnational corporations in Financing Apartheid*, SEM 5/79

Vella Pillay, *Transnational Capital and the Growth of the South African Corporate State*, SEM 2/79

Christabel Gurney, *Recent Trends in the Policies of Transnational Corporations*, SEM 7/79

Brian Bolton, *The Role of Transnational Corporations in the Transfer of Technology, Know-how and Personnel to South Africa*, SEM 6/79

Amon J.Nsekela, *Partners in Apartheid*, SEM 8/79

Elizabeth Schmidt, *The Sullivan Principles: Decoding the Corporate Camouflage*, 4/80

Beate Klein, *Bricks in the Wall*, 15/81

Beate Klein, *Bank Loans to South Africa 1979-mid.1982*, Special Issue, December 1982

2. WCC-related (in date order)

The Race Race, ed. John Vincent (contains a report of the Notting Hill Consultation), SCM Press 1970

Incommunication, Risk 9.2

Time to Withdraw, WCC 1973

E.Adler, *A Small Beginning. An Assessment of the First Five Years of the Programme to Combat Racism*, WCC 1974

Breaking Barriers – Nairobi 1975, WCC 1976

Kenneth Slack, *Nairobi Narrative*, SCM Press 1976

A.Kirby, *South Africa's Bantustans*, WCC 1976

The World Council of Churches and Bank Loans to Apartheid, WCC 1977

Ecunews 32, 1979

PCR Information, nos.1-13

B.Rogers, *No Peace without Justice*, PCR 1980

3. Organizations based in Britain

The Anglican Pacifist Fellowship – publicity leaflet
The Anti-Apartheid Movement
David Hemson, *Foreign Investment and the Reproduction of Racial Capitalism in South Africa*, Anti-Apartheid Movement 1976

4. British Council of Churches (in date order)

Violence in Southern Africa: A Christian Assessment. Report of a working party appointed by the Department of International Affairs of the BCC and the Conference of British Missionary Societies, SCM Press 1970
1970 BCC files on the Special Fund of the PCR (now in the archives of the School of Oriental and African Studies)
Investment in Southern Africa, April 1973
Emigration to Southern Africa, November 1973
Kenneth Sansbury, *Combatting Racism*, BCC 1975
1978 BCC files on the Zimbabwe report
Political Change in South Africa: Britain's Responsibility, 1979
Lesslie Newbigin, *The Other Side of 1984*, BCC 1984

5. Catholic Institute for International Relations

War and Conscience in South Africa. The Churches and Conscientious Objection, CIIR 1982

6. Christian Concern for South Africa (CCSA: in date order)

R.Stares, *ICI in South Africa*, 1977
Britain's Economic Links with South Africa, 1979
Barbara Rogers, *A Code for Misconduct*, 1980
Speaking Out. Secret Interviews with Black Workers in South Africa, 1980
Arms for Apartheid, 1981
Oil and Apartheid. The Churches' Challenge to Shell and BP, 1982

7. The Church of England

The Church of England and the World Council of Churches, Bocardo Press 1979
Facing the Facts. A Working Party chaired by Peter Wheatley, CIO 1982
Barbara Rogers, *Divide and Rule*, IDAF 1976
Apartheid. The Facts, IDAF 1983

Index